Florida's "French" Revolution, 1793–1795

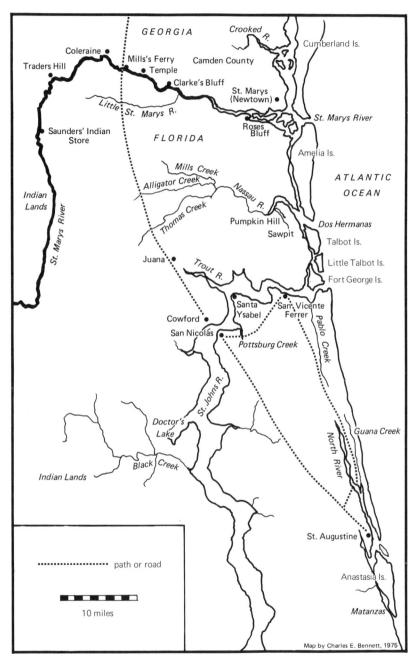

GEORGIA

Coleraine

Traders Hill

Mills's Ferry
Temple

Clarke's Bluff

Camden County

Crooked R.

Cumberland Is.

Little St. Marys R.

St. Marys
(Newtown)

St. Marys River

Saunders' Indian
Store

FLORIDA

Roses
Bluff

Amelia Is.

Mills Creek

Alligator Creek

Nassau R.

ATLANTIC
OCEAN

Indian
Lands

St. Marys River

Thomas Creek

Pumpkin Hill

Sawpit

Dos Hermanas

Talbot Is.

Little Talbot Is.

Juana

Trout R.

Fort George Is.

Santa
Ysabel

San Vicente
Ferrer

Cowford

San Nicolás

Pottsburg Creek

Pablo Creek

St. Johns R.

Doctor's
Lake

Guana Creek

North River

Indian Lands

Black Creek

.... path or road

▮▯▮▯▮▯▮▯▮
10 miles

St. Augustine

Anastasia Is.

Matanzas

Map by Charles E. Bennett, 1975

Northeast Florida, 1790–95

Florida's "French" Revolution, 1793–1795

CHARLES E. BENNETT

A University of Florida Book
UNIVERSITY PRESSES OF FLORIDA
Gainesville 1981

University Presses of Florida is the central agency for scholarly publishing of the State of Florida's university system. Its offices are located at 15 NW 15th Street, Gainesville, FL 32603. Works published by University Presses of Florida are evaluated and selected for publication by a faculty editorial committee of any one of Florida's nine public universities: Florida A&M University (Tallahassee), Florida Atlantic University (Boca Raton), Florida International University (Miami), Florida State University (Tallahassee), University of Central Florida (Orlando), University of Florida (Gainesville), University of North Florida (Jacksonville), University of South Florida (Tampa), University of West Florida (Pensacola).

Library of Congress Cataloging in Publication Data
Bennett, Charles E., 1910–
    Florida's "French" revolution, 1793–1795.
    "A University of Florida book."
    Bibliography: p.
    Includes index.
    1. Florida—History—Spanish colony, 1784–1821.
I. Title.
F314.B39   975.9′03   81-7431
                            AACR2

TYPESETTING BY WILLIAMS TYPOGRAPHY
CHATTANOOGA, TENNESSEE

PRINTED IN U.S.A.

Dedicated to the memory of
Carita Doggett Corse,
distinguished historian,
treasured friend

Contents

Acknowledgments

MANY years ago, the late Judge Burton Barrs of Jacksonville encouraged the author to study the history of East Florida during the American Revolution, a field in which the judge had published *East Florida in the American Revolution* (Jacksonville: Cooper Press, 1949). From this prompting there grew a strong interest concerning some of the participants in that period of history, particularly the patriots Elijah Clark and John McIntosh.

The first outcome of that research pertinent to the subject matter of this book was an appendix, "The French Republic of Florida," added by the author to *Southernmost Battlefields of the Revolution* (Bailey's Crossroads, Va.: Blair, Inc., 1970). The further pursual of this field of study resulted in the present volume.

This book owes most to Richard K. Murdoch of the University of Georgia and to his work *The Georgia-Florida Frontier, 1793–1796* (Berkeley: University of California Press, 1951), an extremely thorough and authoritative volume. Professor Murdoch encouraged the author and generously made constructive suggestions.

The primary source of manuscript material for this work was a microfilm in the Charles E. Bennett Collection of the Manuscript Division of the Library of Congress, entitled "Criminales de oficio contra Don Juan Mac Intosh . . .," reproducing original documents in pormenor 16, legajo 166, Archivo General de Indias, Papeles Procedentes de Cuba, Seville. There is also a typescript of these documents in Box 293 of the East Florida Papers in the Manuscript Division of the Library of Congress. The typescript was completely translated from its Spanish text because the 1977 microfilm reveals that substantial deterioration has occurred in the original documents since the date of the typescript production in 1924 by Charles H. Cunningham at the Library of Congress. Thus the typescript was used to fill in passages from the original documents that are eroded or illegible because of discoloration.

Other manuscript material came from photocopies in the Library of Congress made from the original documents described in the footnotes. All other manuscript source materials were secured from photocopies of the original manuscripts in foreign depositories (for example, the Cochrane Papers in the National Library of Scotland); in each such case the photocopies have now been deposited in the Charles E. Bennett Collection in the Manuscript Division of the Library of Congress.

Three persons who gave much encouragement and help in this work were Luis Arana, historian for the National Park Service, St. Augustine; Ofelia Recio, a recent emigrant from Cuba, Falls Church, Virginia; and Bessie Lewis, historian and consultant at Fort King George, Darien, Georgia.

For the writer this book has been an exciting adventure—about exciting adventure. He hopes its readers may find it so too.

Charles E. Bennett

ONE

Prologue–Changing Frontiers in the New World

WHEN on 27 March 1513 Juan Ponce de León discovered Florida—and on 2 April landed on the coast somewhere between present-day Jacksonville and St. Augustine—he named the land Florida, after the religious period of its discovery, *Pascua Florida*. As far as he was concerned, this new land and all the lands to the north were now Spanish. The king of Spain was agreeable to that; and the Pope had already given his blessings.

Ponce attempted in 1521 to strengthen the Spanish claims by settlement on the lower Gulf coast of present-day Florida.[1] The settlement failed, as did a 1526 Spanish colony under Lucas Vásquez de Ayllón, near the mouth of the Pee Dee River in South Carolina. Neither Ponce nor Ayllón long survived their efforts at settlement. Ponce died of complications from an arrow wound, and Ayllón died of fever and was buried at sea.

Tristán de Luna y Arellano brought his colony for the Spanish king to Pensacola in 1559, endured great hardships for two years, and was supplanted by Angel de Villafañe, who was then ordered to colonize Santa Elena (Port Royal, South Carolina). He landed at several places on the east coast and everywhere claimed title for Spain, but he quickly abandoned settlement efforts in the north and finally in July of 1561 settled his followers on the Caribbean island of Hispaniola. Following all of these failures and after successes in Mexico—beginning with the 1519 settlement of

1. Charles Norman, *Discoverers of America*, p. 12. The other data in these introductory pages are largely from this volume when not otherwise noted. Complete publishing information for all references is in the bibliography.

1

Veracruz by Hernán Cortés—Spain in 1561 was considering abandoning all the northern lands that are now the United States.

France took quick advantage of such Spanish indecision. After all, reasoned Catherine de Médici, queen mother of France, had not French fishermen fished off the coast of America for many years before the Spanish had made any efforts there? And then in 1524 Francis I, king of France, had sent Giovanni da Verrazano to explore those Atlantic seaboard areas. He had ably done so. And in the decade 1534 to 1543 there had been other French efforts by Jacques Cartier and Lord Roberval in the northern American wildernesses. So the French called the eastern seaboard of northern America by the name of New France. Jean Ribault led an expedition that visited the lower St. Johns River and went on to establish a small colony at Port Royal, South Carolina, in 1562. Too small to have much chance of success, it failed; and the handful of survivors took to the sea without a compass and were rescued after they had been driven to devour one of their fellow voyagers.

Undeterred, France dispatched René Laudonnière in 1564 with a colony of several hundred settlers to what is now Jacksonville, Florida. There they founded La Caroline, named for Charles IX, boy king of France. When these French settlers came, there were no settlements of Europeans in what is now the United States. This was never again to be the case. Spain reacted to the French intrusion with understandable vigor. Before the end of the next year she had bloodily run up the Spanish flag over La Caroline, named it San Mateo, and placed the new Spanish colony's capital at a place thirty-five miles to the south. There Pedro Menéndez de Avilés in 1565 established St. Augustine, the oldest city existing in the United States today. It is noteworthy that when Pensacola was finally settled in 1698, it was to forestall French settlement in that area.

The English were the next to challenge the Spanish, basing their claims on the discoveries of John and Sebastian Cabot in the late 1490s. England first made an unsuccessful settlement effort in 1583, with an expedition led by Sir Humphrey Gilbert to Newfoundland. In 1585 Sir Walter Raleigh's Roanoke Island settlement failed also; it was followed in 1587 by the more famous failure of "the lost colony" in present-day North Carolina. England at last gained its permanent toehold in 1607 with Jamestown. From then on, American colonial border disputes played their part in the tensions between England and Spain.[2]

In 1702 the Carolinas' English governor, James Moore, personally led troops into Florida but failed to take the fortress at St. Augustine. He returned to attack the Indian allies of Spain in Apalachee in 1704, and Spain made an abortive retaliation on Charleston in 1706. With the establishment of Georgia by the English in 1733, friction between the countries and between their colonies intensified. Within the next decade Georgia's leader, James Oglethorpe, twice attacked Florida, and Spanish Florida made a retaliatory attack on British Georgia in 1742. Spain and Britain were at that time engaged in a war precipitated in 1739 by the loss of an ear of a British mariner—Robert Jenkins—at the hands of a Spanish official. The war was first called the War of Jenkins' Ear but later merged into the War of the Austrian Succession.

Great Britain captured Havana in 1762, in the Seven Years War; the next year Spain reluctantly deeded Florida to Britain in order to regain the Cuban city, a precious jewel in the Spanish treasury. The British divided the territory into East and West Florida, the Apalachicola River separating the two provinces.[3] The following twenty years were prosperous British years for Florida despite the American Revolution and two sizable expeditions of patriots into Florida, one in 1777 and the other in 1778. The first ended in the battle of Thomas Creek in what is now Jacksonville and the latter ended just to the north in the battle of Alligator Bridge, about a mile north of present-day Callahan.[4]

2. Only a few of these conflicts are mentioned in the text; for a full discussion of them see Verner W. Crane, *The Southern Frontier, 1670–1732.* For instance, there was a major Spanish attack upon the English at Charleston in 1676 and another upon the Scotch at Port Royal three years later; and there were substantial English penetrations of northeast Florida, notably by Colonel John Barnwell in 1708 and by Colonel John Palmer in 1727. For a brief discussion of these events see ibid., p. 81, and Pleasant D. Gold, *History of Duval County, Florida,* pp. 42–50.

3. J. Leitch Wright, Jr., *Florida in the American Revolution,* p. 2.

4. These two Florida engagements are treated at length in Charles E. Bennett, *Southernmost Battlefields of the Revolution.*

These were the most southerly battlefields of the Revolution in the continental United States, at least on the eastern seaboard. Some historians support the 1781 battle of Pensacola as being the most southerly of the Revolution. Pensacola is farther south than Jacksonville or Callahan and did fall in 1781 to Spain in a major Spanish-British battle; and there were small skirmishes elsewhere in West Florida and in the lower Mississippi valley. But it must be remembered that Spain, unlike France, was not an ally of the thirteen colonies. Her contemporaneous war with Britain, though helpful to the colonies, was designed to regain the Floridas for Spain and not to free them.

The 1783 peace treaties did return Florida to Spain, and the Spanish continued the British governmental arrangement of two provinces, East and West Florida. The terms of the treaties carefully ensured the ancient French fishing rights on the northern Atlantic seaboard; France had already lost most of her colonial holdings in North America, having ceded Louisiana to Spain in 1762. The treaties, however, left many boundary matters unsettled. The eastern states of Virginia, North and South Carolina, and Georgia claimed sovereignty westward across the Appalachian Mountains and to the Mississippi River.

But Spain also claimed substantial areas east of the river, and many Indians not only claimed such lands but extensively occupied them. Even when Indians specifically "sold" lands, they often asserted later that they had meant only to convey to others the right to share, not the right to exclude Indians from their traditional uses of the lands for hunting, nomadic food gathering, and agriculture. When white speculators tried to buy up the land of the great Indian warrior Tecumseh after the Revolution, he asked: "Sell the country? Why not sell the air, the clouds, the great sea?"

In the northern areas to the west of the Appalachians, Great Britain maintained forts pressing the Canadian border down into areas firmly claimed by the United States—for example, Detroit. One of the reasons why Great Britain delayed closing these forts was her reluctance to abandon her former Indian allies, who feared that they might lose their rights to lands in those areas. A more compelling motive for the British was to retain leverage for demanding better treatment of British subjects and other loyalists.

The greatest irritant to the western settlers was the adamant refusal of Spain to allow free access to transportation down the Mississippi River. The American settlers were willing to accept almost any political arrangement if only this access could be gained.

According to the 1783 treaty Britain ceded to the United States the land north of a line running from the Mississippi River eastward along the thirty-first parallel to the Chattahoochee River, thence south to the junction of the Flint; and thence eastward again to the source of the St. Marys and along the course of the stream to the Atlantic Ocean. Spain did not agree to this, instead claiming all the land south of the Tennessee River and west of the Appalachian Mountains. She claimed in the west not only Pensacola but also other Spanish settlements at such places as Natchez and Nogales (Vicksburg). Some of the settlements to the east of the river were heavily populated by British loyalists, the Tories. Spain's treaty with Britain, unlike the Anglo-American treaty, left uncertain the exact northern line of the Spanish Floridas.

Spain relied heavily upon her Indian allies to prevent American settlement in the lands east of the Mississippi, thus thwarting U.S. claims. One of Spain's ways of keeping friendly relationships with the Indians was the fostering of Indian commercial trade through the Scottish trading firm of Panton, Leslie and Company. This firm, with roots established while Britain owned the Floridas, enjoyed a monopoly under Spanish protection in return for supplying the Indians and encouraging the natives to resist Anglo-Saxon migration from the eastern seaboard. Spain would have welcomed a Spanish-based successor to this firm, but none could be found to do the job efficiently.

In 1786 Spain's representative in the capital city of Philadelphia, Diego de Gardoqui, approached John Brown, who represented the Kentucky District of Virginia in the Congress, suggesting that if the westerners would pull away from the new nation, traffic on the Mississippi would be opened to them and recognized in a formal alliance with Spain.[5] Thus the "Spanish Conspiracy" was born. In 1787 James Wilkinson, formerly a patriot general in the Revolution and at that time a merchant in Kentucky, took an oath of allegiance to the Spanish king and promised to bring Kentucky over to Spain. But Kentucky's convention voted in 1789 to stay in the union, ending the first phase of the Spanish Conspiracy.

Governor John Sevier of the abortive State of Franklin (later Tennessee) wrote to the Spanish authorities suggesting that Franklin might ally itself with Spain—a plan that quickly collapsed. The entire Spanish Conspiracy expired when North Carolina in 1790 turned its western lands claims over to the United States. This cleared the way for the new State of Tennessee to achieve what Franklin had never achieved: full statehood within the framework of the union.

British officials also made overtures toward filling the vacuum of governmental leadership in the Spanish-claimed lands east of the Mississippi, to which many Tories had fled during and after the Revolution. As a result William Augustus Bowles, with the blessings of the British governor of the Bahamas, arrived in Florida in 1788 with a plan to set up an Indian state in the Floridas and extending northward into the land that is now Alabama. His venture ended in failure a few years later; but in the meantime he had been declared by an aggregation of Indian chiefs to be the director general of the State of Muskogee, an allegedly sovereign territory that included parts of Florida, Georgia, and Alabama.[6]

Early in 1790 Dr. James O'Fallon, a physician and brother-in-law of Kentucky's General George Rogers Clark, was appointed agent for a land-speculating company chartered by Georgia. He planned an independent country in the company's lands lying in areas claimed by Georgia but not relinquished by the Indians. President Washington signed a proclamation on 19 March 1791 forbidding any such effort, and the plan was thwarted. This was but one of many speculative ventures in the

5. Thomas P. Abernethy, *The South in the New Nation, 1789–1819*, p. 46.
6. Ibid., p. 244.

William Augustus Bowles, painted by T. Hardy, engraved by T. Grozer. Courtesy of the National Portrait Gallery, Washington, D.C.

western lands; among persons involved in them were Patrick
Henry, Senator William Blount, and Thomas Carr. The latter two
projected settlements at Muscle Shoals. Henry was involved in
the ventures of the Virginia Yazoo Company, composed primarily
of Virginians but dealing in Georgia lands. The land venture of
O'Fallon was but one of his several imaginative proposals. For
example, in 1788 he had offered to settle and rule for Spain all land
between the St. Marys and the St. Johns. Four years earlier John
Cruden, living on the St. Marys and signing himself "President of
the British-American Loyalists," had tried to achieve autonomy
for the same area under either the British or the Spanish flag.[7]

Spain's feeble claims to sovereignty east of the Mississippi
only mildly disturbed politicians; but the use of Indian allies to
discourage all western migration in Indian-claimed areas greatly
alarmed almost all frontiersmen, particularly in southern Georgia,
where the Indians claimed land all the way to the coast. Anglo-
Saxon migration southward across the St. Marys into Spanish
Florida was an alternative expansion suggested by Spain. When
the British gave up Florida in 1783, almost everyone in East
Florida moved away. Spain felt strongly the need to encourage
even the Anglo-Saxons to immigrate into her regained lands in
Florida.

The transition from British to Spanish reign in the area between the St. Marys and the St. Johns was marked by unrest and
turbulence. Nicholas Griner, the commander of the Spanish garrison on the St. Marys, wrote to the governor on 10 November
1784 that "the number of outlaws between the towns of St. Johns
and St. Marys is about sixty families. Among them some might be
useful to our nation; but the others, the sooner we drive them out
of the province, the better, as they are men who have neither God
nor law, and men who are capable of the greatest atrocities." A
final warning was given to the outlaws to depart on 5 April 1786,
but Griner reported that things were even worse on 5 December
1786: "The inhabitants have openly declared against us but con-

7. Wright, *Florida in the American Revolution*, pp. 136, 137, 142; Helen H. Tanner,
Zéspedes in East Florida, p. 159; Abernethy, *The South in the New Nation*, p. 79.

Chief Hopothle Mico at the signing of the Treaty of New York, 1790, by John Trumbull. Courtesy of Fordham University, New York City.

ceal themselves in the wilderness on the banks of the St. Johns as far as St. Marys, controlling the province."[8]

Georgia authorities were constantly trying to negotiate with the Indians to allow white settlements in the west. The Treaty of Galphinton in 1785 was the joint creation of the Georgia government and certain minor Creek chiefs. It provided that the Indians would move to the west of the Oconee River and west of a line

8. Gold, *Duval County*, pp. 61, 62. Richard Lang, a major figure in the events to follow, already resided in this area at that time. See Wilbur H. Siebert, *Loyalists in East Florida, 1774 to 1785*, 2:7.

from the Oconee's junction with the Altamaha to the headwaters of the St. Marys River. The St. Marys, by that treaty, became for the first time the southern boundary of Georgia without any Indian buffer zone north of Spanish Florida. But the central government of the United States disapproved of state treaties with Indians; and the dominant Creek leader, Alexander McGillivray,[9] also disapproved of the Galphinton treaty. So a lesser Indian removal was arranged in the 1790 Treaty of New York, executed by McGillivray with the government. The St. Marys remained Georgia's southern boundary, however.

In the meantime, on the northern shores of the St. Marys River at Buttermilk Bluff, or Wright's Landing, near the river's mouth, the new town of St. Patrick was established in 1788—shortly following the 1787 designation of the older St. Patrick on the south side of the Satilla as the first county seat of Camden County. By 1792 the official county seat was moved to the St. Marys location and the new town was called thenceforth St. Marys. The Spanish persistently called it New Town, or Newton.[10]

9. A volume of revealing documents relative to McGillivray is John W. Caughey, *McGillivray of the Creeks.*

10. The founding of St. Marys is discussed in detail in Marguerite G. Reddick, *Camden's Challenge: A History of Camden County, Georgia*, pp. 6, 145, 146. See also Richard K. Murdoch, *The Georgia-Florida Frontier, 1793–1796: Spanish Reaction to French Intrigue and American Designs*, p. 4; Janice Borton Miller, "Juan Nepomuceno de Quesada: Spanish Governor of East Florida, 1790–1795" (Ph.D. diss.), p. 211.

TWO

Anglo-Saxons Invited to Spanish Florida

ST. MARYS, Georgia, by whatever name—Buttermilk Bluff, Wright's Landing, St. Patrick, or the name used by the Spanish, Newton—posed a real threat to Spanish Florida in the last decade of the eighteenth century. In its good harbor an aggressive fleet could assemble for an attack on Florida. St. Marys could be a base for pushing westward the Indian allies of Spain. As Georgia's most southerly outpost it furnished a place where revolutionary forces could assemble unnoticed among the population, and from which criminal elements could run across the Florida border in plundering raids and return to safety. The town stared across the St. Marys River at strategic Amelia Island, which the Spanish had from time to time garrisoned with troops. Moreover, other Anglo-Saxon communities springing up along the northern banks of the river extended the dangers westward, notably at Coleraine and Temple.

Spanish nationals remained reluctant to settle north of the St. Johns River. The British had abandoned their plantations on the lands from the St. Johns River to the St. Marys River, and a repopulation of these lands seemed essential to Spain's interests. So Spain in 1790, following her recently liberalized immigration rules for the Mississippi Valley and in order to give more security to Florida's northern border, issued an invitation to aliens to come to East Florida, but under specific restrictions. They had to swear allegiance to the Spanish crown and become Spanish subjects.

Though not required to become Catholics, they would not be allowed to practice openly any other religion. Each family would be granted 100 acres for the head of the family, 50 for each family member, and 50 for each slave. They would be required to build adequate houses and to cultivate their parcels of land for ten years, whereupon an outright deed to the land would be given.[1]

Many Anglo-Saxons came to Spanish Florida during this period, some of them from as far north as Virginia but most directly from Georgia. Among the family names were: Ashley, Atkinson, Blunt, Cryer, Hogans, Hollingsworth, Jones, Lang, McIntosh, McQueen, Plummer, and Wagnon. Four of the settlers who arrived in Florida about this time were of particular importance in the events that were soon to follow: John McIntosh, Richard Lang, John Peter Wagnon, and William Jones.

Traditionally the McIntosh family was opposed to Spanish colonialism in Florida, and they were by nature pugnacious. John's grandfather, John McIntosh, Mor,[2] had been captured when he fought under Oglethorpe in Florida in 1740 and had been freed two years later after imprisonment in Spain. John's uncle, General Lachlan McIntosh, once had commanded the continental troops in Georgia and had killed Georgia's President Button Gwinnett in a duel. John himself had won the hand of his beloved wife, Sarah, following a bloody duel (fought with swords) and a long and tender nursing back to health by his betrothed.

The younger John McIntosh had been a Georgia hero in the American Revolution. When challenged in 1778 to surrender Fort Morris (a small earthen fort on the harbor shore at Sunbury, Georgia), he sent a laconic message to the much more numerous British forces: "Come and take it!" Bluffed, the British withdrew. He had been a member of General Robert Howe's staff in the Florida expedition of 1778. After the American Revolution he settled at St. Marys; by 1791 he was back in Florida, this time as a settler and planter on the banks of the St. Johns River. One of his

---

1. Rembert W. Patrick, *Florida Fiasco: Rampant Rebels on the Georgia-Florida Border, 1810–1815*, p. 50.
2. Ibid., p. 19. The word "Mor," sometimes placed after the first name, is a Gaelic word, variously spelled, denoting "great," "esteemed," or "senior."

plantations, which was to be his principal residence, was on the south side of the river, eight miles downstream from the Spanish military post San Nicolás.[3] This plantation was called by the Spanish Cerro Fuente ("Spring Hill"). When Mrs. McIntosh wrote from there she headed her letters "Bellevue," apparently the name of the house.

The natural leadership of John McIntosh was immediately recognized by the Spanish authorities; he was given a magistrate's position for a broad area in the St. Johns River valley. Spanish documents of the time refer to him as lieutenant governor of East Florida in the St. Johns district. He owned land in various places in Florida but his most strategically placed plantation, and one of his favorites, was at Cowford, on the north bank of the St. Johns directly across from San Nicolás—about where the Jacksonville City Hall stands today.

McIntosh was one of the first three settlers at Cowford, which became Jacksonville in 1822. Thomas Philpot had settled there by 1772 with a store and ferry house, but the place was overrun by the patriots in 1776 and then abandoned.[4] McIntosh and Robert Pritchard[5] both came in 1791, Pritchard settling at the bend of the river to the west of the McIntosh lands. Both soon

3. The McIntosh Spring Hill plantation has been located erroneously by many historians at various locations, even on the eastern side of the river to the south of the center of Jacksonville's population today. From the testimony taken about the capture of San Nicolás, it is clear that Spring Hill was on the southern bank of the river. Mrs. McIntosh's correspondence suggests that the plantation was about eight miles downstream from San Nicolás, near San Vicente Ferrer on the south side of the river. Moreover, there are documents that prove the location precisely. Specifically, the western boundary of the plantation is shown as the eastern boundary of F. P. Fatio's New Castle plantation in a map printed in "Florida Private Land Claims," 2:282, Record Group 49, Archives of the United States; that line is known to all title researchers and is in the official land maps of Duval County, Florida. These documents show that line to be approximately 140 feet east of present-day Buckskin Trail, East. Moreover, the eastern line of the McIntosh plantation is shown as the western boundary of the lands claimed by Andrew Atkinson just west of San Vicente Ferrer; the documents recording these boundaries are under the claims of George Gibbs and Andrew Atkinson, items 1E and 2S (2 February 1792) in "Spanish Land Grants in Florida," vol. 1, Unconfirmed Claims, Florida Department of Agriculture.

4. A map of about 1772 depicts Philpot's ferry house at Cowford (Pleasant D. Gold, *History of Duval County, Florida*, p. 52).

5. Pritchard is discussed in T. Frederick Davis, *History of Jacksonville, Florida, and Vicinity, 1513 to 1924*, pp. 40, 51.

took up residence elsewhere, McIntosh first and then Pritchard. Mr. and Mrs. Zachariah Hogans began the permanent settlement of what is now downtown Jacksonville in 1816, launching the village of Cowford and the City of Jacksonville.[6]

None of them, of course, were the first whites to settle on the land occupied later by Jacksonville with its greatly expanded city limits. René Laudonnière, governor of La Caroline in 1564–65, had been the first.[7] Indians who had once generously populated the area had been pushed westward from this coastal region by 1791.

Richard Lang had come to Florida without benefit of Spain's 1790 invitation. The records show that the Executive Council of Georgia discovered that on 18 June 1784 Lang was in jail in Savannah, charged with committing a felony in South Carolina, and on that date he was ordered removed to Charleston to stand trial. He escaped and promptly went to Florida. He may have arrived just before Governor Vincent Manuel de Zéspedes, who did not take over the reins of government from the British until 27 June 1784. Lang had probably visited Florida before his imprisonment in Savannah. By 1786 he had acquired land on the south side of the St. Marys, and his name appears in a 1787 Florida census.[8]

Governor Zéspedes considered Lang a troublemaker, along with an associate of his in the same neighborhood, Daniel McGirtt. Born in the Kershaw District of South Carolina, McGirtt had been a scout for the patriots at the beginning of the American Revolution. His superior officer at St. Illa, Georgia, had coveted his mare, Gray Goose, and had had McGirtt whipped and imprisoned; but the prisoner escaped and, with his brother, joined the British in Florida. Toward the end of the war they plundered in Georgia; after Spain took title to Florida at the end of the war,

6. Hogans is discussed in Gold, *Duval County*, p. 65, and Davis, *History of Jacksonville*, p. 51.

7. Charles E. Bennett, *Laudonnière and Fort Caroline: History and Documents* and René Goulaine de Laudonnière, *Three Voyages*, p. xvi.

8. See Allen D. Candler, comp., *Revolutionary Records of the State of Georgia*, 2:661; Wilbur H. Siebert, *Loyalists in East Florida, 1774 to 1785*, 2:7; Folks Huxford, *Pioneers of Wiregrass Georgia: A Biographical Account of Some of the Early Settlers . . .*, 5:256.

they plundered in Florida. Daniel was captured in 1783 and imprisoned for five years; released, he returned first to South Carolina and then to Florida, where he continued to make trouble for the authorities.[9]

Toward the end of 1787 Richard Lang was a candidate to supplant Henry O'Neill, a former British officer, as the Spanish magistrate for the St. Marys River valley. Eighteen men on the border submitted a petition endorsing Lang's candidacy. O'Neill was murdered in May 1788; the Spanish suspected followers of Lang and McGirtt of being the felons. Nevertheless, the governor uneasily appointed Lang to the position he had sought.[10]

Lang's principal place of residence in Florida was called Casa Blanca ("White House"), a 400-acre plantation on the south bank of the St. Marys River at Mills's Ferry (now Kings Ferry).[11] It was an important frontier location, for even during the American Revolution the ferry was the northern Florida terminus of a trail or crude road from St. Augustine to Georgia. On that road the battle of Alligator Bridge had taken place in 1778; and General Howe had headquartered himself near that ferry at the British Fort Tonyn, which his Continentals had taken on 29 June 1778. Lang also owned Florida land on Pigeon Creek five miles west of Coleraine.

The Spanish authorities gave Lang the title of "justice of the peace" and "commander of the militia" in the region lying between the St. Marys and Nassau rivers. Originally his jurisdiction extended to the St. Johns; but Carlos Howard was later given the superior military command of all of the northern frontier, with a military command post at St. Johns Bluff (called by the Spanish San Vicente Ferrer). Lang retained his subordinate authority in

9. See Siebert, *Loyalists in East Florida*, 2:328; Gold, *Duval County*, p. 53; Louise F. Hays, *Hero of Hornet's Nest; A Biography of Elijah Clark, 1733 to 1799*, p. 40.

10. Helen H. Tanner, *Zéspedes in East Florida, 1784–1790*, p. 189. Jan H. Johannes reports that O'Neill's widow, Margaret, was given substantial land grants on the mainland near Amelia Island and that the community name of O'Neill in that area perpetuates the name of this family (*Yesterday's Reflections, Nassau County, Florida: A Pictorial History*, pp. 329, 330).

11. Richard K. Murdoch, *The Georgia-Florida Frontier, 1793–1796: Spanish Reaction to French Intrigue and American Designs*, p. 156. The date 4 April 1792 is given as the date of Lang's grant to this land (Johannes, *Yesterday's Reflections*, p. 82).

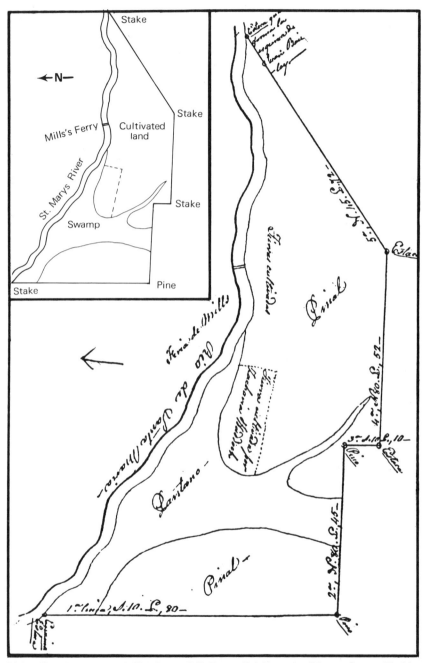

Richard Lang's property at Mills's Ferry, 1817. From official records of Nassau County, Florida.

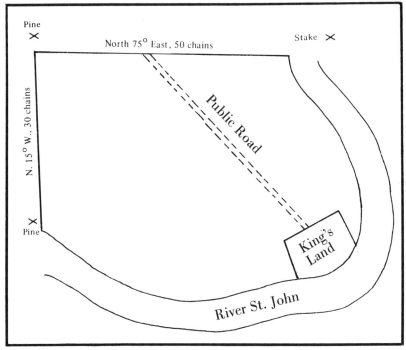

William Jones's property at San Nicolás, 1793. From *American State Papers*, ed. Asbury Dickins and James C. Allen (Washington: Gales and Seaton, 1859), class viii, vol. 4, p. 379.

the St. Marys and Nassau valleys after Howard's appointment; but another, Nathaniel Hall, was given similar responsibilities near the mouth of the St. Marys.

John Peter Wagnon was another veteran of the American Revolution; he and John McIntosh had fought together with distinction. Wagnon was allowed by the Spanish to buy a house in St. Augustine, on Hippolyte Street.[12] A two-story structure, it was purchased by Wagnon in 1793 from Andrew Dewes. The year before, William Jones had been granted land on the south side of the St. Johns River, at the bend in the river as it turns and flows eastward to the Atlantic Ocean. His land abutted on the east the lands of the Spanish Fort San Nicolás and lay just across the river

12. Murdoch, *Georgia-Florida Frontier*, pp. 72, 157.

from the Cowford plantations of John McIntosh and Robert Pritchard.

When McIntosh, Lang, Wagnon, and Jones made their various ways to Florida, they could hardly have anticipated that political affairs in faraway France would unite them in adventure and substantially affect their lives; but such was to be the case.

THREE

The Coming of Minister Genêt

THE end of the American Revolution left the French treasury depleted, partly because of the tremendous assistance given to the thirteen American colonies in revolt and partly because of royal extravagance through several generations. The tax-burdened middle classes and the poor began their ten-year revolution against the French government in 1789. It started with merely reducing the powers of the king; but by 1792 the king was imprisoned, all powers had been vested in the National Assembly, and the National Convention had been created to draw up a new constitution. The 1792 meeting of the Convention declared France to be a republic; the meetings continued until 1795.

Jacques Pierre Brissot de Warville was one of the principal leaders of the Girondists, the majority party in the Convention, which advocated exporting the Revolution and actively sought war. He had traveled in the United States in 1788; in 1791 he published in Paris his observations, *Nouveau Voyage dans les Etats Unis*. In it he discussed particularly the unrest caused by Spain's closure of the Mississippi, commenting on the attitude of western Americans:

> They are determined to open it with good will or by force; and it would not be in the power of Congress to moderate their ardor. Men who have shaken off the yoke of Great Britain and who are masters of the Ohio and the Mississippi

cannot conceive that the insolence of a handful of Spaniards can think of shutting rivers and seas against a hundred thousand free Americans. The slightest quarrel will be sufficient to throw them into a flame; and if ever the Americans shall march toward New Orleans, it will infallibly fall into their hands.[1]

In 1792 General George Rogers Clark and his brother-in-law, Dr. James O'Fallon, put together a plan for an attack on Louisiana under the French flag. Clark had won important victories in the western campaigns of the American Revolution; he had exhausted his personal funds in the cause. Now he was disturbed by the indifference the new government was showing to western settlers.[2] O'Fallon wrote of their plan and their desire for French support to his old friend Thomas Paine, former revolutionary leader in America and by then a member of the French Convention. Paine replied from Paris on 17 February 1793 that the matter was under consideration in France, before the Executive Council of the Republic. Earlier, on 2 February 1793, General Clark had written to Edmond Charles Genêt, prospective French minister to the United States.[3]

Brissot had nominated Genêt for the position in America; as expected, instructions for Genêt's mission in the United States outlined the fomenting of revolution in Spanish America. Thomas Jefferson, then secretary of state, was told by a reliable infor-

1. Quoted in Frederick J. Turner, "The Origin of Genêt's Projected Attack on Louisiana and the Floridas," p. 654. During the period 1793–96, Republican France was increasingly relying on the talents of Napoleon in her efforts to replace royal establishments in Europe with new republics. On 22 December 1793 Napoleon, aged 24, was made brigadier general; his first significant acts were to protect the National Convention in 1795, establish a republican regime in Lombardy, and create the Cisalpine Republic in 1796 (*Encyclopaedia Brittanica* [Chicago: Encyclopedia Brittanica, Inc., 1977], 12:832–33). For a discussion of the French-inspired and French-imposed republics in Europe in the late eighteenth century, see R. R. Palmer, *The Age of the Democratic Revolution* (Princeton, N.J.: Princeton University Press, 1964), pp. 180, 186, 265–70, 295, 549. Palmer observes that France was spreading revolution in Europe primarily as a weapon against her enemies.
2. See *Encyclopaedia Brittanica*, 2:967.
3. Genêt's participation in the French efforts in Florida are fully discussed in Meade Minnigerode, *Jefferson, Friend of France, 1793: The Career of Edmond Charles Genêt.* . . . See also *Encyclopaedia Britannica*, s. v. "Genêt, Edmond Charles."

mant, Colonel W. S. Smith, that the revolutionaries "meant to begin the attack at the mouth of the Mississippi, and to sweep along the bay of Mexico, southwardly, and that they would have no objections to our incorporating into our government the two Floridas."[4]

Having good reason to understand that France was actively considering becoming again a colonial power in America at the expense of Spain and that the United States might benefit as a side result by the acquisition of the Floridas, Secretary of State Jefferson, with the approval of President Washington, on 23 March 1793 drafted instructions to U.S. representatives in Spain against signing any treaty guaranteeing Spanish colonies in America. The Jefferson draft shows a proposal, later expunged, to give such a guarantee if it could be done in exchange for a cession of the Floridas to the United States.

Just as discontent along the Mississippi with the Spanish control of commerce on the river was heavily relied upon there, so in Florida the French revolutionary forces capitalized on an existing deep-seated local frustration with Spanish commercial policies dictated from Madrid. There was a very general dissatisfaction in East Florida about the shortage of commodities for purchase and the lack of the benefits of competitive free enterprise. On 10 January 1793 a sizable cross-section of the leadership of East Florida submitted a lengthy petition for corrections to be made, stressing the relative success of the previous British colonial policies and the poor conditions which had followed under Spanish policies, which granted virtual monopoly in the lucrative Indian trade to the Scottish firm of Panton, Leslie and Company, with principal stores at St. Augustine, Pensacola, and St. Marks. Administration stalwarts like Andrew Atkinson and Juan McQueen signed it and so did potential rebels like J. P. Wagnon and John McIntosh.[5]

Spain was fearful that a policy of freer trade would, by

4. Turner, "Origin of Genêt's Projected Attack," p. 655.

5. Archivo General de Indias, Santo Domingo, 87-3-22, enclosed in Quesada to Gardoqui, 10 January 1793, St. Augustine. Microfilm in P. K. Yonge Library of Florida History, University of Florida, Gainesville.

lessening the profits of Panton, Leslie and Company, reduce total imports to a dangerous level incapable of being offset by imports from other sources. Moreover, the helpful hand of Panton, Leslie and Company in Indian affairs might be weakened. An order was approved in Madrid on 9 June 1793 that, while making minor adjustments, very much maintained the status quo. Many of the East Florida settlers, and many in the States, saw the Spanish government's position only as a selfish one. Frustration with the 1793 order was generally shared by most of the leaders of the Florida rebellion of 1793–95; and it aroused considerable grass roots support for rebellion because the shortage of consumable goods was felt by everyone.

Minister Genêt left France in February of 1793; but, sailing against adverse winds, he arrived on 8 April at Charleston rather than at the more appropriate and ultimate destination of the capital city of Philadelphia. During March, France had declared war on Spain, thus making easier Genêt's task of finding American recruits to aid the esteemed ally, France. President Washington's policy was one of complete neutrality, however; and Genêt immediately became a problem for the American president.

The Girondists, who had been dominant in French politics and had launched Genêt on his American mission, fell from power at the hands of more radical elements in the French Convention in June of 1793, thus making the efforts of Genêt less secure and less authoritative. Although he pressed forward with his original plans and instructions, the broad vision of liberating Spanish colonies in South America was to be postponed to await the outcome of operations in Louisiana and the Floridas.

With the coming of Genêt there simultaneously sprang up in America local societies strongly supportive of the new French republic. Often they were called "democratic" societies. Earlier there had been democratic societies in America to stimulate strong adherence by politicians and others to the basic rights of man. Similar societies existed in France and England, formed to commemorate England's revolution of 1688, which had expelled an English tyrant and enthroned a prince of popular choice, William II.

In America, the Sons of Liberty had been organized in 1765, and during the Revolution the Committees of Correspondence had furnished unparalleled philosophical and political leadership for the war and for the government. Patron saints—inspirers—of the democratic societies after the Revolution were Locke and Rousseau, particularly the latter. The arrival of Genêt in America not only gave great impetus to all such societies but also increased popular concern for liberty—not only in America and in France but wherever it might bloom. Jefferson wrote: "All of the old spirit of 1776 is rekindling."[6]

Substantial opposition to the policies of these societies came from those who strongly supported President Washington's policies of conservatism and strict neutrality. Various conservative societies were established to support the administration. From the development of these societies of opposing views eventually emerged the two-party system of American politics.

Soon after his arrival in America, Genêt made contact with General George Rogers Clark. The general was to lead the main attack by Kentucky frontiersmen against New Orleans and Louisiana. William Tate, a distinguished Virginian now of South Carolina, was to lead a force down the Tennessee River to the Mississippi and cooperate with the Kentucky forces.[7] Colonel Samuel Hammond, another Virginia patriot now of Georgia, was to command the attack on St. Augustine in coordination with General Elijah Clark of Georgia, who was to attack West Florida as well.[8] Clark had led the attack against the British in Florida at the battle of Alligator Bridge in 1778.

6. Quoted in Eugene Perry Link, *Democratic-Republican Societies, 1790–1800*, p. 46 (an excellent study of the political and philosophical societies of this era).

7. Tate was active in the democratic societies of both states and was a trustee of Wythe Academy of Virginia and of Weemsborough Academy of South Carolina. See Link, *Democratic-Republican Societies*, p. 171.

8. Hammond (1757–1842) was born in Richmond County, Virginia. He served as a lieutenant colonel for the patriots in the American Revolution. A member of the U.S. House of Representatives from 1803 to 1805, he was a partner of the trading firm of Hammond and Fowler. From 1805 to 1824 he was military and civil commander of the District of Upper Louisiana; thereafter he moved to South Carolina, where he was surveyor general in 1826 and secretary of state in 1831. See *Webster's Biographical Dictionary* (Springfield, Mass.: G. & C. Merriam Co., 1943) s. v. "Hammond, Samuel." Elijah Clark migrated from North

Jefferson knew many of the details of the planning from the very start; and in the beginning he seemed quite sympathetic and was of substantial assistance to Genêt. The primary motivation of Jefferson was the possible acquisition of the Floridas for the United States. Supporters of the French venture included those who wished to aid the French Republic in establishing sovereignty in the lands that were to be taken, and those who supported the idea of independent countries adjacent to the United States, all to remain under the influence of France. Many were convinced that the Floridas after gaining independence would ultimately become a part of the United States.

At the request of Genêt, Jefferson wrote a letter of introduction to Governor Shelby of Kentucky on behalf of André Michaux,[9] a French botanist who was planning to travel in Kentucky, ostensibly for scientific studies. The letter was intended to give Michaux some standing with the governor—not only in the field of botanical research but also in the field of politics—by informing him that Michaux possessed the good opinion of Genêt, who desired Jefferson to make Michaux known to Shelby. Both Michaux and Genêt thus profited by the letter, which by implication gave some sanction to the deeds of both Frenchmen.

In the southeast the able French consul at Charleston, Michel Ange Bernard de Mangourit,[10] handled political and other matters directed against Spanish rule, in Florida particularly. His

---

Carolina to South Carolina and then to Georgia before the American Revolution, in which he was a hero; he was famous as an Indian fighter. (Others sometimes spelled his name "Clarke," but not Elijah.) See Louise F. Hays, *Hero of Hornet's Nest; A Biography of Elijah Clark, 1733–1799*, especially pp. viii, 296.

9. Michaux (1746–1802) was a French botanist; he traveled in the Tigris and Euphrates valleys (1782–85), in the United States (1785–96), and in Madagascar (1801–2). He collaborated with his son François. André Michaux's works were published in French (*Histoire des Chênes*, 1801) and Latin (*Flora Boreali-Americana, 1803*). François' works were published in French as *Voyage à l'Ouest* (1804) and *Histoire des Arbes* (1810–13), translated as *The North American Sylva*. See *Webster's Biographical Dictionary*, s. v. "Michaux, André."

10. Mangourit (1752–1829) was a diplomat and writer. See Larousse, *Grand dictionnaire universel du XIX siècle* (Paris, 1860–90), s. v. "Mangourit, Michel Ange Bernard de." A useful listing of French consular officers in the United States in the 1790s is in M. S. Fletcher, "French Consular States Agents in the United States, 1791–1800." Mangourit biographical data is from *American Historical Association Report* (1903), p. 930.

most active lieutenant was Major C. M. F. de Bert,[11] a French veteran of the American Revolution. De Bert wrote to Mangourit on 13 February 1793 about French troubles with Spain, American reactions to them, and current turbulences in Florida, covering the most sensitive information in his report by the use of the following secret code words:[12]

Later in the year Mangourit sent Citizen Fremin, a subordinate French consular officer at Savannah, to the St. Marys and St. Johns rivers to cruise about in a small vessel in order to pinpoint the location of the Spanish defenses.[13]

In August of 1793 Mangourit wrote to Genêt that General McIntosh in Georgia was doing all he could for the cause.[14] (The reference was certainly to Lachlan McIntosh[15] rather than to his nephew John, whose highest title at that time was colonel and who was already a resident of Florida.) He added that Major de Bert, William Tate, Elijah Clark, Stephen Drayton (the South Carolina governor's secretary), and the brothers Samuel and Abner Hammond were busy about this work.[16] Clark, major

11. De Bert fought under Casimir Pulaski during the American Revolution. In the 1790s he served under Mangourit as an assistant French consular officer at Savannah. He was active in the recruiting and organizing of the Florida project. See Richard K. Murdoch, "Citizen Mangourit and the Projected Attack on East Florida in 1794," particularly p. 526; see also Link, *Democratic-Republican Societies*, p. 136.

12. The original letter, the property of the Boston Public Library, is partly reproduced here by courtesy of the Trustees of the Boston Public Library.

13. See Richard K. Murdoch, *The Georgia-Florida Frontier, 1793–1796: Spanish Reaction to French Intrigue and American Designs*, p. 26.

14. Frederick J. Turner, "The Mangourit Correspondence in Respect to Genêt's Projected Attack on Louisiana and the Floridas."

15. Lachlan McIntosh (b. 1725, Scotland) came to Georgia in 1736, fought in the American Revolution in the South and North, and was made brigadier general on 16 September 1776. He wintered with Washington at Valley Forge in 1777–78 and was captured by the British at Charleston in 1780. See *Webster's Biographical Dictionary*, s. v. "McIntosh, Lachlan." The quotation concerning him in the text is from Turner, "Mangourit Correspondence."

16. The Hammonds were assisted in recruiting by their uncle LeRoy, who had been a colonel in the patriot forces of the American Revolution. When the French intrigue failed,

Edmond Charles Genêt. Courtesy of the Library of Congress, Washington, D.C.

general of the Georgia militia at the time, resigned his Georgia commission to accept one as a major general for France. Such a commission could be given by the French army or navy to nonnationals to award a temporary status or protection. Others with new French commissions were Abner Hammond, colonel of cavalry, and Brigadier Generals William Tate and Samuel Hammond.

The Hammonds operated an Indian trading firm, Hammond

Abner Hammond returned to mercantile and political pursuits in Georgia, living his last years in retirement in Milledgeville. See Murdoch, *Georgia-Florida Frontier*, pp. 25, 28, 40, 114; Hays, *Hero of Hornet's Nest*, p. 359.

and Fowler.[17] One of their strong interests in the matter was their desire to supplant Panton, Leslie and Company and to take over the lucrative Florida Indian trade. Local discontent with Panton, Leslie enhanced the prospects of Florida recruitments for rebellion. Despite repeated petitions for a much freer trade in Florida[18] (in part supported by the Spanish governor), Spain had not responded.

An event occurred in 1793 that embarrassed the success of the French project and brought to bear the heavy hand of President Washington. Genêt proposed to fit up a fast sailing corvette called the *Petite Démocrate* and provide her with ample armaments for use in southern waters in support of the plot. However, this plan violated Washington's orders against the arming of privateers in U.S. waters. Jefferson asked Genêt to take no steps until the president returned from Mount Vernon to Philadelphia and the matter could be discussed more fully on a cabinet level. Jefferson then reported to the cabinet that Genêt had agreed not to move the ship immediately. But Genêt changed his mind, renamed the ship *Cornelia,* after his fiancée in New York, added guns, and sailed off on a cruise. Washington was infuriated, not only because of the sailing but also because of statements attributed to Genêt, reported by Jefferson to the cabinet, that if Washington did not assist in the project Genêt would take his appeal from the president to the people.

Genêt went to President Washington in an effort to win his point. The president was courteous but gave him no encouragement. The French minister, in an effort to placate, stressed that the newspaper accounts had inaccurately quoted his criticisms. Genêt recorded that Washington "simply told me that he did not read the papers and that he did not care what they said concerning his Administration."[19]

17. Murdoch, *Georgia-Florida Frontier*, p. 26; Turner, "Mangourit Correspondence," pp. 572, 591.
18. See Arthur Preston Whitaker, *Documents Relating to the Commercial Policy of Spain in the Floridas* . . ., pp. 185, xxxvi; Janice Borton Miller, "Juan Nepomuceno de Quesada: Spanish Governor of East Florida, 1790–1795" (Ph.D. diss.), p. 199.
19. Minnigerode, *Jefferson, Friend of France*, p. 270.

On 15 September 1793 Washington asked France to recall Genêt; the new power structure in France honored this request on 22 February 1794. However, Genêt did not go back to France and did not, for a time at least, even retard his efforts to carry out his original plans. His lieutenants, both French and American, did not allow his recall to interfere with their own activity. In fact, Mangourit at Charleston was attempting to speed the operations along, and Major de Bert, French consul at Savannah, was actively enlisting followers and organizing the expedition.

The attack on St. Augustine was set for 10 April 1794. Genêt pursued efforts to find more ships to send to the St. Marys River for a coordinated land and sea attack. Michaux was at Charleston and the leaders in Georgia claimed to have thousands of men, under the leadership of General Samuel Hammond, ready for entry into Florida. A formal declaration of independence was prepared for Florida, promising ultimate independence under French protection and featuring in its heading the words "Equality" and "Liberty." Its salutation was "from the free French to their brothers in Florida."[20]

A new French minister, Antoine Fauchet, was sent to America bearing orders to arrest Genêt and send him back to France to face trial—orders based on Washington's request for his recall. However, Washington mercifully refused to permit the extradition and Genêt remained in America, became a naturalized American citizen, and eventually abandoned the active leadership of the revolutionary plans he had nurtured.

On 6 March 1794 the newspapers printed Fauchet's proclamation that every Frenchman was forbidden to violate the neutrality of the United States and that all commissions tending to infringe upon that neutrality were to be revoked and returned.

Though France, under pressure from the United States government, had officially repudiated Genêt and the use of the French flag in the planned revolutionary efforts in North America, she still stood to gain by any harassment given to Spain, a nation with which she was at war. So French agents in America

20. Turner, "Origin of Genêt's Projected Attack," p. 654.

continued to give quiet and ambiguous encouragement to the American rebel movement. In the Mississippi Valley the venture lost steam, partly because Spain liberalized slightly its rules for Mississippi River commerce; but the borderlands inhabitants in the Southeast, bolstered by French immigrants from the Caribbean and by French veterans of the American Revolution, still found the French flag a useful shield in rebellion against Spain in Florida. The Americans involved in these adventures reasoned for the most part that the U.S. avowal of neutrality was just window dressing since any new French republic in America would be U.S. territory as soon as the Spanish flag could be lowered.

In Florida there were subjects of Spain who were enthusiastic about the idea of freedom from Spanish rule. One of those counted upon by Samuel Hammond, Elijah Clark, and their associates was Colonel John McIntosh, with his strategically located plantation on the north side of the St. Johns River in what is now downtown Jacksonville. McIntosh carried on an extensive correspondence with General Samuel Hammond and with John Peter Wagnon, the Georgian who had served under McIntosh during the American Revolution and who had resided in St. Augustine since 1792.

When Abner Hammond came to Florida early in 1794, ostensibly to visit his wife and his father-in-law, William Jones, the Spanish authorities suspected that his real motive was to support the French revolutionary effort in Florida. He and Jones, along with McIntosh, Wagnon, William Plowden, and Richard Lang, were accused of crimes of rebellion against Spain. Abner Hammond and McIntosh were imprisoned in Morro Castle in Cuba. Lang, Wagnon, Jones, and Plowden were released after a few months' incarceration in Florida. Major de Bert, the veteran French military and consular officer involved in the Florida activities, wrote to the French consul at Charleston on 15 February 1794 that most of the persons imprisoned were "not in on the secret but from their known sentiments they were counted upon for help."[21]

21. Ibid.

The McIntosh plantation, Cerro Fuente, was ransacked and all correspondence and papers were seized. Knowing that her letters to her imprisoned husband would be read carefully by the Spanish authorities, the colonel's wife, Sarah, wrote cautiously to him that she had obtained the return of most of his letters and papers "except your agreement with Mr. Wagnon to bring in your cattle from Georgia and four letters from Colonel Samuel Hammond which he [the governor] informed me he had forwarded to the Captain General." She stressed that "this was far from being unpleasant, knowing full well the contents" to be innocent business and simply correspondence among old friends.[22] McIntosh and Hammond were not released for about a year, after a brisk correspondence to secure this end by Mrs. McIntosh, who was almost totally blind. She even invoked and secured the assistance of President Washington.

On the *affaire Genêt* Washington did not content himself with proclamations of neutrality and the official repudiation of Genêt's plans by the French. He arranged for the presence of troops to enforce neutrality at the Georgia border. There were rumors of Spanish troops moving northward toward the St. Marys while Captain Jonas Fauche, commanding American troops, marched south to the same destination. Fauche later wrote: "Before this, General Clark had withdrawn his garrisons; and at the aforementioned approach, his troops dispersed."[23] The French warship *Las Casas,* which had arrived at Amelia Island on 9 April, pulled away to return to Charleston before the end of the month; Clark withdrew his troops to Indian lands to the west of Georgia; and the French-inspired Florida revolution almost died aborning in 1794.[24]

As we shall see, Washington's opposition and France's official repudiation failed to put a stop to revolutionary activities in 1794.

22. George White, *Historical Collections of Georgia*, p. 552.
23. Fauche to Joseph Bevan, 5 February 1826, Joseph Bevan Papers, Georgia Historical Society.
24. The activities of *Las Casas* at Charleston and St. Marys were supportive of the rebellion (Murdoch, *Georgia-Florida Frontier*, pp. 13, 34). The warship withdrew from the Amelia Island support position in April 1794 (ibid., p. 165).

The end would not occur before shots were fired under the French flag in 1795. Meanwhile, the Spanish were investigating these activities and collecting testimony from their prisoners: John McIntosh, Richard Lang, John Peter Wagnon, William Jones, William Plowden, and Abner Hammond. Their depositions and the other documents presented in the following chapters give the background for the story of Florida's French revolution.

FOUR

Captain Lang and Colonel Hammond Expose the Rebellion

AS the Spanish investigations into the rebellion continued during 1794, documentary evidence was submitted to the governor of East Florida, Juan Nepomuceno de Quesada.[1] Quesada was in poor health in the early 1790s and made many efforts to retire. He was allowed to retire officially as of 30 April 1795 (to be succeeded later by Bartolomé Morales) but was unable to turn over the reins of government permanently until well into 1796.[2] The document

1. The common source for most of the documents pertaining to the French-induced rebellion against the Spanish government of East Florida presented in this volume is a single bundle (a *legajo*) of official papers (in this case a "litigation") preserved in the Archivo General de Indias, Papeles Procedentes de Cuba. These documents in legajo 166, *pormenor* ("subsection") 16, were located from a study made of Roscoe R. Hill's *Descriptive Catalogue of the Documents Relating to the History of the United States in the Papeles Procedentes de Cuba Deposited in the Archivo General de Indias at Seville* (p. 98). Most of the original documents are recorded in Spanish; these are printed here in translations by Charles E. Bennett. The original English-language documents from the legajo are identified as such in the source note, which appears in square brackets [ ] immediately above the first line of the document itself. Sometimes the next line is a heading [printed in *italic type* in this volume] that was entered for cross-reference by the clerk in the original document.

Copies of these documents are to be found in Box 293 in the East Florida Papers, Library of Congress, and there is a complete microfilm of all of legajo 166 in the Charles E. Bennett Collection of the Manuscript Division of the Library of Congress.

As this volume is being readied for the printer, the University of Florida's P. K. Yonge Library is preparing a calendar of their Spanish colonial documents, an expanding microfilm collection, which includes the East Florida Papers. That calendar may permit the later identification of still more documents bearing upon the French intrigue of 1794.

2. See Janice Borton Miller, "Juan Nepomuceno de Quesada: Spanish Governor of East Florida, 1790–1795" (Ph.D. diss.), for general biographical information; see also Richard K. Murdoch, *The Georgia-Florida Frontier, 1793–1796: Spanish Reaction to French Intrigue and American Designs*, p. 140.

bearing the earliest date of those collected in legajo 166, 29 December 1793, was generated by Captain Richard Lang, commander of the Spanish dragoons in the St. Marys Valley (see chapter 2). It is a formal statement taken by Lang from Ruben Pitcher, an immigrant from the United States who had settled near the St. Marys in 1790. Pitcher was an early collaborator in the French intrigue, returning to Georgia in 1793 as one of Samuel Hammond's principal recruiting agents.[3] Lang forwarded Pitcher's statement to Lieutenant Colonel Carlos Howard, commander of Spain's northern frontier in East Florida.

Howard, according to Luis de las Casas, Spain's governor of Cuba, was "an individual of mature judgment, capable, well informed, and one who has earned the esteem of the two governors under whose orders he has served." Of Irish descent, Howard had thirty years of military service behind him when he began his administrative duties in East Florida, first for Governor Zéspedes, then for Governor Quesada. He had fought for Spain in Brazil, at the Rio de la Plata, in the expedition of Havana in 1780, and in Santo Domingo. He then became an officer of the Irish infantry regiment stationed at St. Augustine. Zéspedes gave him the title of secretary of the government.[4]

[AGI, PC, leg. 166, pormenor 16, p. 64]

December 30, 1793

Sir:

I have transmitted to you a copy of Mr. Ruben Pitcher's statement, of which matter I expect to have a fuller account in a few days, which I will communicate either to you or his Excellency the Gov [ernor], as I intend to get to town on Saturday next if nothing unexpected happens.

3. Murdoch, *Georgia-Florida Frontier*, p. 156.
4. Lawrence Kinnaird, ed., *Spain in the Mississippi Valley, 1765-1794*, 2:34; Miller, "Quesada," p. 91; Helen H. Tanner, "Zéspedes and the Southern Conspiracies," p. 17. In 1797 Howard was sent on a reconnaissance of the upper Mississippi when it was feared Britain might attack Louisiana from Canada. Later he was made commanding officer of the Fixed Regiment of Louisiana. See Arthur Preston Whitaker, *Documents Relating to the Commercial Policy of Spain in the Floridas* . . ., p. 238.

I have further to inform you that I have made a confidant of Pitcher, begging you and his Excellency not to make it known where the intelligence comes from. He has proposed to me that he enlist with their forces to find out all the schemes and plans; and I will communicate anything that comes to my notice.

I hope you will excuse haste. I have some accounts of three Indians being at Mrs. Neely's house, she talking with them, giving them potatoes. I wish to go to see what they are about and what they say. I am with respect and affection, your humble servant

Richd. Lang

[AGI, PC, leg. 166, pormenor 16, p. 64]

Statement mentioned in the preceding letter:

Personally appeared before me Ruben Pitcher who, being duly sworn, says and deposes on his oath that he is informed by good authority that an expedition is forming against the Province of East Florida.

He further says that he has had some conversation with some of the recruiting officers; that they had enlisted in the County of Camden, Georgia, upwards of thirty men to plunder Florida.

He further says on his oath that he is informed that Colonel Samuel Hammond is to command the land forces; and that there are in Newton three frigates ready for the expedition.

He further says on his oath that Lieutenant Hardee,[5] the recruiting officer for said expedition, tried to enlist him for the intended expedition.

The deponent further says that he was informed that a vessel had arrived at the Newton landing, with provisions and a large number of entrenching tools.

He further says that he has every reason to believe that this said vessel is intended for this expedition.

5. John Hardee came from a prominent Camden County family, several of whom fought in the American Revolution. Their coastal plantation in the northern part of Camden County was called Rural Felicity (Marguerite G. Reddick, *Camden's Challenge: A History of Camden County, Georgia*, pp. 4, 22, 30, 54). Johannes reports that a distinguished descendant of his, Dr. Charles Hardee, settled on the Bell River near Amelia Island in the 1800s (Jan H. Johannes, *Yesterday's Reflections, Nassau County, Florida: A Pictorial History*, pp. 133–34).

He further says that he was informed that a late survey of the works of St. Augustine was taken together with the situation of the town.

The deponent further says that he is well informed in Camden County that the abovementioned Hammond is to recruit a force of 700 men there to take the oath of allegiance to France and then to plunder and take the Province of East Florida, with the assistance of the three frigates, which are to strike at the same time as the land forces do.

The deponent further sayeth not.

Ruben Pitcher

Sworn before me this 29th day of December, 1793.

Richard Lang

This is a true copy of the original that is actually in my possession.

Richd. Lang

Lieutenant Colonel Carlos Howard responded to Richard Lang in a note dated just one day after Lang's letter to Howard.

[AGI, PC, leg. 166, pormenor 16, p. 66]

Amelia Island at 11:30 on the night of December 31, 1793

Richard Lang.

Dear Sir:

I have just this instant received your letter of yesterday, which I shall use appropriately, with appreciation for its promptness. At the same time I want to inform you that the matter you talk about has been made public in the State of South Carolina, where the main agents have been arrested and condemned by a decree of the Governor. Such decree has been published in the newspaper of Savannah on the 19th of last month.

In any case, you and Captain Hall would do well to warn the people about this.

I am,

C. H.

P.S. You should also find out the reason for the visit of the Indians. These are copies translated from the originals that are in my possession.

Amelia Island, January 1, 1794

Carlos Howard

A week later, on 7 January 1794, Lieutenant Colonel Carlos Howard wrote to Governor Quesada. His letter enclosed two important statements taken by Howard from Abner Hammond, sergeant major of Georgia militia in Camden County, Georgia, and commissary general for the French-backed rebels in Florida.

[AGI, PC, leg. 166, pormenor 16, p. 53]

Official letter of Lieutenant Colonel Carlos Howard accompanying the testimony heretofore taken by him from Abner Hammond; and another paper which he submitted to him.

Confidential:

Señor Governor:

Day before yesterday at noon I received a letter from the American Abner Hammond asking me to go talk with him on Cumberland Island,[6] where he had some interesting things to tell me affecting the well being of Spain and the United States.

So, consequently, I went there in the afternoon; and, walking alone with me, he told me that the matter he wished to discuss with me was of such a nature as to require that I would, on my word of honor, never say that he gave me such information. I gave it to him in a formal way, not without thinking that the matter would be relating to the enlisting already known about; and so it was. But, finding out later that he had the full secret of the infamous conspiracy, I thought

---

6. Cumberland Island is the most southerly island in Georgia, just across the St. Marys from Amelia Island in Florida. It was the site of a sixteenth-century Spanish mission. Fortified by Oglethorpe in the eighteenth century, it was well populated before the town of St. Marys was established (Reddick, *Camden's Challenge*, p. 211). Most of it is now a part of National Park Service holdings, i.e., the Cumberland Island National Seashore.

of the little value that would come from reference to a simple conversation and how much more important it would be if all were documented.

I suggested this to him, adding that for better achieving the honorable ends he had in mind it would be best for him to accompany me to my post so we could discuss the matter more deliberately. He accepted this upon condition that I would give him a pass to St. Johns[7] and to St. Augustine, because he wanted to see Your Excellency. This is exactly what I wanted. He accompanied me to this post; and that same night I wrote down his sworn statement, a translated copy of which I enclose for Your Excellency, numbered one, and the second, a translation of the paper he wrote and signed the next morning.

There is no doubt that everything said is the straight truth; and, when supplemented by the copy of the original propositions made by the French agent De Burte, which Hammond will present to Your Excellency, it will constitute a convincing and detailed account of this evil plot.

I say that I am certain as to the truth of the testimony. What seems to confirm the good intentions of the witness is the clear proposition[8] set out in Number 2 that is about placing the provisions and war supplies of the conspiracy so that they can fall into the hands of the government, thus wrecking the projected expedition. But at the same time, I must confess that the confidence I now have in the man is more apparent than real, and it will remain so until I see all the preparations of the plotters completely under our control.

I do not like Hammond's proposal (although I have concealed my feelings from him) that before taking any steps against them, they be allowed to gather in Temple all of the supplies. It would seem to me to be more natural and less likely to arouse the suspicion of the conspirators if Hammond, returning from St. Augustine where at the latest he should be on the 14th, could cleverly tell his confederates and spread around in this river valley the news that he had gained the permission he sought from the Spanish government (because of the scarcities which have brought about the rebellion) to bring in a certain amount of provisions and farm equipment by means of an

7. There was a St. Johns town at the bluff in the late 1700s, but here the term was used to describe the lower St. Johns River valley, which today comprises most of Duval County.
8. Printed below at p. 44.

inner passage to the St. Johns River.[9] Consequently he could start sending in shipments without delay and deposit them in places which Your Excellency may deem safe and close at hand for easy seizure. The permit for the introduction should be put in writing and limited to small amounts.

In order to satisfy Hammond and with his knowledge, I shall let everything pass through here in all quantities; and the excess over Your Excellency's licensed amounts will always be a sufficient excuse for the Royal Estate to take it all over whenever desired.

If Hammond acts accordingly in good faith, the greatest difficulty I foresee is finding enough small vessels to provide transportation for these goods. Such are in very short supply in this river.

Everything considered, I feel that the disclosure of the plot in Carolina, and the recommendation afterwards made by the Legislature of Georgia in the middle of last month and to their Governor on the same matter, must have weakened, if not killed entirely, the plans of the conspiracy; and I firmly believe that even in the event that the plot had not been uncovered, [not even] a third of those enlisted would have come together inside the Indian Line.

That the project was formed and was intended to be carried off I am sure; but I still consider it to be the fruit of the thoughtless fanaticism, temerity, and impudence that distinguish the rebellious Ambassador Genêt and his diabolic masters, the National Convention.

It is appropriate to add that I learned through a conversation with Abner Hammond that the French commissions or certificates would not be handed over to the leaders in the conspiracy until they are outside the boundaries of Georgia, with the idea that this would exempt the behavior and the people from all the responsibilities to the laws of the United States.

In order to assure keeping the secrecy that I had promised Hammond, before trusting the words of his statement, paper, and letter to the clerk whom I was obliged to use, I formally swore him [the clerk] to secrecy about the whole affair as a Christian and loyal subject.

I have the intention, if Your Excellency approves, to write

9. The inner passage, or inland waterway of today, had been but slightly improved at the time. Some work on it was done by patriots during the American Revolution (Charles E. Bennett, *Southernmost Battlefields of the Revolution*, p. 17).

another letter to the Governor of Georgia letting him know the contents of the recent statement and naming all the conspirators, without omitting same Don Abner as Commissary elect of the expedition.

God keep Your Excellency many years,

Amelia Island, January 7, 1794

Carlos Howard

Juan Nepomuceno de Quesada

The first of Hammond's statements transmitted to the governor by Howard's foregoing letter was given orally to Howard and recorded by the Spanish officer. The second was written by Hammond himself. It offered what had been suggested previously, a betrayal of his associates. The means of accomplishing the betrayal were outlined and the motives for it stated.

[AGI, PC, leg. 166, pormenor 16, p. 40—in English]

Statement by Abner Hammond concerning a conspiracy formed against the two Floridas and Louisiana.

Number 1.

Charles Howard, Lieutenant Colonel of his Majesty's Army, Captain of Grenadiers in the Third Battalion of the Regt of Cuba, and Temporary Commandant of the Spanish frontier on the River St. Marys in the Province of East Florida——On the fifth day of January of the year 1794 in the Island of Amalia of the abovementioned province, on the aforesaid frontier and river personally appear'd before me one Abner Hammond Esqre major of the militia in Camden County of the State of Georgia, who in presence of two assisting witness, Justo López and Emmanuel Bernal, being duly sworn on the Holy Evangelists, in consequence of his professing the Protestant religion, declareth spontaneously, and at his own request and desire by virtue of the said oath, as follows.

That previous to his the deponents departure from his residence at Temple on this River of St. Mary, which departure was on the first day of last November he had reports of men there being enlisting the States of Georgia and South Carolina under French commissions for the purposes of levying war against His Catholic Majesty's possessions, particularly against East and West Florida and the Louisiana; but of this deponent did not make any account or give faith to at that time, but upon his arrival at Augusta the seat of government in Georgia he found it to be true, having been invited to engage in the business by various persons already concerned in it, in the first instance by Mr. De Burte agent for the French Republick, and who had formerly serv'd in the American Army in the Regiment Pulawski, Colonel Samuel Hammond, who was to have the command of the troops to be rais'd in Georgia, Colonel Henry Hampton, a member of the Senate of said State, as was the abovemention'd Samuel a representative, and several other individuals of respectability, whose names deponent considers superfluous to specify; the above persons, after disclosing the business, propos'd to deponent to engage in it, which he declined, insisting insisting [*sic*] strenuously on the risquiness of the attempt and that such a proceeding militated flagrantly against the honour and laws of the general government of the United States; but the arguments made use of by deponent were of no avail and were laughed at and even caused a dispute and dissatisfaction between deponent and his brother, the above [mentioned] Colonel Samuel Hammond.

From these circumstances after two days weighing the matter, deponent judged that the best method he could adopt to keep himself out of trouble, to reclaim his brother Samuel, and to [*sic*] his duty to his country, would be to shew an appearance of his being convinced by the arguments urged to him and share with the proposals to obtain a fuller knowledge of the general tendency of the designs, to be the better able to free his brother, his country and himself from the disagreeable consequences which must inevitably attend so wild and unlawfull a project; in consequence of which accession of deponent to their proposals, they laid open their whole plan to him, and appointed him commissary of stores for the intended expedition, part of which stores, consisting of forty-five barrels of flour, ten of pork, and five of beef, with one dozen of shovels, one dozen of spades and four dozen of hoes, and four hundred and twenty-seven gallons of rum, are actually lodged at deponent's house at Temple brought round from Savanah in the schooner *Lively,* Captain Sherman, the same one that Mr. Oliver[10] is said to have freighted to carry him and his party from Cumberland to Augustine. Deponent adds the leaders of the expedition are to send forward to Temple as much greater [a] quantity of provisions and military stores, arms and ammunition to be sent to the same place but none are being forwarded as yet. That number enroll'd are said to be six hundred, the commander to be the abovementioned Samuel Hammond the second in command Henry Kerr,[11] late Colonel of militia in Green County and the third a Mr. Oliver,[12] whose Christian name deponent is unacquainted with but comprehends he was formerly settled in Charleston in the mercantile line. Deponent further adds that there are captains and subalterns appointed, but does not know the name of any of them, except having heard, since his return from Savannah, four days ago and by land that Mr. William Knecblack[13] of Camden County is one of the captains. Deponent further adds the officers and men were to be pay'd cloath'd and ration'd on the same footing as the federal Troops of the United States. That when the whole will be ready to be carry'd into execution, the people enroll'd are to march in small partys to the place of rendezvous (the particular spot deponent is unacquainted with, nor does he think it is fix'd upon as yet). However he believes it will be somewhere within the Indian Line, near the fork of the Oconees, to be the sooner clear of the State of Georgia and from there to fall down towards the head of St. Marys, and there enter East Florida there to find some [illegible] provisions at Temple; it being encharged to deponent to procure beforehand a permitt from the Spanish government to transport the greater part to the river at St. Johns under the appearance of disposing of them there at public market, to the [illegible] to which deponent agreed, tho firmly resolved to disclose the whole to the Spanish government.

Deponent being asked if any part or the whole of the above had

10. This was probably Captain Pedro Oliver, a Spanish officer who was given the task of trying to dissuade the Indians from giving up the lands agreed upon in the U.S. treaty of 1790, New York (Murdoch, *Florida-Georgia Frontier*, p. 46; James F. Doster, *The Creek Indians and Their Florida Lands, 1740–1823*, 1:164).

11. Colonel Henry Kerr of Greene County, Georgia, raised many recruits for Samuel Hammond (Murdoch, *Georgia-Florida Frontier*, p. 27).

12. This Mr. Oliver was originally from Greene County, Georgia; he moved to Charleston and from there recruited men for Samuel Hammond (ibid.).

13. William Niblack was a leader in Camden County affairs and was instrumental in establishing St. Marys as the county seat (Reddick, *Camden's Challenge*, pp. 5, 6, 22).

come to the knowledge of the executive government of the State [of Georgia]——sayeth that he believes that the government had come to the knowledge of part, but not of the whole, and that said part was not known by government, until after deponent left Augusta, which was to the best of his recollection the fifteenth of last month a day more or less. Deponent further sayeth that at Savannah he heard from good authority that the affair had been brought forward at the assembly, deponent does not recollect by whom, but that in consequence a motion was made to adopt the same measures to stop the progress of so vile a proceeding as had been adopted for the same purpose at South Carolina but the motion was overruled. All the proponents of it could affect was that a recommendation should be passed to the governour, to [illegible] that he might issue a proclamation forbidding the enlistment of men under a foreign authority, and further the assembly voted that the governour should use such means as were legally permitted to quash any such enlistments.

Deponent being asked if said expedition against the Spanish dominions are to be supported by any naval force——sayeth he was inform'd by the abovemention'd French agent that it would be supported by seven, or [illegible] arm'd frigates, but deponent does not know where said armed force was to come from or be collected.

It is remarked that deponent in the beginning of his declaration said the ringleaders of the enlistments had in view the invasions of the two Floridas and the Louisiana, yet farther on in his declaration he specifys the design to be particularly against East Florida. He is therefore asked how he can account for that difference. Deponent says that the partys enlisted in South Carolina were of an understanding with that of Georgia and the two had combin'd their operations; for the better effecting of which Colonel Tate of the South Carolina party had repair'd to Augusta whilst deponent was yet there and it was agreed that the South Carolina corps should assemble at the Muscle Shoals on the Tennessee to proceed against West Florida and the Louisiana. [Illegible] from Carolina being to be joined by parties from the Western [sic] Country and Kentucky; and that the whole was to be commanded by General Clarke; the Georgia corps being to act separately against East Florida as declared above. And farther deponent sayeth that he had in his hands at Temple a copy of the original proposals made by aforesaid French agent to deponent's brother Samuel, which copy deponent is ready to produce to Colonel Howard or his Excellency Gov. John [Nepomuceno] de Quesada to which purpose he wishes to go to Augustine.

Deponent being ask'd if any of the people of Coleraine, or of his own stockade at Temple are concerned in the business and particularly if a Lieutenant Hardy or an Ensign Howard[14] are of the number——sayeth that since his return he has heard that Hardy, and the abovementioned Knecblack were concerned in the business, also one Brown[15] at the Station of Satilly, but deponent does not believe that Howard is concern'd, and deponent has also heard that one Hampton of Coleraine is likewise concern'd; deponent here recollects that he this day wrote to Knecblack and Hardy to meet him tomorrow at Temple, on purpose to enquire as party concern'd, how far they are engaged in the business, deponent being persuaded that they are not engaged in the same party that he is and wishes to know who may be their employers: and further deponent sayeth not, except that what he has declared above is truth and nothing but the truth by virtue of the oath he hath taken, and that he is thirty-two years of age, in testimony whereof he signs this his declaration after having read it word by word to his own satisfaction in presence of the abovenamed witnesses.

A. Hammond
Carlos Howard
Justo López
Manual Bernal

January 7, 1794

[AGI, PC, leg. 166, pormenor 16, p. 444—in English]

Abner Hammond's paper written in English and signed in his own handwriting, on the morning after the night he gave his statement to Carlos Howard.

Number 2.

It might appear presumptious in me (after the information given) to pretend to advise what measures might best be taken, that I

---

14. William Howard, a U.S. army officer stationed in Georgia, assisted in the enlistment for the French intrigue (Miller, "Quesada," p. 242).

15. Jacob R. Brown served under William Tate (Louise F. Hays, *Hero of Hornet's Nest; A Biography of Elijah Clark, 1733 to 1799*, p. 243).

therefore must submit to the superior judgment of his Exclncy the Governor and any measures adopted by him will be readyly agreed to by me [if] they do not extend to discover my having given information of the business which to me would be dangerous and prejudicial to the measures to be taken to prevent the progress thereof.

As a considerable quantity of provisions more are to be ship'd to me, I should judge that when the whole may be receiv'd I might be permited to send them for sale to St. Johns, where they may, from some information given by some other person, be siez'd on by the government as property of the French Republick, in which case I should expect that my expences and trouble in the business would be paid by the government and, as I have given recepts and shall be oblig'd to give others for all I may receive, I shall expect that the government will indemnify me for any damage therefrom and the french property being put into their hands by me will judge the propriety of what would be a proper disposial thereof.

As the whole of the provisions are to be rec'd by me and stored previous to any movements being made by the troops and as they are to wait my advice when the provisions are ready, it may be so fix'd that the first advice I give them will be that I have been admited to send the provisions to St. Johns and that after their being stor'd there a suspicion had arisen or some information been given and that the provisions a[re] seized on by the government & remov'd to St. Augustine, which will put a stop to the movement of the men, not being able to procure supplies.

As I am to be in Augustine it is my wish that the communications there be had through some good and confidential person; perhaps Father O'Riley[16] would be the most [proper] person, I being acquainted with his brother, and with the uprightness of his own charactor.

And for my own safety as well as to have it in my power more effectually to prevent the intended business it is my wish that the information from me be known to as few persons as possible.

Amelia—6 Jany., 1794—

A. Hammond.

16. Father O'Reilly spoke four languages and taught in the school at St. Augustine (Miller, "Quesada," p. 110). Variant spellings of proper names have been preserved in this study unless otherwise noted.

[AGI, PC, leg. 166, pormenor 16, p. 82—in English]

A letter from Abner Hammond to Richard Lang of 1st November.

1 Nov. 1793

Dear Sir:

I herewith send a letter for Mr. Jones which I will thank you to send by the first safe hand and the mare also.

I have engaged the wagon for Mr. Jones if the money can be sent soon to Capt. Dawson, of which I inform Jones by the letter to him & you may also inform him if he sends the money shortly he can have her. I am in haste, just setting out for Augusta.

Remain dr sir

Your most obt servt

A. Hammond

Captn Lang

Royal House, residence of the Spanish governors at St. Augustine. From a 1764 watercolor, courtesy of the National Park Service.

FIVE

Council of War, 16 January 1794;

Statements by Hall, Arons, and Cryer

AT the Royal House in St. Augustine, the governor's mansion on the plaza, Governor Quesada called the following officers together in a council of war on 16 January 1794. Colonel Bartolomé Morales, commander of the Third Battalion of the Cuban Infantry Regiment, had been intendant of Louisiana before coming to St. Augustine in 1791. During the governor's frequent illnesses, Morales was called upon to act in his stead. Captain Juan Remedios, the ranking artillery officer in East Florida, and Pedro Salcedo, another captain of artillery, were also present. Pedro Berrio was the ranking officer of the engineers in East Florida and regularly advised the governor on the improvement of defenses, particularly those of Amelia Island.[1] Gonzalo Zamorano was the colony's accountant; when the governor was ill, Zamorano assumed his duties in fiscal matters.[2] Manuel Rengil held the title of government secretary of East Florida.

The council of war decided that John McIntosh, Richard Lang, Abner Hammond, William Jones, John Peter Wagnon, and William Plowden should be arrested for their suspicious behavior in connection with the rebellion. John McIntosh, because of his responsibilities as lieutenant governor for the St. Johns River district, had apparently violated his trust by not reporting the

1. Richard K. Murdoch, *The Florida-Georgia Frontier, 1793–1796: Spanish Reaction to French Intrigue and American Designs*, p. 168.
2. Ibid., p. 163.

rebellion promptly. Although Richard Lang, captain of one of the companies of dragoons on the St. Marys River, had originally insisted on the fortifying of a house at San José on the upper St. Marys, he had then suspiciously urged abandoning it despite its strategic location at an entry into Florida.[3] Abner Hammond was ordered arrested because of his failure to report the progress of his plot to subvert the rebellion. William Jones, father-in-law of Hammond, and William Plowden[4] were apprehended under more general allegations of suspicion.

That same day the governor received an unsigned letter making secret accusations against McIntosh, Jones, Plowden, and other Americans residing in the St. Johns River valley, and asserting that they could be expected to join the rebellion and that the people in the St. Marys and Nassau valleys were mostly Tories, who could be expected to resist an American-supported rebellion. Lang was also implicated because of his close friendships with people in the St. Johns area. This unsigned letter was probably written by Captain Nathaniel Hall, commander of the Spanish militia in the lower valley of the St. Marys. In the proceedings he was noted as being present at a meeting wherein he submitted a statement. Evidence concerning his identity is to be found in the language of an order of 20 January based on the conclusions of the council of war. Hall also gave a formal statement under oath on 17 January and wrote a letter to Carlos Howard dated 19 January, both of which are included in this chapter along with statements by other Florida residents, George Arons and Thomas Cryer.[5]

3. The exact location of San José has not been pinpointed, but it seems probable that it was either across the river from Coleraine, a major point of entry, or more likely about five miles to the west, since Lang said it was about ten miles from Florida settlement and that location would be ten miles west from Lang's house. The latter location became the major entry into Florida in the later years. A detachment of Spanish dragoons was ordered there on 16 January 1794 (Janice Borton Miller, "Juan Nepomuceno de Quesada: Spanish Governor of East Florida, 1790–1795" [Ph.D. diss.], p. 242).

4. Plowden had settled in St. Augustine around 1791 and purchased a large house there in the Calle de Marina. He fled to Georgia because of the exposure of the intrigue, and his properties were confiscated (Murdoch, *Florida-Georgia Frontier*, p. 157).

5. Cryer had been granted 500 acres south of the St. Marys on 6 November 1790 ("Spanish Land Grants in Florida," Florida Department of Agriculture, 3:30; Murdoch,

The statement by Arons gave many details of the planned invasion and quoted Ruben Pitcher as saying that Richard Lang had been planning to leave his Spanish post as militia captain on the St. Marys but was dissuaded by John McIntosh, who had urged Lang "instead to keep his commission because very shortly this province would be free and independent; and then he would command this river and McIntosh the St. Johns." Thomas Cryer stated in his testimony about John McIntosh that Ruben Pitcher had said of McIntosh "some months ago" that he "knew and participated fully in the plot of the Georgians."

[AGI, PC, leg. 166, pormenor 16, p. 19]

Two articles, beginning and end of the Council of War.

At the Council of War held on the day of this writing, in the Royal House which serves as the residence of the governors at St. Augustine, East Florida, those present were Don Juan Nepomuceno de Quesada, Colonel in the Royal Army, Governor of said City and Province, who, as president, authorized the council and as committeemen convened by him, Colonel Bartolomé Morales, Commander of the Third Battalion of the Regiment of Infantry of Cuba: the Captains of the Royal Corps of Artillery, Pedro Salcedo and Juan Remedios; Pedro Berrios, engineer; Gonzalo Zamorano, Comptroller of the Royal Treasury; and myself, Manuel Rengil, Interim Secretary of this government; so that the following could be accomplished in the council meeting:

Said President reported all the secret and clandestine information that he had received from the shores of the St. Johns and St. Marys rivers, all relating to the enlisting of a group of Americans, certain people from the State of Georgia, on the boundary of this province under commissions and directions from the French with intent of attacking this province; he read several paragraphs of letters and other documents relating to the same matters, and all that

---

Florida-Georgia Frontier, p. 175). Jan H. Johannes identifies Cryer's holdings as the lands that the British set aside for their new communities of New Bermuda and Hillsborough on the St. Marys River, the latter having been settled by John Bethune and others from the Isle of Skye in 1772 (see *Yesterday's Reflections, Nassau County, Florida: A Pictorial History*, pp. 101–3).

he had written about the matter to the Governor of Georgia and to the Spanish and English ministers established in various places around the United States, demonstrating to them a justified suspicion and mistrust of certain Americans recently admitted as subjects of his Majesty and established in this city and on the shores of said rivers.

Everything being fully considered under mature reflection and with a view to the risks that such proceedings entail and with the determination to prevent and avoid such in every way possible, the council unanimously and with common accord, without dissent, agreed and decided upon the following things:

Article I

With regard to the fact that John MacIntosh, who is authorized the title of Lieutenant Governor in the District of the St. Johns River, has violated government regulations by giving open protection to Diego Allen[6] and John Peter Wagnon, men known to be perverse and under suspicion, and that he has also failed to communicate to the government as he should the schemes that are being plotted in the State of Georgia, which are public knowledge and notorious along the entire length of that river and, moreover, that he has seen and dealt with Abner Hammond, one of those planning to invade this province and in charge of collecting supplies for said expedition, and brother of the main leader of it:

For these acts and others described by the President at said meeting, he is suspected of conspiring with enemies of the State; and it is ordered that he be arrested this night while he is in this city without a license from the government and without any excuse that could justify his so coming, thus increasing the suspicion against him.

Because of similar reasons for suspicion, Richard Lang, Captain of one of the companies of dragoons on the St. Marys River, should also be arrested, since he, having fortified a house at the expense of the Royal Treasury at the upper part of said river (at a place called San José) all because of concern expressed by the inhabitants there and mainly by said Lang, now insists that it be abandoned under frivolous pretense; and in addition said house is on the entry into this province, and to this may be added that he

6. Allen wanted to trade with Indians in Florida, and McIntosh was accused of encouraging this violation of rules (Miller, "Quesada," p. 239).

communicated with said Abner Hammond before coming to this city where he now is. And other reasons for mistrust were stated by the President against said Lang.

William Plowden should also be arrested because of the mistrust and suspicion which the President has and has made known against him.

It is ordered that these three men be put in separate cells and without communication until examined by the government, removing from them all the papers they possess; and that somebody be sent to the house of John MacIntosh to pick up the papers he may have there so they can be scrutinized and examined.

Article II

In view of the fact that Abner Hammond had suggested to Carlos Howard that he would negotiate with the Governor about taking to the St. Johns River the military supplies and food which were planned for use in the invasion of this province from the State of Georgia; and also about designating the spot or spots where they could be gathered together so that after they had been assembled the Spanish Government could confiscate them as being French, and that he stipulated the fourteenth of this month as the latest date to arrange this, and it being already the sixteenth without finalization and he being still on the St. Johns River negotiating and conferring with residents there who are suspect to the government (among them John MacIntosh and William Jones, a rebellious man of restless disposition and father-in-law of said Hammond), said Hammond because of his acts is under suspicion of conspiring with residents along said river while pretending to come in good faith to deal with the Governor: and it is believed and presumed that his devious intention is to lull the government with attractive offers, while truly collaborating with his confederates. It is ordered that someone trustworthy go to the home of William Jones, taking with him enough escort to arrest said Abner Hammond and said William Jones, his father-in-law, bringing them to this city with all the papers that can be found.

That the detail, having accomplished this, go on to the home of Richard Lang and pick up and bring back to the Governor all the papers that are found there so they can be inspected too.

Conclusion of the council.

The preceding points were determined and unanimously ap-

proved for the better service of the King; and after being signed by
the President they were also signed by the other members. I certify
to this in St. Augustine, January 16, 1794.

> Juan Nepomuceno de
> Quesada
> Bartolomé Morales
> Pedro José Salcedo
> Juan Remedios
> Pedro Diaz Berrio
> Gonzalo Zamorano
> Manuel Rengil

[This document] reproduces the two articles, conclusion, and
preamble of the original meeting which were given to me to produce
this testimony and which I returned to the Secretary of Government;
and in accordance with orders I attest to it in St. Augustine, Florida,
today, January 22, 1794.

> José de Zubizarreta,
> government reporter

[AGI, PC, leg. 166, pormenor 16, p. 12]

Copy of the secret accusation.[7]

East Florida, January 16, 1794

To His Excellency the Governor:

Dear Sir:

In regard to what I mentioned to Your Excellency this morning I
am of the opinion that if a group of Americans were to come to take
over or plunder this province many of the residents of the St. Johns
area instead of defending the country would go against it and maybe
would join them: like MacIntosh, Plowden, Goodwin,[8] Jones, Sterling[9] and a majority of those that came lately from the United States.

7. This letter was probably written by Nathaniel Hall.
8. The house of Francis Goodwin was searched and suspicious materials were found
there. He left the province but was allowed to return and reoccupy his old plantation,
Strawberry Hill (Murdoch, *Georgia-Florida Frontier*, pp. 107, 171).
9. Francis Sterling married Mary Lang, second daughter of Richard Lang, about 1790

As to the people of the St. Marys and the Nassau, who were mainly British subjects before, it is evident that in general they hate the Americans, and consequently they would defend the Province.

Concerning Captain Lang, he appears to be very close to the people of the St. Johns mentioned above, but that may not mean there is anything wrong intended; but if so I will discover it, and will send the appropriate message to Colonel Carlos Howard; and I will do likewise with any other thing that I hear of that would be harmful to the Province.

Sir, the most obedient friend and humble servant of Your Excellency.

Certified that the foregoing is a faithful copy of the original in the secretariat temporarily under my charge and its signature is concealed in accordance with the stipulation in the Order which heads [the report of] this business.

Saint Augustine, Florida, January 21, 1794

Manuel Rengil

[AGI, PC, leg. 166, pormenor 16, p. 67]

Order.

Amelia Island, January 16, 1794.

Carlos Howard, Lieutenant Colonel of the Royal Army, Captain of the Grenadiers of the Third Battalion of the Regiment of Infantry of Cuba and Interim Commander of the Spanish frontier:

With reference to Samuel Russell,[10] Orderly of the Militia of this river valley, having come last night to tell me that George Arons, a local resident, had told him various things about the covert enlisting of people in Georgia for hostilities against this province; and that Arons had a neighbor in Georgia who had told him about this so that Arons could protect his property; that this information was given by

---

(Folks Huxford, *Pioneers of Wiregrass Georgia: A Biographical Account of Some of the Early Settlers* . . ., 5:256). He should not be confused with Thomas Sterling, a Spanish justice of the peace (see p. 85 in this volume).

10. Samuel Russell settled on the south side of the St. Johns River in the early 1790s and afterwards sold the 650-acre tract to Francis Richard (Pleasant D. Gold, *History of Duval County, Florida*, p. 68). Russell was in the Spanish militia (see p. 57 in this volume).

his neighbor in gratitude for Arons having saved his life some years before; and upon the Orderly's asking Arons why he did not report it to me, he responded that he was ready to do it when I would call him; so consequently I sent the Orderly to bring him to me; and in the meantime I ordered this document signed with two witnesses to have it ready so that when the aforesaid Arons appeared I could examine him about the matters mentioned above. Consequently I've ordered it drawn up and signed with witnesses.

Carlos Howard

Justo López

Manuel Bernal

[AGI, PC, leg. 166, pormenor 16, p. 4]

Statement by Nathaniel Hall.

St. Augustine, Florida, January 17, 1794.

Juan Nepomuceno de Quesada, Colonel of the Royal Army, Governor, Commanding General, Royal Protector and Administrator of the Royal Estate in said City and Province for his Majesty: Since the prompt return to the St. Marys River of the Captain of Militia of that area, Nathaniel Hall, is important, given that Richard Lang, also Captain of Militia on that river, has been imprisoned by order of His Lordship in the fortress [the Castillo de San Marcos][11] of this place, and it being necessary that said Hall testify about some aspects of the imprisonment of Lang, and of others. Hall was ordered to appear before His Lordship and Manuel Rengil, secretary of this government, and took an oath by God and by all that he believes

---

11. St. Augustine was originally fortified in 1565. The fort was made of wood and was followed by eight other wooden and earthen forts. When Charleston was settled by the English in 1670, the need for a stronger fort seemed evident. Spain built the present *coquina* fort in the period 1672–95, replacing the last wooden fort. It withstood a 50-day siege by John Moore's Carolinians in 1702 and repeated efforts by Oglethorpe in the 1740s, including a 38-day siege. After the British capture of Charleston in 1780, the South Carolinians brought to the Castillo as prisoners were Lieutenant Governor Christopher Gadsden and three signers of the Declaration of Independence: Arthur Middleton, Edward Rutledge, and Thomas Heyward, Jr. The signers had the freedom of the town, but the lieutenant governor was imprisoned. See Luis Arana and Albert Manucy, ''The Building of Castillo de San Marcos'' (manuscript).

in the Bible according to his Protestant beliefs and under this he promised to tell the truth of what he knew and was asked; and he responded as follows:

Asked what day he had left the St. Marys River, if alone, or with others:

He said he had left there last Saturday, the eleventh of this month, alone, and that he arrived in the nighttime near the St. Johns River and that at about half a mile from its bank he went to sleep in the field, and that the next morning he crossed the river by the pass of San Nicolás,[12] from whence he went to the house of William Jones, who has charge of it.

Asked about whom he found there, whether he went somewhere else, and with whom did he come from there to this city:

He said that he found Mr. Hammond in the house, a resident of the State of Georgia and the son-in-law of William Jones; that having asked him about Captain Lang, whom he expected to find there because of a message left for him on the 8th of this month at the St. Marys by Mr. Blunt, an inhabitant there, they told him that Lang had been waiting for him some two or three days but that during this time he had gone to the other side of the river to the residence of Mr. Thomas Sterling, with whom he had some things to discuss. That when Lang had come back to the house of Mr. Jones and found out that the witness [Hall] had not yet arrived, he went to the residence of John McIntosh, from whence he came back again at around 10 or 11 o'clock that same morning, in a boat accompanied by the said McIntosh, Mr. Cay, his foreman, and William Lee.[13] Having asked Lang if he was going to the city, he was told it was too late and that he would wait until the next day; and in truth the next morning they started on their way to the city—the said McIntosh, Lang, Daniel Johnson and the witness—and at about 18 miles from the city they met up with Mr. Prither, and they all arrived in the city together.

Asked if he thought that said Daniel Johnson was a companion

12. The pass of San Nicolás was at the bend of the St. Johns where Fort San Nicolás was built. It was planned about 1740 because of threats of English invasions at that time, but it was not built until late 1791 or early 1792 (Gold, *Duval County*, p. 47). Its later history is described in T. Frederick Davis, *History of Jacksonville, Florida, and Vicinity, 1513 to 1924*, pp. 36, 37, and in James Ward and Peggy O'Neal, "Time Traveler."

13. William Lee had a plantation on the south side of the St. Johns, and since he was a suspect in the intrigue, his effects were searched (Murdoch, *Georgia-Florida Frontier*, pp. 106–7).

of the people that came with him or if his coming was only to solicit from the government a pass to look over his properties (which he did secure); if in the time he stayed at the Jones residence, in the Road District, or in the time they stayed in this city [St. Augustine] he had heard any conversations about the rumors that were going around of attacks against this province, and if he knew the reason why Hammond did not accompany him as he said he would; and all the rest he could contribute to clarifying what was sought to be accomplished by an act so harmful:

He said he believes Johnson does not contemplate any other thought but that which he manifested because he does not suspect him of any wrongdoing; that in the time that he stayed at the Jones residence he heard no other revelations except the ones Lang submitted to His Lordship and he thinks these are the same things which he said he wrote about to Lieutenant Colonel Carlos Howard, though the witness did not see the letter. And that in the city he was not able to find out anything more, even though they were always in the city together. But this was not unusual because they all lived in the same house, although the others sometimes went their separate ways to visit Leslie[14] and Fatio[15] whom the witness does not visit. This is all he can say about this matter; and he signed under oath before His Lordship with the said Secretary, to which I testify.

> Quesada
> Nathaniel Hall
> Manuel Rengil

Before me, José Zubizarreta, government reporter

---

14. John Leslie was a partner in the firm of Panton, Leslie and Company; he was elected 16 March 1781 as a representative in the General Assembly of East Florida (Wilbur H. Siebert, *Loyalists in East Florida, 1774 to 1785*, 1:169, 2:276). The other members of this firm were William Panton, William Alexander, and Thomas Forbes. They had a business house in London with branches at Charleston and Savannah, and early in the American Revolution they moved from Savannah to the St. Johns River. Later they established their headquarters at St. Augustine and Pensacola and maintained branches at St. Marks and Mobile (ibid., 2:365).

15. Francis Philip Fatio, Sr., was born in Switzerland in 1724 and died in Florida in 1811. He moved from Switzerland to England and there became interested in land investments, which brought him to Florida in 1771. He wielded wide influence in the British and second Spanish occupations of Florida.

[AGI, PC, leg. 166, pormenor 16, p. 67]

Statement of George Arons.

Amelia Island, January 18, 1794

Before me, the said Lieutenant Colonel Carlos Howard, and two witnesses in my presence, appeared George Arons, brought there by the orderly of the militia, Samuel Russell; and Arons, having taken the oath upon the cross and by the Holy Trinity, as is done in his homeland of Alsacia, offered to tell the truth as to the matters about which he was to be questioned, and interrogated with respect to the particulars which the foregoing order embraces, he said the following:

1st. Asked if he had talked with the orderly of the militia, Samuel Russell, about some enlistment of people being made in Georgia and what it is that he knows about the matter:

He said that it is true that he had talked about the enlistings to said Russell last Tuesday and that he had told him at the same time that he was coming to tell me what he had heard, but first he wanted to bring his slaves to safety; that he told the orderly to come to give advance notice. And he added that now that he has been called before me, what he knows of the matter is that fifteen days ago, more or less, he went with Richard Lang to the house of Mr. Wright (the one that has been the chief constable in Camden County), located between the stockades of Temple and Coleraine in Georgia and about half a mile from the house of said Lang, and that in Wright's house Lang had a long private conversation with an American called Ruben Pitcher, of which he could not hear a word; but afterwards he went to the front yard where the two were talking and asked if the conversation were over; to which Pitcher responded by asking the witness [Arons] if he did not know the dangers threatening his Province of East Florida, with the witness answering back that he did not know of any danger at all; to which Pitcher replied that an invasion of Florida was planned and that recruitments were being made in Georgia, particularly inland.

In due time the recruits would march in small platoons, assembling together in Indian Territory, and once assembled, would attack Florida by the Lachua side[16] and from there head toward St. Johns;

16. That is, from the Indian lands to the west of St. Augustine.

comprising altogether between five and seven hundred men, well mounted and armed with sabers and pistols, with intent to move on to St. Augustine to take the city and fort by assault.

Consequently Pitcher insisted that the witness spend the night with him, from which he excused himself saying that there were things to do at home; and the witness added that, as he was walking down to the pier to go on the boat accompanied by the owner of the house, Wright, he asked Wright about what had he heard Pitcher say, and asked confidentially for advice; and he received the reply that these things seemed to be true and about to be carried out, but that it was too bad that the plans would be executed despite whatever opposition from the government of Georgia, because the majority of the people were inclined to go ahead with them.

2nd. Asked if Richard Lang heard or was present during anything of what is stated by the witness:

He said that he is positive Lang did not hear anything of what happened between the owner of the house and the witness when he went down to leave; that he does not know whether Lang heard what Pitcher told the witness, but he is certain he could have as he was present during the conversation.

The witness added that last Sunday Pitcher came to his house and told him that he came on request of Simeon Dillingham,[17] a resident of Temple and close friend of Abner Hammond, to warn him to take care as to what he does and to guard his property because he was in danger of an attack from the other side of the river, that is from Georgia.

Pitcher also said that Dillingham was sending this message to the witness because of friendship and gratitude for favors received, but he emphatically wants his name not to be mentioned to anybody; because if news spread of him, Dillingham, giving such information on Hammond, he would have to suffer the consequences.

Pitcher added of his own accord that already in Temple there was a stock of food supplies, arms, military supplies, and entrenching tools for the expedition, that two more boats loaded with similar things were expected, and that Colonel Hammond and his brother

---

17. Simeon Dillingham was a voting resident of Camden County, Georgia, in 1788. He was instrumental in establishing St. Marys in 1788, including the signing of papers in 1787. He was a member of the Georgia Constitutional Convention of 1789 (Marguerite G. Reddick, *Camden's Challenge: A History of Camden County, Georgia*, pp. 5, 145, 146).

Abner had already received five thousand pounds sterling from certain Frenchmen to buy said supplies.

That Samuel Hammond was to be commander-in-chief of the troops and that the second in command would be Colonel Kerr,[18] and they would have as agent or commissary of supplies the said Abner; that the land troops would be supported by three frigates with all the supplies already anchored at Port Royal or Beaufort, in South Carolina, between Savannah and Charleston, and that the battery on Amelia Island would be attacked by surprise when least expected unless Spanish or British warships prevented it, which event would be the only thing to fear for that could spoil the success of the expedition.

That it was known that there were only a small number of people, such as one hundred and fifty, in St. Augustine; and even in case of failure to take the city by assault, it would be taken by starving them as it is known there is only food for one month there.

3rd. Asked if he had heard or knew that there were some in this province participating in or with knowledge of the premeditated expedition:

He said that he thinks in the St. Marys River valley the people in general have an idea of the matter, some more and others less, and that he thinks that some are thinking of leaving the province to be safe in the United States.

4th. Asked if he knows who they were:

He said that he does not know with certainty, but he does not doubt that the majority of them consider it, and that a little time will tell who they are.

The witness added that he had pressed Pitcher to know if there were any of the ones from this side, or of the St. Johns, who joined with the bad intentioned ones in Georgia, and that Pitcher resisted telling him; but that finally he said that he was sure that John McIntosh of the St. Johns River knew of the matter some six weeks ago, and that some time ago when it was said that Richard Lang was going to leave his post as captain of the Militia, McIntosh had advised him not to do that, but instead to keep his commission because very shortly this province would be free and independent and then he would command this river and McIntosh the St. Johns.

18. The spelling of this man's name is Carr at this point in the record; but to avoid confusion, since it is clearly the same man whose name elsewhere is given as Kerr, the latter spelling has been used here.

And the witness added that he presumes that another who must know of the plot is William Jones, inhabitant of said river valley, because he is the father-in-law of Abner Hammond; and the witness added that if what he has said about McIntosh becomes known it could be dangerous to himself, so to prevent that he wants to persuade Ruben Pitcher to come and say the same things before me.

Also the witness has no doubt that John Peter Wagnon also knows everything because he came back by himself Sunday from Georgia, saying at Thomas Cryer's house that he was only coming for his wife and family and that he would be back in this river in eight days to move away from the province; for which purpose he had a boat and people waiting for him at Newton even then; and that said Cryer can inform me further on this; and that Richard Lang can further inform me on the whole matter, since Pitcher has told the witness that all he knows about the matter has come from Lang.

Here the witness remembered that Pitcher told him that he had heard Abner Hammond refer to being with Colonel Howard and that the latter had pressed with great zeal to discover his thoughts but that Hammond had known how to avoid his efforts and wiles; and that the witness does not know anything more about the things he has been asked about, but all that he has stated so far is the truth under the oath he has given in good faith, and that being forty-seven years old he signs the statement in front of Justo López and Manuel Bernal after its being read by me, word for word in the English language, which, although he is not from that nation, he understands best.

Carlos Howard

George Arons

Justo López

Manuel Bernal.

[AGI, PC, leg. 166, pormenor 16, p. 130]

A letter of Captain of the Militia Nathaniel Hall to Carlos Howard, dated January 19, 1794.

Dear Sir:

I have to inform you that when I was examined in St. Augustine I stated that I thought the people of St. Marys and Nassau would fight for their province if they were ordered to; and I am still of that opinion if they are ordered to while still in this country; but after my return home I have been informed that John Bailey,[19] Frank Sterling,[20] and Walter Drummond, with the Motes, are all about to move away to Carolina.

I was a little suspicious of these men before, because they had offered their pigs and cattle for sale; and I mentioned them to you, Colonel, in my last letter. When I was interviewed in St. Augustine I did not think of these men, but before I got home I remembered that and hurried and walked fast, until at 10 at night I reached home, and I went out early in the morning and soon I [was informed by] Lieutenant Hogan y Ricardo [that] they were going to leave the province, positively. And as I have found mistakes in what I had said and pointed out my errors, I hope to be forgiven.

You asked me to tell you where Wagnon had crossed the river and what route he took for St. Johns. I understand that he went by water, and going first to Mr. Talley he got a horse and then hurried on so fast toward the castle that he tired out his horse before coming to the St. Johns, leaving it at San Nicolás, where he got another horse from Jones, which he rode to the city.

I hope you will place this letter in the hands of the Governor as soon as possible. In doing so you will highly oblige his most obedient and sincere friend and humble servant,

Nathaniel Hall

P.S. Mr. Daniel Burnett[21] told me today that there is a certain Mr. Hampton living in Coleraine who owes him 10 pounds, which debt he contracted in East Florida, and that Atkinson,[22] who lives in this province, owes Hampton enough to pay said Burnett; and Mr. Burnett would like to know if that could be obtained from Mr. Atkinson or frozen in his possession. You could kindly let me know if something can be done about this matter.

19. John Bailey married Elizabeth, the eldest daughter of Richard Lang (Huxford, *Pioneers of Wiregrass Georgia*, 5:256). He owned lands just east of Lang's, where Fort Tonyn had stood, now called Woodstock (Johannes, *Yesterday's Reflections*, p. 119).

20. See note 9 in this chapter.

21. Burnett was a member of the family of David Burnett, who had two sons in the Spanish militia (Murdoch, *Georgia-Florida Frontier*, pp. 86, 167).

22. Andrew Atkinson, a native of Northampton County, Virginia, came to Camden County, Georgia, as a settler in 1785 and to East Florida in 1792. He was soon a captain in the

62   *Council of War,*

[AGI, PC, leg. 166, pormenor 16, p. 73]

Statement by Thomas Cryer.

Amelia Island, January 20, 1794.

Before me, Carlos Howard, Lieutenant Colonel of the Royal Army, Captain of the Grenadiers of the Third Battalion of the Regiment of Infantry of Cuba and Interim Commander of the Spanish Frontier, in the presence of two witnesses and of myself, appeared Thomas Cryer, resident in the St. Marys River valley, for the purpose of being examined with respect to the statement made by George Arons on the eighteenth of the current month about the enlistments being made in Georgia, which statement was sent to the government yesterday; and being present the said Thomas Cryer gave his oath on the four gospels by which he promised to tell the truth on the points he would be questioned about.

1st. Asked if he has heard or knows of enlistments of people being made in Georgia for the purpose of harassing this province; from whom and when did he hear such things:

He said that it is true that he has heard of such enlistings from two different people, both Americans, one called Ruben Pitcher and the other one Mr. Lewis,[23] whose first name is not known to the witness; that the first one he heard these things from was the said Pitcher, who on the eleventh of the current month, arrived at the witness's house and told him as a friend to pick up his things as soon as possible and take them to safety because groups of people were forming in Georgia and Carolina under the pretext of marching against the Indians, but with the real purpose of attacking this province.

He said that it was not the purpose of those people to unite themselves inside the limits of Georgia or Carolina but inside the Indian territory, or this province, so as to avoid incurring the penalties of the laws in those states.

Spanish militia and was praised by Quesada; a loyal supporter of the Spanish government, he married an illustrious Spanish woman. He visited Coleraine to gain information on the French intrigue and was sent to Georgia to deal with Georgia officials. In 1820 he was living in Philadelphia (Murdoch, *Georgia-Florida Frontier*, pp. 94, 104, 108, 161; Miller, "Quesada," p. 230). He owned substantial real properties in Florida, including 450 acres at Shipyard, now partly included in the Fort Caroline National Memorial at Jacksonville (Gold, *Duval County*, p. 88). Calypso Island in those government lands is at the mouth of Shipyard Creek.

23. This was possibly the Lewis who served under Elijah Clark in the American Revolution and for a time was on the Executive Council of Georgia (Louise F. Hays, *Hero of Hornet's Nest; A Biography of Elijah Clark, 1733 to 1799*, p. 141).

That the governors of both, especially that of Carolina, were very opposed to such a treacherous attempt; but that nevertheless the conspirators were determined to follow through with their ideas, considering themselves once out of the United States to be subjects of the new French republic; that the people of Georgia were to be led by Colonel Samuel Hammond and Colonel Kerr; and that the brother of said Hammond, Abner Hammond, was in charge of supplies for the expedition and had received and deposited lately in his stockade at Temple a large supply of barrels of flour, beef, and pork meat, one hundred and seventy bushels of corn, a number of casks of rum, various entrenching tools, and seventy swords; and he adds that to buy such supplies and some others yet to come, the French ambassador gave Samuel Hammond several thousand guineas. The witness said that he definitely heard them mentioned.

The witness went on to say that what he heard from the said Mr. Lewis was on the twelfth of this month when he arrived at the witness's house (accompanied by John Peter Wagnon, who had arrived from Georgia in a boat with three Negroes with the plan of removing his wife, and quitting the province to go and live in Augusta, from whence he had just come); and the witness, then remembering what Pitcher had said about the enlistments, anxiously asked Wagnon what he knew of the matter, and was answered that he hadn't heard a word of such an enterprise; but Mr. Lewis having answered that there was in fact such business underway, Wagnon added to the witness: "Yes, yes there is something going on and you can be sure it will be carried through"; Wagnon said no more about the matter, and having finished lunch (he had arrived at such a time) he started on his way to the St. Johns and from there to St. Augustine seeking his wife, with whom he promised Mr. Lewis to return in eight days. And Lewis, to whom the boat belongs, told him he would not extend the wait with the boat one day longer than eight days.

Wagnon having departed, the witness again talked about the enlistments to Mr. Lewis, who expressed surprise that this matter had been discovered by the residents of this river valley.

The witness answered that it was not remarkable at all, because it was well known in the river valley that there was an accumulation of food stuffs and war supplies being assembled in Temple for the expedition; and likewise that they expected two other boats loaded for the same purpose; and Lewis said that perhaps there was no need for immediate concern for the time being because the troops were not going to move until the middle of March or the beginning of April, and right then the waters of the Altamaha River were so swollen that they were not passable.

Lewis added that anyway nobody need fear for his properties, because as soon as the troops entered the province and the three French frigates blocked the harbors, particularly St. Augustine, edicts would be published assuring the peaceful and full possession of property for all who would join the invaders and also full pardon to all the refugees for their crimes or debts (which kind of people comprised, as is well known, the majority of the population of the province); to this the witness replied that they would never be able to capture the fortress of St. Augustine because it was too strong.

Lewis answered that nevertheless it would eventually be taken because it was well known that they did not have supplies for three months, and consequently the Spanish would have to surrender because of hunger; Lewis concluded by saying that to this the circumstance must be added that the invaders will find many friends in the countryside; with this Lewis said goodbye and left in his boat for Newton to wait there for Wagnon's arrival, and he has not seen him since.

2nd. Asked if he has heard of or knows any of the inhabitants of this river valley or of the province in general who are participating in the plot of the enlistments:

He said that he knows generally that almost all of the inhabitants of this river valley know by now and are very apprehensive about what is being contrived in Georgia; but that he does not know or has not heard that any of them, or of the province in general, are accomplices in the plot, with the exception of the magistrate of the St. Johns River, John McIntosh, who according to information given the witness by the said Ruben Pitcher, knew and participated fully for some months in the plot of the Georgians; and the witness added, if this be so, it must be since the said John visited said state in September or October; that is the most the witness remembers about the matter; and what he has said is the truth under oath; and being sixty-two years old he signed this statement in the presence of Justo López and Manuel Bernal, after having it read to him by me, word for word in his native language, which is English.

Carlos Howard

Thomas Cryer

Justo López

Manuel Bernal

Castillo de San Marcos, modern-day St. Augustine. Courtesy of the National Park Service.

SIX

Order of Imprisonment; Lang's Testimony

ON 20 January 1794 Governor Quesada moved to carry out the conclusions of the council of war held on 16 January by ordering the swift arrest of John McIntosh, Richard Lang, Abner Hammond, John Peter Wagnon, William Jones, and William Plowden. The seizure of papers in the homes of the accused men was ordered as well as the taking of testimony. The first of the accused to be interrogated was Captain Lang, who testified on 21 January in his prison cell in the fortress at St. Augustine, the Castillo de San Marcos. He gave details of his knowledge of the plans of the rebels, and his affidavit cited "Rubin Pitchard" as his chief informant.[1]

[AGI, PC, leg. 166, pormenor 16, p. 1]

Florida 1794

Official Criminal Papers

Against John MacIntosh, Lieutenant Governor of the St. Johns River; Richard Lang, Captain of the Militia of the St. Marys River;

1. Although the document spells the name of the informant as "Pitchard," the text of the deposition indicates that the reference was to the same man who signed his name "Pitcher" in the statement given before Captain Lang on 29 December 1793. Variant spellings of proper names in the documents have been preserved in this study, unless otherwise noted.

John Peter Wagnon; William Jones and William Plowden, new settlers and residents on both rivers: On suspicion of conspiracy and subversive negotiations with the Americans and the French, who together planned in the States to invade this province from Georgia; in which action is included Abner Hammond, subject of said States and working with the invaders in the post of Commissary General— in charge of provisions for the expedition that was to be undertaken—under suspicion also of deception in his entry into said Province, and that which he sought for all the provisions with ostensible loyalty.

Order. St. Augustine, Florida, January 20, 1794

Don Juan Nepomuceno de Quesada, Colonel of the Royal Army, Governor, Commanding General, Royal Protector and Administrator of the Royal Estate of this City and of this Province for his Majesty said:

That on information—circumstantial and proved by documents—provided with due caution by Lieutenant Colonel Carlos Howard, Captain of Grenadiers of the Third Battalion of the Regiment of Infantry of Cuba and Interim Commander of the Spanish Frontier on the St. Marys River in this Province, and on other information received from reliable sources, His Lordship [the governor]:[2] knows about the conspiracy plotted against this Province, Louisiana and the other Florida by a certain number of Anglo Americans established in the States of Georgia and South Carolina, who by violating their official laws and their friendship with our Sovereign, enlisted themselves with some of the French Convention circulating in those States. These, it was said, have influenced them to invade this Province, and the others already mentioned.

That His Lordship, in the attempt to take the precautions for the defense of his Province which his responsibility and zeal for better service for the King dictate, has come to suspect, not without foundation, that Richard Lang, John MacIntosh, William Plowden, William Jones, and Abner Hammond, all Americans and, except for the last one, residents of this province and subjects of his Majesty, had sinister communications and plots among them; and perhaps were joined by Samuel Hammond, resident of Augusta and named to the command of the troops that are being enlisted in Georgia, brother

2. *Su Señoria*, often abbreviated as "S. S." in the documents.

of Abner, son-in-law of Jones. That His Lordship, moved by zeal and better calculation, divulged his suspicions against said persons, and his reasons for the same, in a Council of War that he called together for this purpose among others. And the members by unanimous decision determined on imprisonment for all; and upon this being verified, and with the gathering up of the papers that were found, His Lordship so ordered and included the arrest of John Peter Wagnon, also American, who, having left for Georgia without a passport, he arranged to have arrested when he came back, having a suspicion about him similar to that about the others.

It had to be ordered and was ordered: that, in his presence and that of the counsellor, the documents be examined by the public interpreter after his authorization and oath; and that with appropriate discrimination an inventory be made of those papers adjudged to be pertinent to this investigation. The reporter will assist throughout this matter, and will keep those papers not pertinent until further action by the Tribunal.

That the Interim Secretary of the Government add a certified copy of the secret accusation made to His Lordship, which, keeping confidential the identity of the author [probably Nathaniel Hall], as it will also be in that copy, was examined in the aforementioned Council of War and contributed to its decision.

That also it will be put in these proceedings, after these matters, that it was decided to imprison the said persons and to gather up their papers; and that the testimony include the heading and conclusion of the said decision.

And finally, that having certified the arrest of the said culprits and having taken care of the matters supplied and the statements of the persons named by His Lordship concerning the things that can be adjudged relevant to these proceedings or in any way related to them, the prisoners' statements be taken as to whatever particulars His Lordship may determine; among them, what will result from the statement supplied by the Captain of the Militia of the St. Marys River, Nathaniel Hall, which will also be included. In view of this and from what by then has come out, other suitable orders will be entered.

And by this document which His Lordship executed with the concurrence of his lieutenant and general counsellor it was so ordered; and each signed under oath.

Juan Nepomuceno de Quesada.

Attorney José de Ortega[3]

Before me, José de Zubizarreta, reporter

The matter of the suspension of the examination of papers seized from prisoners; and accusation by the accused Richard Lang before His Lordship.

St. Augustine, Florida, January 20, 1794

For the purpose of the examination of the papers as provided under the preceding order, the public interpreter, Miguel Iznardy, in the presence of His Lordship and of the counsellor and before me as the scribe, was examining one of the two packages of papers that were found in the home of William Jones, to give notice to the Court of Justice about their contents, as proposed, and to inventory the pertinent ones. And, being engaged in this business, notice was received by the said interpreter, Miguel Iznardy,[4] that Richard Lang, one of the prisoners, begged to see him right away. Motivated by this request, and in case what he wanted to say might be pertinent to the inquiry underway, His Lordship, with the agreement of the counsellor, ordered that the interpreter with me, the reporter, determine what Lang wanted. And when we returned immediately to report that what he wanted was to talk alone with the Governor accompanied by the said interpreter, it was agreed to get on with it without delay but that he be persuaded to talk to His Lordship in front of me without giving up in our insistence unless he absolutely refused. And although at first he insisted that I retire, in the end he took the advice of His Lordship.

His Lordship, having been informed by the interpreter about the

3. Ortega was a highly competent lawyer of unquestioned integrity. He had held the important post of director of tobacco in the Spanish government (Janice Borton Miller, "Juan Nepomuceno de Quesada: Spanish Governor of East Florida, 1790–1795" [Ph.D. diss.], p. 99). Quesada complained of his arrogance but the Spanish authorities justified his actions, although they admitted that he was headstrong. It was suggested that a solution might be to send him to a more populous location where the presence of other lawyers might restrain him (Arthur Preston Whitaker, *Documents Relating to the Commercial Policy of Spain in the Floridas* . . ., p. 243). He was acting governor of Florida for a brief time in 1796. An important area on the St. Johns River bears his name, as does the Ortega River, a tributary of the St. Johns.

4. Iznardy was the government interpreter, captain and owner of a schooner, and captain in the Spanish militia (Miller, "Quesada," p. 179).

statements that Lang made, which in many ways confirmed the suspicions upon which this investigation is based, retired with the interpreter and me and made the necessary preparations, Lang having agreed to testify under oath.

Signed by the counsellor as to the part that he witnessed, and the said interpreter, to all of which I testify.

Quesada

Attorney Ortega

Miguel Iznardy

Before me, José de Zubizarreta

[AGI, PC, leg. 166, pormenor 16, p. 15]

Legal ratification by means of a formal statement of Richard Lang concerning the verbal accusations he made before His Lordship.

St. Augustine, Florida, in the same day, month, and year [21 January 1794].[5]

For the purpose of receiving the statements from Richard Lang anticipated under the previous order, His Lordship went to the fortress of this place, where [Lang] is being held prisoner, accompanied by the general counsellor and by the public interpreter and by the reporter and being in the said fortress, there was brought to our presence the said Richard Lang, who (through the interpreter) was put under oath, which he made by God Almighty and the Sacred Bible of the Protestant faith, which he professes. And he promised to speak the truth of whatever he knew and was asked, and being asked as to what he had said to His Lordship yesterday afternoon about the information he had concerning the enlisting on the prodding by the French of certain Americans in the States of Georgia and South Carolina to come against this Province:

He said that it had been fifteen days since Rubin Pitchard, formerly a neighbor of his and a resident of this Province, and since then a fugitive in Georgia, had informed the witness of the organization at Newton, to which he had gone to find out if it were true that

5. This date is taken from a purely procedural paper, not included here, that immediately preceded the document translated in the text.

troops were gathering there against this province; that he had heard this rumor earlier from John Bayley, American resident of that place; that the enlisting there was a fact not only against this province but also against Louisiana and Pensacola, which were to be invaded by the American and French residents; and that they are recruiting in the areas of Cumberland[6] and Kentucky.

That the said Pitchard added that in a few days, he would give the witness other particulars which he did, coming to the home of the witness, at about eight o'clock, and saying that he had received a letter from Dillingham (one of the recruiting captains in the State of Georgia), including an official French subaltern's commission for him, so that he could enlist as such with those forces.

That the said Pitchard informed the witness at that time that the number of those troops were eleven hundred in landing forces ready to come in three frigates, now at anchor and alerted to sail from Port Royal;[7] and another seven hundred on horses, these led by Brigadier General Samuel Hammond as commander-in-chief; one brigade of them commanded by his brother Abner; and another by Colonel Kerr.

That he also had said that the invasion was to be ready in three or four weeks. And the witness, having talked about this matter with said Abner Hammond in the home of William Jones, his father-in-law, then Hammond confirmed to the witness the news of the invasion, saying he believed it was true because the Frenchmen wanted a port to land their plunder.

That, talking to the witness about 15 days or more ago in American stores on the other side of the St. Marys River, there was one Henry Wright who asked the witness how many troops and prisoners were here and how long the fortress could resist a siege.

That the witness, having answered by exaggerating all the matters of strength inquired about, turned the conversation to what the witness had heard about Abner Hammond wanting to sell his food supplies and goods on the St. Johns River for the king, to which Henry [Wright] told him not to believe such a thing because the food and war materials were not his and that he was just an agent for the French to buy them.

That, while this conversation was going on, Rubin Pitchard came in and told the witness that he would advise him of the day and

6. Later called Tennessee.
7. In South Carolina.

time that [the troops] would march, because he had to know; and that from what he understood it was not the intention to come down the St. Marys River, but to cut through, and make the trip as if they were going toward Indian [territory], attacking from west of the city.

That this is all he knows of the matter that was asked about and precisely what he told His Lordship yesterday; and that everything is the truth under the weight of the oath he took; and having read his statement (translated into English by said interpreter, which is the language of the witness), he said that it was faithfully and legally translated and he affirms and ratifies it; that he is fifty years old, and he signed with His Lordship and with the counsellor and with the said interpreter, to which I testify.

> Quesada
> Attorney Ortega
> Richard Lang
> Miguel de Iznardy

Before me, José de Zubizarreta, government reporter

SEVEN

21 January Council of War; McIntosh's Testimony

THE preliminary investigation having clearly revealed to Governor Quesada the necessity for immediate defense precautions, he urgently called together another council of war in his residence on the plaza in St. Augustine. This conclave of 21 January 1794 was presided over by the governor and included Colonel Bartolomé Morales and Captains Pedro Salcedo and Juan Remedios—as well as Pedro Berrio, Gonzalo Zamorano, and Manuel Rengil.

The council of war provided for a coordinated plan of defense for the Province of East Florida in the face of the growing evidence of imminent attack. It ordered Carlos Howard to remove the battery of two cannon from Amelia Island to San Nicolás, on the south side of the St. Johns River. Personnel from the St. Marys region were consolidated with the troops at San Vicente Ferrer in order to strengthen the more realistic defense line provided by the broad waters of the St. Johns. San Nicolás was ordered to be manned by troops from both San Vicente Ferrer and St. Augustine—augmented by local militia.

The militia on the St. Marys and St. Johns rivers and at St. Augustine were called up for full active duty. Every man over fourteen years old was called into military service; any who refused were required to leave the province. Negroes, whether slaves or free, were called up for work duty. Captain Miguel Costa's sloop *Maria* was ordered to sail swiftly to Havana to

73

John McIntosh, Mor. From a miniature painting, courtesy of
Walter Dunwody.

notify officials there of the crisis and to take to prison John
McIntosh and Abner Hammond, who were considered the most
dangerous rebel leaders.

All residents of the province living north of the St. Johns
were ordered to move south of that river, bringing with them all of
their possessions and burning their buildings behind them so they
could not be used by the revolutionaries. This tactic vacated
immediately such strategic locations as the McIntosh plantation
on the north side of the St. Johns at the cow ford, and the fortified
house of Richard Lang on the south side of the St. Marys at Mills's
Ferry. It also made unnecessary the difficult defense of the
marshes, hammocks, islands, and waterways in the land north of
the St. Johns.

This order is referred to many times in today's chains of title to lands in Florida. In one of them the order was referred to as an incident of "Wagner's War,"[1] probably a reference to the name of John Peter Wagnon. About forty families moved out of Florida because of this command. At the conclusion of this chapter there is a statement made on 23 January by John McIntosh and a contract between Wagnon and McIntosh; together with a 23 June 1793 letter from Samuel Hammond to John McIntosh, which speaks of Hammond's current and growing military leadership in the troubled times "with the Indians." In that letter Hammond said: "The troops will not march without me and I have been overpersuaded to take command again." Correspondence between Hammond and Mangourit indicated that Hammond intended to use military forces to "wipe out Panton and Leslie's stores."[2] The Spanish authorities may well have believed that Hammond's letter to McIntosh in referring to "Indian" troubles was just using the phrase as a cover for a reference to the rebellion—a conjecture that would probably have been entirely correct.

[AGI, PC, leg. 166, pormenor 16, p. 17]

In the meeting of the Council of War today held in the Royal House that serves as the residence of the Governors of this Province of East Florida there came Juan Nepomuceno Quesada, Colonel of the Royal Army and Governor of this city and said province, who presided over the council members assembled by him: Colonel Bartolomé Morales, commander of the battalion which guards this city; Pedro Salcedo and Juan Remedios, Captains of the Royal Corps of Artillery; Pedro Berrio, artillery engineer; Gonzalo Zamorano, accountant of the Royal estate and me, Manuel Rengil, Interim Secretary of this government, all to perform our duties in this Council of War.

After said President produced a letter of Carlos Howard, Com-

1. See Pleasant D. Gold, *History of Duval County, Florida*, p. 67.
2. Hammond to Mangourit, 5 March 1794, Samuel Hammond Papers, Boston Public Library.

mander of the Indian and American Frontier, and a sworn statement of a resident of the St. Marys River and another secret statement by an individual in whom he has confidence, in all of which are contained positive reports to the effect that there are now being enlisted in the State of Georgia some seven hundred cavalrymen to enter this province, at the same time that three French ships appear nearby with 1,100 men with a plan to attack under orders from Samuel Hammond, American and Brigadier General, who is named chief of said expedition, which is to take place within three weeks, we unanimously and of common accord resolved and agreed to the following measures:

1. That Carlos Howard should retire from Amelia Island, embarking in the vessel *San Agustín* with two cannon that are now placed in the battery there, together with all the military supplies that are on the island and burning everything else under his command that could be of use to the enemy, because the site cannot be defended on account of its location and distance from this city, with the few troops available; that he should join the troops at San Vicente Ferrer on the St Johns River, taking command of the troops there and at the [post] on the sand bar, and advise the residents of the St. Marys and Nassau rivers to the north of the St. Johns River that anyone who wants to stay in the province and take up arms in its defense should within eight days retire to the southern side of said river with all his property, including boats and canoes, which it is indispensable that they keep on the said bank [of the river], within a week, burning behind them all their houses and ranches.

2. That having united with the forces now detached at San Vicente Ferrer, Commander Carlos Howard should post the troops and boats that are under his command at the places he deems most appropriate to prevent the enemy from crossing the river in case such anticipated effort takes place.

3. That with the two cannon taken from Amelia Island they should form a battery at San Nicolás to stop the enemy from penetrating that area and that it is to be manned by the Subaltern from San Vicente and ten soldiers and two gunners from said post and by a sergeant, a corporal, and another ten men from this city together with a company of militia or of Negroes if it can be formed; and that so that said Subaltern can retire in case of being attacked by superior forces, and can ask for all necessary assistance from Carlos Howard,

to whom he must be subordinated, he shall designate the boats to be taken with him.

4. That men of the Companies of Militia of the St. Johns and St. Marys rivers in whom the officers have confidence shall be called under arms with appropriate salaries; and that, as to the suspicious ones or ones not wanting to comply with what they have sworn to, those are to be told to leave the province within three days and that this should be enforced without exception. That all of the militia to take up arms will take orders from Carlos Howard and will be employed in any matter of service which may occur, but that they are mainly to oppose the intentions of the enemy.

5. That because of the scarcity of men in the Battalion of Cuba and the large number of detached troops, it will be reinforced by eight men and a corporal from each of the three companies of urban militia of this city, paying only those men who actually are used for each day of service.

6. That the guards should be reinforced for the fortress, the bakery, and the gunpowder magazine.

7. That the Governor should publish a decree ordering every man over fourteen years of age who does not want to take up arms in defense of the province to leave it within five days.

And that all the residents who have Negroes to put to work provide these as soon as possible under the assurance that they will be paid their wages.

And that all free Negroes who are in the province are to come immediately to such service, and anyone who does not do it should be punished by order of the Governor.

8. That in consideration of the small number of cells this fortress has, of the war supplies that they contain, of the fact that they must be used for housing troops in case of the attack that is expected, and that five cells are now occupied by prisoners, there should now be sent to Havana both Abner Hammond and John MacIntosh, who are men of great reputation and power, bringing together the other four in the same cell, at an opportune time.

9. That, finally, the Governor should reiterate his official communications to the Captain General, with a copy of these latest reports because they leave no doubt of the imminence of an attack upon this province; and not only for this purpose but also for conveying said prisoners, the sloop of Miguel Costa should be commis-

sioned because it is faster than the sloop of Juan Bautista Ferreira, which is about to leave for the Port of Havana.

The nine preceding points were the agreements and unanimous accords dictated in the best service of the King; that after these expressions by the President, they were signed and agreed to by all Council members as follows:

St. Augustine, Florida,
January 21, 1794

Juan Nepomuceno de
Quesada

Bartolomé Morales

Pedro Salcedo

Juan Remedios

Pedro Diaz Berrio

Gonzalo Zamorano

Manuel Rengil

[AGI, PC, leg. 166, pormenor 16, p. 20]

Statement by John McIntosh

St. Augustine, Florida, January 23, 1794.

Don Juan Nepomuceno de Quesada, Governor and Commanding General, went to the Castillo de San Marcos of this city, accompanied by the general counsellor and the public interpreter and me, the government reporter, all to receive the statement of John McIntosh, whom His Lordship ordered brought before him. And by means of the interpreter the witness was put under oath before God Almighty and the Holy Bible of the Protestant faith which he professes, by which he swore to tell the truth of what he knew and was asked, and so the following ensued:

1. Asked if he knew or had heard of the expedition that is planned against this province in the States of Georgia and South Carolina, what is the date set, number of troops enlisted, military supplies, provisions and ammunition accumulated:

He said he did not know any more of what he was asked, than

that which he had already told His Lordship on the night of the fifteenth of this month, that is to say, that he had heard vaguely of the expedition.

2. Asked if he does not remember that he has had two conversations with His Lordship about that subject, one on the morning of the fourteenth and the other on the night of the fifteenth in the presence of John Leslie. That in the first one (after trying to excuse himself with His Lordship about the trip to Georgia by John Peter Wagnon, sent there by the witness without any permission from the government, and the showing of a letter from his brother about sending some cattle) he inadequately responded to His Lordship on the details of the expedition even though given ample freedom in the questioning. And that on the second visit, which was on the night of the fifteenth, he was accompanied by John Leslie (who tried to excuse with His Lordship this mistake of the witness in not telling him in the previous visit of the information on the proposed expedition) and the witness told His Lordship about it by means of Leslie, who speaks Spanish. The witness was asked to say therefore if he does not remember these things and if he wants to take back now what he had said, having now recalled what he did then, so that it can be attested to judicially:

He replied that things were true as referred to in the question, and that it is also true that if on the first of the two occasions referred to he did not tell His Lordship all the news given on the second occasion through John Leslie, this is because he thought it warranted discretion, and he could not use discretion with the commander of the battalion present and since people were always coming in and going out; but that he, having left the house of the Governor, had talked to Leslie and told him what he knew and asked him if he thought His Lordship had the same information, to which Leslie had answered that he thought the government knew but nevertheless he thought it the duty of the witness to inform about it also as a precaution; and that as a result he went back to the Governor and by means of Leslie, who tried to excuse said oversight, he told him about it; that his information came from some people on the St. Johns River, although he does not remember their names; that the previously mentioned Hammond (whose first name he does not know and who is the son-in-law of William Jones, a resident on the St. Johns River) had accumulated on the other side of the St. Marys a large amount of provisions, the same things he had up for sale at his father-in-law's house for the residents on the river; but that the defendant thinks that it was not for that purpose that they had been gathered, believing that they were instead for the planned invasion, because of their excessive quantity.

He said that he also informed His Lordship of what he knew of that, that is to say, that he heard that they had enlisted from 1,500 to 2,000 men, and that there were three ships cruising before Britford,[3] ready for the expedition and said to be connected with it; but he does not remember if he said then to His Lordship that he also had heard that their leaders were in prison in the Carolinas; although, by the latest information he had received from Georgia through John Peter Wagnon (who had just returned from there), he had understood that the enlisting of the troops is not against this province, as thought, but rather for establishing a new country or body politic in the western part of Georgia.

3. Asked if the latest news that was communicated by Wagnon had been written or by word of mouth:

He replied that the information was oral at the time he received two letters brought from Georgia.

4. Asked if he knows who is in charge of the command of said expedition, if those enlisted in it are infantry or cavalry, and if he knows anyone in command, from having seen him, talked with him, or having communicated with him by mail:

He said that he knows nothing with certainty on these questions, but he thinks His Lordship told him that a brother of Hammond was in command of the troops. That he does not know him [Abner] and consequently he is not in touch with him.

5. Asked about how long he had known of the expedition and if concerning it, its progress, its present status, and the circumstances which he has now mentioned, he talked with other people in the city or province, with whom, and what they had said:

He said that he remembers that in the Clark Inn he had talked to Andrew Davies[4] about said expedition, and that the witness said that he knew all the residents of this province would suffer many difficulties which would not occur in the city, and that Davies expressed the opinion that he thought said expedition would not materialize.

6. Asked if he were a friend of Hammond, son-in-law of Jones,

3. Undoubtedly Beaufort, South Carolina, was referred to, as other evidence shows that French naval support was located there.

4. Davies, a lieutenant in the Spanish militia, had responsibilities on the St. Johns.

of whom he has spoken, if it had been long since he had seen him, where and with what purpose, if he discussed with him the conspiracy against this province and, if so, did he speak about the selling of the goods that he had talked about before, and if he gathered that there was something sinister intended in the proposal of selling them:

He said he was not a friend of Hammond, whom he hardly knows by sight; that the one he does know and has spoken to is his brother Samuel, but that he did first see him [Abner] on the San Nicolás road when the witness last came to his city; and that on the road the witness said to him that he would be glad if on his return he would visit him for two or three days; but he replied that he did not know if he would have any free time.

7. Asked if Samuel Hammond with whom he keeps in touch has written to him lately or at some other time concerning anything related to the planned invasion, and if so, what and when:

He said that Samuel Hammond has never written him a word related to the said invasion.

8. Asked if John Peter Wagnon, who he says has informed him lately of how things are in Georgia, carries a government passport to go there, and the motive for his trip:

He said that Wagnon had a government passport to go to Georgia, the same one he [McIntosh] carries (dated April of '91, a very few days after he was admitted to be a subject);[5] that the witness while on the road to Georgia with some of his Negroes was using the passport that His Lordship had given him with which to bring back part of his cattle; that he was informed on the way by Andrew Atkinson, Captain of the Militia of St. Johns, that the wife of the witness had arrived from the State of Georgia where she had gone to be cured of some illness; that this information caused him to return to his home to be with her and there he found Wagnon and Francisco Sterling, who was coming to the city; and that he [Wagnon] in the presence of Sterling asked the witness how much money he would give him for going to Georgia to bring back the cattle, and they having agreed on $110, the witness did not hesitate to commission him to do it, thinking he was authorized by the passport in which His Lordship gave him leave to go with three or four white men; that he told the Governor of this event caused by the arrival of his wife, telling him by way of Thomas Sterling, who was going to the city.

5. April 1791 was apparently the date of the McIntosh official permit to settle in Florida.

9. Asked, if on the day he asked for the permit from His Lordship to bring in the cattle, was he not denied this on the terms he wanted it (that is to be able to send the person he would choose); being told by His Lordship that it had to be a personal pass; the witness saying he did not know whom he was going to send and being told by the Governor to go back home, from whence he could advise him of the person he had chosen so that he could send him a personal permit; that the witness said he would go personally; and from all of that should he not have come to the conclusion that one had to give the names of people in the permits to avoid such fraud as the one Wagnon wanted to work with his permit of April of '91:

He said that although everything is true as expressed in the question he thought however that he could substitute himself for another person because of the specifications in the permit that two white men could accompany him.

10. Asked if he knew Diego Allen had enlisted in the expedition against the province after he escaped from here, protected by the witness and William Jones and John Peter Wagnon:

He said he does not know if Allen enlisted, and that it is not true that he had escaped from the province under the witness's protection, because he was away at the time.

11. Asked if the government (having had to make the determination to deprive Allen of all contact with the Indians because it was harmful) did not place him under the care of the witness as a Judge on the St. Johns River, making him stay near the witness and telling the witness, among other things, under no circumstances to let him join the Indians; and did not the witness, notwithstanding this, allow or overlook his going to them on two occasions; so His Lordship, being suspicious of the witness, commissioned Andrew Atkinson to arrest Allen; and that the witness, having verified this, pressed for his immediate release, and not having accomplished his purpose, asked to be permitted to take him before His Lordship, who freed him on the ardent petition of the witness and Thomas Sterling; not punishing the disobediences and misdeeds of Allen, but complying with their requests, being confident of their promises that they would answer for Allen's conduct to allow him to establish himself at Matanzas from then on; but was not the result of all this, during the voluntary absence of the witness to Georgia and the illness of Sterling, that Allen escaped in the meantime assisted by William Jones who bought his things and by John Peter Wagnon who also helped:

He said it was true what is being said about when Allen was to be established and true about the witness being in charge of not letting him visit the Indians, and that he nevertheless went two times; but the first time he was authorized by His Lordship so that he could go get the things he had left there and when the second visit was made the witness was very ill and unconscious.

That it is not true that he pressed Andrew Atkinson to free Allen, but it is true that he asked him to turn him over to His Lordship as was verified, pleading for him along with Thomas Sterling, who wanted to answer for Allen on the matter of his second visit to the Indians, blaming himself for it; and that he does not remember Sterling ever talking to him about the last recommendation of His Lordship about Allen's conduct after he told him to go live in Matanzas, because he would never obligate himself to answer for his conduct or the fulfillment of that command.

And at this point His Lordship ordered the hearing suspended, to continue it later if necessary; the witness had all this read to him, translated to his language by means of an interpreter.

He said that there is an exception to the response to the fourth question, for he had thought that the Governor had informed him that Samuel Hammond was commissioned to lead the expedition and that he now thought it was Richard Lang who gave him this information, and that everything else in the statement is in accordance with what he has said; and it is affirmed and ratified; and that he is thirty-eight years old and signed with His Lordship and with the Counsellor and the Interpreter, on oath.

> Quesada
> Attorney Ortega
> McIntosh
> Miguel de Iznardy

Before me, José de Zubizarreta, government reporter

[AGI, PC, leg. 166, pormenor 16, p. 81—in English]

One of the letters cited as disclosing the undertakings, written by Samuel Hammond to John McIntosh, and reading as follows:

Savannah, 27th June, 1793

Dear McIntosh:

Since I wrote to you last I have had a severe attack of the fever of which I am now, thank God, fully well relieved.

I spent yesterday afternoon with Mrs. McIntosh and am happy to find that she is mending fast and that she is in good spirits. She really appeared quite cheerful. The inflammation has entirely subsided and the film in one of her eyes is grown so thin that the color of the eye is easily discovered. Doct. McLeod appears very sanguine & on his judgment I back my hopes principally. Yet should he fail of success I think there may be found men whose particular study has been the occular system, who must have greater knowledge than McLeod and thro whose means I am persuaded she may be perfectly restored. She has now a [illegible] issue on the back of her neck which she says give her little or no pain or inconvenience, although she has suffered considerably with them when with you. This I apprehend naught out of; of the better judgment of the Doct. in whose hands she now is. Your son has grown a stout fellow and is very well. William McIntosh, the old lady, & son request that I communicate their love to you. William M. says she cannot see quite well enough to write you as yet but as soon as she is so far recovered you may expect to hear from her; but hopes in the meantime that you will not conclude she could not get some of her friends to read to her any letters she may have the pleasure to receive from his friends.

We are still in trouble with the Indians. A detachment marched from Savannah yesterday for the frontier, and another goes today, and I shall follow tomorrow. Politics are strangely changed here. I, who never sought the dame of popularity and who six months ago could scarcely make interest enough to keep out of long ships, am now as popular as any of the dons of this place. The troops will not march without me; and I have been overpersuaded to take command again. The bearer will not wait, & I have only time to add that nothing could afford me such real happiness in this world as to be set down in the same neighborhood with you, with our families with us in good health—& that I am with unabated esteem your most obedient humble servant

S. Hammond

[AGI, PC, leg. 166, pormenor 16, p. 81]

*The paper that contains, as expressed, the agreement between John
McIntosh and John Peter Wagnon concerning the transporting from
Georgia to this province of part of the cattle that should have been
delivered by his brother.*

Received of John McIntosh, esquire, a bay gelding valued at
one hundred and ten dollars, for which I oblige myself to go into
Georgia and have all such cattle as may be delivered to me by his
brother William brought to this Province, the expense to be paid by
him, and the business to be compleated in thirty days, provided the
cattle are delivered in twenty days after my arrival. It is also understood that I am not to be liable for any loss or accidents as witness my
hand this 24th Nov. 1793.

J. P. Wagnon
Witness: Thomas Sterling, J.P.,
Justice of the Peace

EIGHT

Hammond's Declaration; Documents of Revolution

ON 24 January the governor, accompanied by lawyer and interpreter, went to Abner Hammond's cell in the Castillo de San
Marcos to interview the prisoner before he was shipped off to the
dungeon in Havana. Hammond volunteered that his wife was still
at her father's plantation at San Nicolás, where she guarded some
very important papers concerning the revolution. He suggested a
procedure to obtain the papers, and José Maria Figueroa, sublieutenant of dragoons, was immediately dispatched for them.
Figueroa returned with some of the papers on 26 January.

The next day, 27 January, the governor interviewed Hammond again at the fortress, this time with documents retrieved
from Mrs. Hammond at William Jones's plantation, among them
the accounts of the rebels' supplies. Although Hammond admitted the importance of these, he said that his wife had not sent
the extremely important document that outlined the French consul's proposals to Samuel Hammond. Abner Hammond then
wrote down what he could remember about these proposals, but
he suggested that the copy he had made of the French proposals to
Samuel Hammond be explicitly requested.

Major C. M. F. de Bert had signed the original document
under instructions from Mangourit (the French consul at Charleston). In that document, as Abner's copy indicated, Colonel
Samuel Hammond was referred to only as "Coll._____." It was

dated 24 July 1793. After a new effort, Abner's original copy was obtained.

Once Abner Hammond's interrogation was completed, he and John McIntosh were finally put aboard the *Maria*, the sloop of Captain Miguel Costa. The sloop sailed for Cuba on 28 January 1794.

[AGI, PC, leg. 166, pormenor 16, p. 28]

Statement by Abner Hammond.

St. Augustine, Florida, January 24, 1794.

His Lordship accompanied by the general counsellor and by the public interpreter, Miguel Iznardy, went for the purpose of getting a statement to the Castillo de San Marcos of this city, where in one of its underground cells there is a prisoner answering to the name of Abner Hammond; and he [Hammond] having read the oath by means of said interpreter, affirmed it by God Almighty and what he believes of the Holy Bible under the Protestant faith which he professes, offering to tell the truth in everything he knows and was asked, in which disposition the following questions were asked:

1. First of all, what was his name, where was he from, what age, occupation and profession did he have:

He said he was a native of Virginia and a neighbor in the State of Georgia (in the environs of the St. Marys River), thirty-two years of age, married and a merchant by trade.

2. Asked how many times he has been in this province, when was each time, if every time that he has come he has notified the government of his motives for coming, and when he was here most recently:

He said he does not now recall how many times he has come to the province; that he came among other times last October and talked with His Lordship as on another occasion when he was in the city; and at other times he had not done this because he did not come to the city first, just as when residents of this place go to Georgia they do not present themselves to that government; and, as he recalls, it was on the tenth of this month when he last came to this province.

3. Asked where or at whose house he stayed on the occasions that he has been in this province or in the city:

He said when he has come to the city he has stayed at Clark's public house and when he has come only to the province he has stayed in the home of his father-in-law, William Jones.

4. Asked if, being the foreigner that he is, the government should not at all times, and particularly now, have knowledge of the business things he came for; requested to tell what they are and the reasons he had to remain silent on them, and maybe he could be excused for what was indicated to be the cause of his imprisonment:

He said that this last time he came to the province it was with the intention of seeing his wife, who is at her father's house, and at the same time to talk with His Lordship and show him certain papers; and for that purpose he obtained a pass from Lieutenant Colonel Carlos Howard, commander of the Spanish post on the American frontier, who, as the witness remembers, told him that by the fourteenth or fifteenth of the month he would present himself before His Lordship, to whom he was writing to that effect, and the witness did not in fact comply with this because, having arrived at his father-in-law's house where his wife was, he found her sick, and so he postponed his coming a few days, bad weather also contributing. But having been arrested on Friday the seventeenth he has not been able to comply with his promise.

5. Asked where the papers were that he said he came to show His Lordship:

He said that he has them at his father-in-law's house on the St. John's River.

6. Asked if such papers were sent sealed to His Lordship; or by another person, and if so, who was it; or if they belonged to the defendant:

He said that they did not come directed to the governor by anyone who sent them; that they were copies of papers that had news of interest to this government, and that the witness had copied them from some originals; that he promised Carlos Howard he would come on the fourteenth to bring the information to His Lordship in order to ratify the statement he had made on the subject before Don Carlos.

7. Asked if he explained in said statement substantially all of the contents of the papers that he spoke of, or if he kept something to say personally or in writing to the Governor:

He said that actually he said everything in his statement before Don Carlos as to the content of said papers; but that at the same time he advised him that in case some other thoughts came to him he would tell them personally to the Governor.

8. Asked if, after the statement which he said he had made before Don Carlos, did he make or sign any other one afterwards; and if there is something he would like to add in order to continue to demonstrate the good faith already indicated in his first statement:

He said that besides his statement, he voluntarily made and signed another paper which he left with Don Carlos so that he could then send a translation of this to the Governor, but that his now confused mind does not remember well what he said, mainly because he has not seen the papers since his imprisonment; that he only remembers that he did not mention in his statement some materials gathered up which later he had found out about.

9. Asked if in support of his intent he wants to write an order to his father-in-law's home so they could deliver up the papers he is talking about or tell them where they are kept so that His Lordship can have them picked up:

He said that the location of the papers about which he is asked is not known to anyone and that because of their importance he has even hidden them from his father-in-law; that if His Lordship deems it convenient to send him to the place where they are, even escorted by 100 men, the witness himself will bring them back and will continue, until the end, the good faith he has demonstrated.

10. Having been shown the original statement that he gave under oath before Lieutenant Colonel Carlos Howard on the fifth of this month and the other paper dated the next day at Amelia Island, asked if they are the same papers he has been talking about in the preceding inquiry, and if the signatures are authentic, and if he verifies the contents, and if he wants this as part of his statement:

He said, having recognized both papers and the signatures at the bottom of them, that they are in his handwriting and script; that he ratifies both as being true in all their parts and that he wants this statement to be added to this record as part of his declaration.

11. Asked if on the fourteenth or fifteenth of this month (by when, following his promise to Howard, he would talk with the Governor and show him the said papers) he had not talked in his father-in-law's house with some people who were coming to the city and who had arrived there on the fourteenth, the day after they had been talking; asked who they were, and if he had used them to send any message to the Governor:

He said that it was true that the stated day he had talked in the house of his father-in-law Jones to Richard Lang, in the presence of John McIntosh, both of whom were coming to town, and that he had asked the former to tell the Governor that he was here with a permit from Carlos Howard to come to talk with him but that he would not take advantage of the occasion to accompany Lang and McIntosh because his wife was ill, but would instead do it a day or two afterwards.

12. Asked if he had spoken to Lang and McIntosh or to anyone else about the expedition which is planned against this province and which was discussed in his ratified statement and also in his other verified paper; and if in conversation with them he had told them about the time and place determined upon for said expedition, and the persons to whose command it was entrusted:

He said that he doesn't think he has spoken to McIntosh of that matter, but he did with Lang, to whom, although he assured him that the expedition was certainly going to take place, he still insisted that he thought it would not take place; but he did not tell Lang the people in charge nor the time it was going to take place, nor does he think he discussed those matters with anybody except Carlos Howard, whom he informed in writing as to what was in the wind, both by his statement and in another paper duly acknowledged along with his signature.

13. Asked if he has anything more to say; or if, continuing his good will toward the Spanish government, he wants to testify as to the whereabouts of the hidden papers so that a reliable person can go pick them up and inspect them, thus contributing to reducing the suspicions that have led to his imprisonment:

After explaining the risks that would imperil his life if he revealed this (making him by this action alone a target for the rebels of the projected expedition as soon as found out), he said that nevertheless, in spite of everything and to give the Governor the fullest impression that his intentions were not corrupt but all in agreement with what he said in the first statement, he was going to write four alphabet letters which would be shown to his wife, whom he believes will immediately deliver the papers, so that, with the appropriate confidentiality, and the fidelity of the person who is chosen to bring them, they may be examined. With this, His Lordship suspended the hearing to be continued if convenient. And the defendant, to whom it was read by the said interpreter by way of translation to his language, said he was in agreement on it and signs and ratifies it with His Lordship and with said interpreter, under oath.

> Quesada
> Attorney Ortega
> A. Hammond
> Miguel de Iznardy

Before me, José de Zubizarreta, government reporter

Florida, January 25, 1794.

In view of the fact that the papers belonging to Abner Hammond referred to at the end of his preceding statement can contribute to changing the projected course of this case, the proceedings will be now suspended until Sublieutenant of Dragoons José Maria Figueroa comes back, to whom His Lordship has given the letter which was written in his presence and before the Counsellor and before myself, the reporter, after being informed by the public interpreter of its contents, by which Don Abner ordered his wife to give to the bearer of said letter the portfolio which the symbols had identified; and in the meantime so that no time will be lost in such an interesting case, the examination of the papers begun previously and suspended for the reasons noted elsewhere will continue.

Hammond is to testify further when Figueroa comes back about details revealed as relevant by the papers, if they are in fact sent, as the letter provided.

> Quesada
> Ortega

Before me, José de Zubizarreta, government reporter

[AGI, PC, leg. 166, pormenor 16, p. 36]

Continuation of the statement of Abner Hammond.

St. Augustine, Florida, January 27, 1794.

Having returned yesterday night, Sublieutenant of Dragoons José Maria Figueroa brought a portfolio with various papers for the purpose of conducting the examination and eliciting the testimony as prearranged in the foregoing order. His Lordship, attended by the general counsellor, by the public interpreter, Miguel Iznardy, and by me, the government reporter, went to the Castillo de San Marcos.

Abner Hammond, being called up, was by means of the interpreter put under oath before Almighty God and by what he believes of the Holy Bible according to the Protestant sect which he professes, under which he promised to tell the truth in what he knows and is asked about. And enquiring officially then, they showed him the portfolio which said Sublieutenant Figueroa had brought back: to see if it were the same that had been requested from the wife by the letter written and entrusted to this courier; and if in it were all the papers mentioned in the witness's foregoing statement for the purpose of testifying as to his conduct and good faith in notification of the Spanish government as to the status and progress of the expedition being mounted against this province from Georgia and South Carolina:

The witness said the portfolio that was shown him was in fact the same one which his letter to his wife had asked to be sent to him, but it was lacking a copy in his own handwriting of the propositions made by M. de Bert, agent of the French Republic, which he had mentioned in his first declaration and which clearly affirmed the said proposals.

That without doubt his wife (notwithstanding his order not to leave out any papers) seeing that one—the main one that he sent for the portfolio for—which contained plans for the invasion of this province, had probably retained it, believing it to be prejudicial to the witness in the hands of His Lordship, by whose order he had been arrested.

That among all the papers in the portfolio and also there for inspection none is pertinent to the aforesaid negotiations except another account in his handwriting which would show the foods and military supplies that by order of the French agent were bought and accumulated in the Temple warehouse and destined for the expedition.

That he had already told about the aforesaid tools, more or less, in his first statement, referring to them in his second, and to prove it he hands in the list that shows all the things bought by the defendant, part of which are stored in Temple, and the other part he is waiting for, for the same disposition.

And His Lordship, having ordered the two statements given before the Commander of the St. Marys River Carlos Howard to be added as exhibits in the case and the aforementioned account, but not adding the other papers contained in the portfolio because they were found not relevant, after ordering their translation by the public interpreter, ordered that the testimony continue.

First: Asked why did the witness suggest that he could almost state in writing the main points that were referred to by the French agent: Does he want to write them out personally, or to give a new order to his wife telling her precisely to send said copy, the one that the defendant thinks has been withdrawn from the portfolio, she thinking, without doubt, that the defendant's order to send the copy was against his will:

He said that actually he knows his wife would be apprehensive about the matter, thinking that this paper she withdrew could damage the defendant, and he fears that even if he writes it for a second time that the same thing would happen; nevertheless he is willing to try it immediately, to prove the truth of all he has said, and also to write out and sign the paper they suggest, outlining the proposals that he remembers to have been made to his brother Samuel by the French agent for the proposed expedition, a copy of which was hidden by the witness's wife.

And His Lordship having decided that he should write both papers he did so, and the Governor took them to make proper use of them, studying their contents as revealed by the interpreter; then he ordered the proceedings suspended to be continued later if needed. And the witness to whom it was read, as translated by the interpreter, said he agreed with the contents of what was stated and signed and ratified the same with His Lordship and the interpreter under oath.

Quesada

Attorney Ortega

A. Hammond

Miguel de Iznardy

Before me, José de Zubizarreta

Lieutenant Figueroa in searching through the portfolio of Abner Hammond had found a paper dated 24 December 1793, in which

Hammond had listed supplies under shipment from Savannah to St. Marys for the use of the French expedition, as follows: 600 pounds of gunpowder, 500 pounds of lead, 12 shovels, 17 spades, 48 hoes, 21 axes, 6 handsaws, 6 drawing knives, 45 barrels of flour, 10 barrels of pork, 4 barrels of beef, 50 bushels of salt, and 427 gallons of rum. Listed in addition were supplies already at St. Marys: 100 more pounds of lead, 400 flints, 60 camp kettles, and 130 bushels of corn. There was a marginal notation of other supplies already at Temple: another 300 bushels of corn, 15 barrels of rice, 12 barrels of bread, 2 pounds of sugar, 16 swords, and 2 boxes of soap. The commodities listed at St. Marys and on the way there were valued at 320 pounds, 19 shillings, and 2 pennies, of which amount the provisions already at St. Marys were stated to be valued at 34 pounds, 25 shillings. At the bottom of the paper there was a statement signed by Abner Hammond in which he promised to dispose of the supplies "according to future orders, providing they escape the dangers of the seas on their passage to the river of St. Marys."

It would appear that a sizable force of men armed with 600 pounds of lead, 600 pounds of gunpowder, and 427 gallons of rum—and with only 2 boxes of soap—could indeed be formidable.

Abner Hammond wrote down what he could recall of his copy of the paper that had outlined for Colonel Samuel Hammond the French proposals for the liberation of Florida. Since the document that he sought to remember was soon obtained and placed in the papers of litigation, it is printed here. Abner's less accurate recollections are reprinted in the appendix of this book.

[AGI, PC, leg. 166, pormenor 16, p. 61—in English]

In consequence of the instructions & authorization from Citizen Consul Mangourit of the French Republick, I, the subscriber have put down the following proposals for the consideration of Coll. ———.

I.

Coll. ——— will endeavor to raise a number of men who are to be march'd into East Florida there to take the oath to the French Republick & in the name of said R[epublic] attempt the reduction of that country.

II.

Coll. _____, & the officers under his command shall be commission'd by the said R[epublic] immediately after their having become French citizens. They & their soldiers shall be under French pay from that moment which is to be continued to them as long as the war lasts or as long as their service will be wanted. They shall be furnish'd during the time of their service with rations, arms & clothing by s'd R[epublic].

III.

Every adventurer engaging upon said expedition shall be entitled to a generous bounty in land the quantity to be specified hereafter: they shall also be intitled, in the Town of St. Augustine, Every one to a lot or lot & house as far as vacant lots together with those call'd Crown property will reach, the officers to make choice by superiority, & the remaining lots to be drawn for by the men & shou'd there not be a sufficient number of lots then the remainder to be subdivided in such a manner as to afford every man a share.

IV.

Proper aid & encouragement will be held out to such inhabitants of the neighbouring & other countries who will wish to become settlers & join during the war in the defence of said country.

V.

The town of St. Augustine and such other places as may insure the possession of E[ast] F[lorida] will be put in a defensable situation & stores will be established which must be plentifully supplid with provisions, ammunition, etc.

VI.

In order to protect the coast & inland navigation against the excurtions of the Bahama & Havannah pirates it will be necesary to provide several arm'd gallies. It will also be of infinate advantage to the Common Cause to have a few armed vessels of such burthen as the Bars of s'd Country will admit.

VII.

E[ast] F[lorida] will be considered a part of the F[rench] R[epublic] during the continuation of the war & as such remain under its immediate protection. At the conclusion of the war the said country is to become independent to all intents & purposes with the provisos of adopting a strictly democratical republican government[,] the rights of man to form the basis of their constitution.

VIII.

Should the province of west Florida and Louisiana shake of [f] the yoke from their present masters & form similar governments to that of E[ast] F[lorida] it will be left at their option to join the latter in forming a Federal government.

IX.

At all events the gov of E[ast] F[lorida] will form an alliance, offensive & defensive with the R[epublic] of F[rance], both countries will try to keep up between themselves that friendly & brotherly intercourse which will forever cement their comon freedom & safety.

X.

As an indemnity to the F[rench] R[epublic] for the expences that will [be] incurred by her for the carrying on [of] the expedition & the defence of the country during the present war the R[epublic] of F[rance] shall be entitled to a moiety of the net proceeds of the sales of all lands called vacant in E[ast] [Florida].

XI.

We mean by vacant land such as are not appropriated to the present settlers nor such as will be granted on bounty to the troops & other adventurers joining during the war as well as those lands that are reservd to the Indians for their hunting grounds or for publick purposes.

XII.

All provisions, navil & military stores as well as other property belonging to the King of Spain taken in E[ast] F[lorida] shall be appropriated to the support & defence of said country and a certain proportion of the cash that may be found in the Treasury is to be allow'd to the Troops who Engage in the Expedition.

XIII.

Such vessels as may be taken in the ports & harbours of said country shall belong one half to the F[rench] R[epublic] & the other half to the troops of the [expedition] & such of said vessels as are armed are to be continued for the defense of said country in its service & the proceeds of the prizes if any taken shall be divided between the abovementioned proprietors or captors according to custom.

XIIII.

The plan of operation being once concerted & fixed upon, there must be made out a list includeing every article required for the execution thereof & proper measures taken to have them provided in due time.

XV.

In order to indemnify the individuals who engage in the proposd expedition in case they should miscarry or in case the countrys should be returned to their old masters at the conclusion of the war, the R[epublic] of F[rance] will grant them a proportion of confiscated property either in the West Indies or in some other of their possessions equivilent to the sacrifices they may have made in their own country.

copy (signed)

C. M. F. de Burt
Savannah, 24th July 1793
C[onsul] of the [French]
Republick

Proposals of C.M.F. de Burt in behalf of the Republick of France

[AGI, PC, leg. 166, pormenor 16, p. 98]

Certification of the transfer and embarkation of John MacIntosh and Abner Hammond.

As it is my duty I certify under oath to having been present on last January 28, at the embarkation of John MacIntosh and Abner

Hammond. It is verified that on said day it took place with ample escort and custody in the government small boat, with the adjutant of this city, José Fernandez, being present for the purpose of transferring them to the sloop *Maria* under Captain Miguel Acosta (then at the point of the bar and ready to receive them and to be underway). To put this on record as ordered I certify to these matters.

Florida, February 1, 1794.

José de Zubizarreta, government reporter

NINE

Gambling for Cigars at Clark's Inn

WILLIAM MacEnnry on 8 February appeared before the governor and testified about the evening of 20 January, when he and others had enjoyed a friendly card game at Clark's Inn, in St. Augustine.[1] The players, who were gambling for cigars, had included John McIntosh and Richard Lang.

Gaming was not illegal in those times, nor was it thought improper. In fact, members of the clergy had participated in the game at Clark's Inn. Besides MacEnnry, McIntosh, and Lang, the other players were Father Francis,[2] Constantine McCaffrey,[3] Father Michael Crosby,[4] innkeeper Jacob Clark, and his wife. The socializing had ended abruptly when McIntosh and Lang were arrested on suspicion of conspiracy under an order entered earlier on the same day.

Andrew Davies, who had also been present at the inn, stated that during the evening McIntosh and Lang had discussed the

1. Jacob Clark was born in North Carolina in 1747 and married Sarah Stephens. He fought at Germantown and Brandywine in the American Revolution. Captured in the battle at Charleston in 1780, he was imprisoned at St. Augustine (Marguerite G. Reddick, *Camden's Challenge: A History of Camden County, Georgia*, p. 22).

2. His full name was Francis Estaban; he was a Franciscan (Janice Borton Miller, "Juan Nepomuceno de Quesada: Spanish Governor of East Florida, 1790–1795," [Ph.D. diss.], p. 115).

3. A young priest sent to Florida in 1791 to assist with the English-speaking subjects (Miller, "Quesada," p. 114).

4. Another young priest sent to Florida in 1791 to assist with the English-speaking subjects (ibid.).

rebellion—with Lang sounding skeptical but McIntosh confident that the revolution would take place. From time to time, Lang and McIntosh had gone out into the patio to discuss matters in privacy.

William Plowden, a prisoner in the Castillo de San Marcos, was later interviewed by the governor in Plowden's cell. He also remembered conversations with Lang and McIntosh at Clark's Inn. He said that the rebellion had been discussed and that Samuel Hammond had been named as the principal leader of the impending attack on East Florida. Plowden said that he had returned from Georgia to his East Florida home at dusk one evening, planning to report to the governor what he had heard in Georgia about the rebellion in Florida. He had been arrested, he said, before he had a chance to see Quesada.

John Peter Wagnon, also languishing in the fortress, told the governor he had gone to Georgia to fetch McIntosh's cattle, but swollen streams had prevented him from bringing the animals back. Wagnon said that early on the evening of the twentieth McIntosh, Lang, and Plowden had come to his house asking whether he had heard any news of the rebellion during his journey into Georgia. Wagnon then told the governor of plans in Georgia to raise troops in Kentucky for the same expedition.

Manuel Solana, sent by the governor with Peter Marrot[5] to Lang's house on the St. Marys to pick up any incriminating papers, reported that rumors of the rebellion were prevalent there.

The governor, meanwhile, continued to gather disturbing evidence. On 6 February, in the fortress guardroom, he interviewed William Jones. Jones told the Spanish official of his own arrest along with that of his house guest and son-in-law Abner Hammond. Hammond, Jones said, had come to Florida to sell to the Spanish government some supplies that had been accumulating in Georgia.

The St. Johns River planter went on to say that Hammond

5. Marrot was government surveyor in East Florida (Pleasant D. Gold, *History of Duval County, Florida*, pp. 66, 67).

had discussed with him the two task forces being enlisted in Georgia, one to come against East Florida and the other to open up navigation of the Mississippi. He said that Hammond had suggested he remove himself to St. Augustine for reasons of safety, since little protection would be available at San Nicolás.

Jones said that Hammond had expressed distress about his brother Samuel being mixed up in the rebellion. Further, Jones said, Hammond had told him that General Elijah Clark would lead an expedition from Georgia against Pensacola to be coordinated with the attack on East Florida.

The next day the governor interviewed James McGirtt,[6] a resident of the St. Johns River valley. McGirtt disclosed that when he had been at Lang's house a fortnight before, William Howard, a Georgian, had come into the house and told Mrs. Lang that "if you had advised me when Marrot and Solana were here, the devil take me if they would have returned the same way they came." McGirtt said that Howard had been very belligerent, boasting that he would get Lang and Hammond out of the fortress within fifteen days.

Robert Seagrove, a trader with the Indians and brother of the U.S. Indian agent for Georgia, James Seagrove,[7] maintained a store at Traders Hill on the Georgia side of the St. Marys River about eight miles west of Coleraine. In a note of 12 February 1794 Seagrove said that a French corsair and his brigantine of sixteen cannon were at St. Marys, hovering off the bar all day; and he expressed the opinion that the ship was there in behalf of the rebellion.

6. James McGirtt joined his brother Daniel in an attack on Wright's fort and in defecting to the British. He became a captain in the loyalist Florida Rangers in the American Revolution. The British governor (Tonyn) later called him and his brother Dan men of "infamous character" (Wilbur H. Siebert, *Loyalists in East Florida, 1774 to 1785*, 1:26, 38, 164, 329; biographical note at 2:328).

7. Robert Seagrove was a brother of James Seagrove, U.S. agent to the Creeks (James F. Doster, *The Creek Indians and Their Florida Lands, 1740–1823*, 1:93, 154). He traded with the Indians at Traders Hill and also at Coleraine, where thirty Indians murdered the storekeeper (ibid., 1:177; Reddick, *Camden's Challenge*, p. 13). The brothers were among the founders of St. Marys (Reddick, *Camden's Challenge*, p. 146; Louise F. Hays, *Hero of Hornet's Nest; A Biography of Elijah Clark, 1733 to 1799*, p. 229).

[AGI, PC, leg. 166, pormenor 16, p. 115]

Statement by William MacEnrry.

St. Augustine, Florida, February 8, 1794.

Before His Lordship the Governor, being accompanied by the general counsellor, appeared William MacEnrry, Irishman and a new settler and resident of said city; who by means of Miguel Iznardy, public interpreter, and before me, the government reporter, took an oath before God and the Holy Cross by which he promised to tell the truth of what he knew and was asked; and he was told to refer to the things that took place in Jacob Clark's house on the night of the imprisonment of John McIntosh, Richard Lang, William Plowden, and others, things which he had told His Lordship about one or two days after their imprisonment:

He said that between nine and ten on the night when they were caught the witness was gambling for cigars with Lang, McIntosh, Father Francis, Constantine McCaffrey, and Father Michael Crosby in the house of Clark, the innkeeper.

That several times the defendant tried to leave but the said priests detained him, insisting he should continue playing because later they would all retire together, since they were all going by the same road.

That to be accommodating he continued a bit longer than he had in mind and in all this time he observed that McIntosh and Lang, who were also gambling with him, got up on two or three occasions and went to the patio of the house, from which the witness guessed it must have been some secret matters they wanted to talk about because they would not talk about them in front of the others playing the game.

That he does not remember that there was anyone else there than those he had mentioned, and that this is the whole conversation as he told the Governor, who, knowing of the witness's presence in Clark's home at the time of the imprisonment, called to ask him what he had seen, which is what he affirms and ratifies. And, having read his statement translated to his language by the interpreter, he said that it was faithfully written as said; that he is fifty-four years old, and signed with the interpreter under oath.

                                                        Quesada

Attorney Ortega

William MacEnnry

Miguel de Iznardy

Before me, José de Zubizarreta, government reporter

[AGI, PC, leg. 166, pormenor 16, p. 99]

Statement by Andrew Davies

In the city of St. Augustine, Florida, February 3, 1794.

Before His Lordship the Governor (being assisted by his lieutenant and general counsellor) appeared Andrew Davies, Lieutenant of Militia of the Cavalry on the St. Johns River of this province, who by means of Miguel Iznardy, public interpreter, took the oath before me, the reporter, in the name of God Almighty and on what he believes of the Sacred Bible under the Protestant religion which he professes, promising to tell the truth in everything he knew and was asked; and pursuing the tenor of the interview of John McIntosh (reported heretofore) and relating in an orderly manner the conversation which is said to have started in front of the witness in the Clark boarding house on the subject of the expedition planned against this province in the States of Georgia and South Carolina:

He said that he has well remembered the conversation at the Clark boarding house with McIntosh in the presence of Richard Lang and another person whom he does not remember; that, initiating it, the witness asked McIntosh if he was sure that this expedition was going to take place, which the public knew was notoriously projected against this province from the States of Georgia and South Carolina; that McIntosh answered affirmatively, basing his opinion on the perseverance and independence of the ones planning the expedition; nevertheless the witness insisted on the opposite opinion, because of the lack of means and of allies to carry out the project; the conversation being restricted to these two points of view (in which Lang indifferently said nothing), each defending his point of view without changing the trend of the conversation to another matter; that this was also the drift of the discussions which the witness had in the St. Johns River valley when he talked with the inhabitants there about the imprisonment of McIntosh, which he heard of there, making him think (he does not know if accurately) that since the government had arrested him there must be something in his behavior that could be prejudicial to him.

That is all he knows and the truth under his given oath. And the defendant (to whom the statement was read as translated by the said interpreter) stated that he affirms its contents and ratifies it; that he is thirty-eight years old and signed with His Lordship, with the general counsellor, and with the interpreter, under oath.

Quesada

Attorney Ortega

And [rew] Davies

Miguel de Iznardy

Before me, José de Zubizarreta, government reporter

[AGI, PC, leg. 166, pormenor 16, p. 102]

William Plowden

City of St. Augustine, Florida, February 4, 1794

The Governor, in continuation of this matter, was assisted by the general counsellor, by the public interpreter Miguel Iznardy, and by me, the reporter, at the Castillo de San Marcos of this city and at the dungeon where William Plowden is imprisoned, who by means of said interpreter was placed under oath before God Almighty and what he believes of the Holy Bible according to the Protestant faith which he professes; and under such oath he promised to tell the truth of what he knew and was asked about. And in consequence he answered as follows:

1st. Asked how long it has been since he first came to this province, and in which part of it he became established, and if on his entry he had sworn to loyalty and being a subject:

He said that it had been three years since he came from Georgia, where he used to live, to settle in this province; and that he had sworn to his loyalty and being a subject and that he is living near the St. Johns River.

2d. Asked if he remembers that a few days before his imprisonment the Governor had called him to ask him who were the two men who came to His Lordship with the purpose of becoming new settlers and subjects and that they asserted that they were coming to live with the witness:

He said that he does not remember being called by the Governor on such a matter; but that he remembers that when he went to the government for another purpose His Lordship spoke to him about them; that they are William Howard[8] and Daniel Bakin [Brackin];[9] that he had stated that he had a contract with the first one to build him a house in Mosquitoes,[10] where the witness planned to establish himself; that he was also asked by His Lordship as to why they did not carry a pass and he said in reply that they did not have it because Richard Lang told Howard that he did not need one since he was coming before the Governor in person with the witness; and that His Lordship suggested that these men should not stay in the province; and that he [the governor] did not admit them and that he told the witness to see that they left there immediately.

3rd. Asked it he knows of a certain expedition coming against this province from the states of Georgia and South Carolina, and what he knows about it, and the ways he found out about it:

He said that while staying in this city, before going to jail, he had heard (he does not remember whether from Richard Lang or from Daniel Hall[11] or both) in Clark's Inn (also with John McIntosh, Prentis Gallop,[12] and others whom he does not remember) that such an expedition was forming and that the leaders would be John Moore[13] and Samuel Hammond, and he said that those present, including the witness, gave their opinions; some expressed the opinion that [given] the little reputation of Moore, [they doubted] he would be chosen by those preparing the expedition, but that the

8. William Howard served in the U.S. army in Georgia and recruited for the French intrigue.

9. Daniel Brackin served in the U.S. army in Georgia and had been allowed by Richard Lang to enter East Florida without papers. He came with William Howard, who also carried no entry papers (Miller, "Quesada," p. 242).

10. In the vicinity of New Smyrna Beach.

11. This was probably a reference to Nathaniel Hall.

12. Prentis Gallop was one of the founders of St. Marys (Reddick, *Camden's Challenge*, p. 146).

13. John Moore was a political leader of Georgia and served in the Georgia legislature (Hays, *Hero of Hornet's Nest*, p. 286).

contrary was said about Hammond; that these were the points discussed in the conversation and that is all he knows about it.

4th. Asked if he has heard whether Howard and Bakin [Brackin], at the time they came here to be admitted as subjects and new settlers, were enlisted for the said expedition and whether they are now:

He said that he did not know anything about them being enlisted nor does he believe that they were when they came over here, because he did not hear a word about it, and does not know what they did later on.

5th. Asked if he has information that Howard or Baquin [Brackin] left the province in compliance with the order of the government; or if both left; and if either have returned he was to say to what location and with what motive:

He said that he knew that Howard had been by the house of the witness on the St. Johns River to pick up his tools that he had left there but he does not know if his companion also did this or if they returned to the province.

That he now remembers that Howard told him that the Governor would admit him to the province with a passport from the Commander of our river; and he also remembers that the same Howard told him that he was a Lieutenant in Georgia, of one of the companies established there against the Indians. And in this situation His Lordship ordered the statement suspended to be continued if found necessary; and the witness, to whom this was read in English by the public interpreter, said that he agrees to it, affirms it, and ratifies it; that he is forty years old and signed it with His Lordship, with the Counsellor, and with the interpreter, under oath.

> Quesada
> Attorney Ortega
> Miguel Iznardy
> William Plowden

Before me: José de Zubizarreta, government reporter

[AGI, PC, leg. 166, pormenor 16, p. 105]

Statement by D. John Peter Wagnon

In the city of St. Augustine, February 5, 1794

The Governor, accompanied by the general counsellor and by the public interpreter, Miguel Iznardy, went to the Castillo de San Marcos in this city and to the dungeon where John Peter Wagnon is imprisoned, who by means of the interpreter swore by God Almighty and by what he believes of the Holy Bible according to the Protestant faith he professes; and under this he promised to tell the truth of what he knew and was asked; and the following questions were put to him:

1st. Asked how long it has been since he became established in this province and if he swore fidelity and to being a subject:

He said that in April it will be three years since he was admitted as a subject and settler.

2nd. Asked how many times he has gone to Georgia or any other American establishment since arriving in this province and if when he went he always carried the proper permit from the government:

He said that at first he was established near the St. Marys River and he went several more times to other parts of it without anybody's permission; that in the same way he has gone two more times after establishing himself on the St. Johns River; one to take his wife under a proper government permit and the other to have dinner with Major Abner Hammond in his house on the other side of the St. Marys River; and lately he has been to Georgia to pick up cattle belonging to John McIntosh, who had commissioned him to do it, telling him he had a license from the Governor to hire white men to carry out the task.

3rd. Asked when was the last time he was in Georgia, how long was he there and what was the day he returned:

He said that he left the house of John McIntosh on November 14, and that he stayed in Georgia until the 12th or 13th of January, when he returned.

4th. Asked if he was returning with the idea of staying here or going back immediately with his wife and family:

He said he came with the determined intention of going back immediately with his family to Georgia.

5th. Asked if he told his ideas of returning to any of the inhabitants of the St. Marys and the St. Johns, and told to state the reason he was determined to go back:

He said that he did not tell anyone of his idea of returning except

William Jones and told him without telling him the reason because he knew beforehand that the witness wanted to return to Georgia.

6th. Asked if he left anyone on the St. Marys River to wait for his return, with a boat or any other arrangement:

He said that he only left a Negro boy in care of an American named Lewis; who accompanied him from Augusta but went back after leaving the witness on this side of the St. Marys River; that the witness gave orders to him to take the Negro boy to the house of William McIntosh, brother of John, where the defendant had left his horses.

7th. Asked if in the most recent time he has been in Georgia, he has heard or found out about the expedition projected against this province, and by what persons, and to tell about the circumstances:

He said that he heard only general talk, so he cannot point out any particular people who spoke about this expedition, which was promoted by the French making tempting propositions to Americans who might enlist.

That, although wise men all said that the expedition was not going to take place because it was not supported by any power capable of sustaining the expenses and that even if it did take place there would only be a few who would come to loot the establishments on the St. Johns and St. Marys Rivers, nevertheless the witness came here with the idea of telling His Lordship about these matters the day after his arrival; and he would have done so except for the rising waters of the rivers.

8th. Asked what day he had arrived in the city and at what time; and if on that day he had spoken to anyone about the details of the said expedition; and to tell where, whether in his house or in any other, and explain:

He said that he arrived in this city at dusk on the date he was jailed; and that soon thereafter John McIntosh, Richard Lang, William Plowden, and James Hall[14] arrived at his house, and the first three named asked him for news, and he told them about what he has just now been answering.

9th. Asked if he has also told these men of his intention to

14. Dr. James Hall was a Revolutionary War veteran of the New Hampshire line, who fought under Lafayette at Yorktown. He received a Spanish land grant in 1790 in East Florida, near Julington Creek, married the widow of Robert Pritchard, moved to Mandarin, participated in the 1812 rebellion in Florida (and was banished for this but later forgiven). He returned to Florida, where he is buried at Mandarin. See Mary M. DuPree and G. Dekle Taylor, "Dr. James Hall, 1760–1837."

communicate with the Governor the next day about these things:

He said no.

10th. Asked if in transit or in the settlements between St. Mary and this city, he gave news of the projected expedition to any of the inhabitants, whose names he will say, telling them of the terrible situation, and that they were going to lose all their properties if they did not move to Georgia, and if the defendant pushed them to leave the province:

He said that it is true that in answer to many people on the way to the city who asked him about the expedition, he told them it was true, but that he did not intimidate anybody with it, much less tell them to leave the province.

11th. Asked if while in Georgia recently he was accompanied by an escort, from one place to another, and why:

He said no.

12th. Asked what was the object of the commission on which he has been lately in Georgia and if it was carried out in every way:

He said that he went to Georgia to bring back some cattle of John MacIntosh, as he has said before, but that he could not do it because of the high waters that prevented it.

At this point His Lordship suspended the statement, to be continued if necessary; and the witness to whom it was read as translated into his language by the public interpreter said that he confirmed it; adding, because of having thought about it just then, that in carrying out in Georgia the commission from John McIntosh he took with him a pass given by the Governor and endorsed by McIntosh for the witness, since it was a personal pass for said McIntosh; and also he adds that he made another trip into Georgia to the wedding of Abner Hammond with a daughter of William Jones; and also upon coming back to this province the last time he stated his intention of retiring to Georgia to Thomas Cryer, a resident of the St. Marys; that he confirms and ratifies everything else in his statement, and he signed with His Lordship and with the general counsellor and with said interpreter, under oath.

> Quesada
>
> Attorney Ortega
>
> J. Wagnon
>
> Miguel Iznardy

Before me, José de Zubizarreta, government reporter

[AGI, PC, leg. 166, pormenor 16, p. 101]

Statement by Manuel Solana [3 February 1794]

On the above stated day, month, and year, before the Governor and the general counsellor, appeared Manuel Solana, resident of this city, who, under oath before God and the Holy Cross, promised to speak the truth of what he knew and was asked; he was asked to expound on the information he obtained and from whom he got it when he was last commissioned by His Lordship to go to the St. Marys River to investigate the outcries which John Peter Wagnon stirred up on his arrival from Georgia, spreading among the inhabitants of that river valley rumors of the American expedition against the province; the witness also to expose Wagnon's purpose of returning here:

He said that some twenty or more days ago the witness, obeying the order of the Governor, accompanied the Captain of this Battalion, Peter Marrot, to the house of Richard Lang on the St. Marys River; that there he found out about things from one of its residents whom he calls Horrin (who afterwards has come to live on the St. Johns River) and from Francis Sterling, son-in-law of Lang, and others from his family (who the defendant says have moved to Georgia); that Wagnon (who some days before had arrived at the said St. Marys River, coming from Georgia) had spread the word among the inhabitants that a certain expedition was being planned, which was soon going to take place, and he had urged them to collect their belongings immediately and flee with them to safety in Georgia, which he said he was going to do, coming for the purpose to the city to remove his wife; and he said he was leaving in readiness on the said river the boat on which he had come, and was leaving his horse on the other side of the Alta Maja ["Big Snake"; now Altamaha] River, near Savannah.

That the said Horrin, who among others heard the conversation to which he has referred, promised to write it down if desired, but was told it was not necessary.

That the witness also knows, because it is well known on the St. Marys River, that upon the arrival of Wagnon to the other side of it, he was escorted there by one military detachment or another of the three stationed on the other side, the American side, of said river.

That is all he knows about the matter, and it is what he reported to His Lordship on his return from his commissioned errand; which he affirms and ratifies under the oath he has taken. His statement having been read to him he said he was satisfied; that he did not sign because he does not know how, and that he is forty-six years old. Signed by His Lordship, with the General Counsellor, under oath.

Quesada
Attorney Ortega

Before me, José de Zubizarreta, reporter

[AGI, PC, leg. 166, pormenor 16, p. 139]

Statement by John Peter Wagnon [19 February 1794]

On the above day, month, and year His Lordship and the counsellor came to the cell of the prisoner John Peter Wagnon, who by means of the public interpreter, Miguel Iznardy, was put under oath before God Almighty and what he believes of the Holy Bible under his Protestant faith, and he promised to tell the truth of what he knew and was asked.

1st. He was asked if, on the night he arrived in this city from Georgia and spoke with John McIntosh, [the witness] had said something to him about the destination of the expedition that was projected against this province; which was the latest one he had been given:

He said that he said nothing to McIntosh except what he has here stated.

2nd. Asked if he heard something in Georgia about the enlistment being made with the objective of creating a new establishment in the western part of said province and if he had told anyone about it:

He said that he had heard of enlistings planned in the State of Kentucky with the purpose of attacking the settlements in the West but he does not remember talking about it to anyone in this province.

That is all he can say about the matter, and the truth under oath, which he affirms and ratifies, affirming that he is as old as he has stated and signs under oath with the interpreter.

Quesada
Attorney Ortega
Miguel de Iznardy
J. P. Wagnon

Before me, José de Zubizarreta, court reporter

[AGI, PC, leg. 166, pormenor 16, p. 110]

Statement by William Jones

St. Augustine, February 6, 1794

The Governor, accompanied by the general counsellor and by the public interpreter, Miguel Iznardy, came to the barracks of this city and to the room of the officer of the guard, where he ordered to appear before him William Jones, a prisoner in a cell in said quarters, to take an oath with the help of the interpreter before God Almighty and what he believes of the Holy Bible in accordance with the Protestant faith he professes; and under the same he promised to tell the truth of what he knew and was asked; and so the following ensued:

1st. Asked how long he had been established in this province, and if he had sworn loyalty and to be a subject when he was admitted:

He said that it has been a little more than two years and that he had taken the oath.

2nd. Asked if he had children or relatives established in any of the American States, and to say who and where they are:

He said that he has two sons and two daughters, the first son being established in Virginia and the other son in Augusta: and of the daughters, one is in this province married to John Daedly and the other, who is now in the house of the witness, married to Abner Hammond, inhabitant and subject of the State of Georgia.

3rd. Asked if, when they arrested the witness in his home, was his son-in-law Hammond also taken:

He said yes.

4th. Asked how long the witness Hammond had been in his house when arrested, and if he knows why he was arrested:

He said that he does not recall whether it was three or four days that Hammond was in his house before he was arrested and he does not know the cause of his imprisonment, but he had heard it said on coming to this city that it was supposed to be because he had been delayed some days beyond the date he had said aboard the packet of the Commander of the St. Marys, Carlos Howard, that he would be in the city to talk to the Governor: and the witness reflecting that he has said, it could have been three or four days that Hammond was in his house before he was arrested, insists he cannot remember the exact number and perhaps it was more days than that.

5th. Asked if he knows about or had heard Hammond say anything about the business that had brought him to this province; and if he has heard it from anyone else he should tell about it:

He said that Hammond had told him the object of his coming was to offer the government at good prices a shipment of flour, pork meat, and beef that a boat from Savannah was bringing him, to which end he asked the witness about the current prices here and said he would sell them at cheaper prices; that's what Hammond told him in reference to this matter.

That he also spoke about certain enlistments in Augusta to come against this province and also to open up passages in Louisiana for the navigation of the Mississippi River, the place of rendezvous being on the bank of the Tennessee River, from whence both enterprises were to take their separate routes.

That a John Mur [Moore] who came to this province with Francis Goodwing [Goodwin] and lived here about six months, was named Sergeant Major of one of the Divisions.

That the government of South Carolina had taken steps in the matter and consequently had imprisoned three leaders of the rebels (two of them being named Teats,[15] and the other one named Drayton[16]) but nevertheless the expedition was now being vigorously prepared and the witness asked his son-in-law what he should do since he did not believe he was protected in the place where he was established; and he was advised to come to this city with his family and live by his work and that of his Negroes; that the witness was going to follow this advice but he had not done so yet because of the high waters on the day when he was arrested.

That among other things discussed with his son-in-law was the fact that three or four days before then Richard Lang had been at his house talking about the projected expedition and had told him that Samuel Hammond, brother of Abner, was involved in it, and that he was to command the cavalry while General Clark was to command the troops that were going to Pensacola; and on this his son-in-law had remarked that he would feel very sorry if his brother Samuel, who until that time had maintained his character as a gentleman,

15. Undoubtedly the name meant was Tate, i. e., William and his brother Robert (Eugene Perry Link, *Democratic-Republican Societies, 1790–1800*, p. 135; Richard K. Murdoch, *The Georgia-Florida Frontier, 1793–1796: Spanish Reaction to French Intrigue and American Designs*, pp. 14, 150; Hays, *Hero of Hornet's Nest*, p. 243).

16. Stephen Drayton, private secretary of Governor William Moultrie of South Carolina (Murdoch, *Georgia-Florida Frontier*, p. 151).

would mix up with these people who in his country were called outlaws.

That having told him that Lang had also informed him that there were 7,000 already enlisted for the expedition, Abner Hammond confirmed this.

6th. Asked if he had not told him other things, in addition to what has already been told, which he wanted to tell the Governor:
He said no.

7th. Asked if he knows that his son-in-law tried to sell to the people of the St. Johns or St. Marys River a store of food supplies and things that he had gathered in his warehouse in Temple:
He said that he does not know about that.

At this point His Lordship suspended the proceedings to be continued if appropriate; and the witness to whom it was read in his language, English, by the interpreter, said he was in accord and ratified it; that he is fifty-eight years old and signs with His Lordship and with the counsellor and with the interpreter, under oath.

                                        Quesada
                                        Miguel de Iznardy
                                        William Jones

Before me, José de Zubizarreta, government reporter

[AGI, PC, leg. 166, pormenor 16, p. 113]

Statement by James McGirtt.

St. Augustine, Florida, February 7, 1794

Before the Governor, being assisted by the counsellor, appeared James McGuirtt, resident in the St. Johns River Valley and a long-time settler and native of South Carolina in the United States, from whence he came to this province, who with Miguel Iznardy, public interpreter, and before me, the government reporter, swore by God Almighty and what he believes of the Holy Bible according to the Protestant faith he professes, under which he promised to tell the truth of what he knew and was asked; and so referring to the conversation he had with His Lordship about an event that occurred on the St. Marys River and in the home of Richard Lang, with William Howard:

He said when he was at Lang's house fifteen days ago, Howard landed there from a boat while others remained behind in it, and as he [Howard] came to the house he told Mrs. Lang in front of the witness: "If you had advised me when Marrot and Solana were here (they were the two in charge of picking up the papers from Lang as commissioned by the Governor), the devil take me if they would have returned the same way they came."

Further, that Howard, on walking into the living room of Lang's house and without lowering his rifle or cartridge pouch with which he landed, again pressed Mrs. Lang to say if she knew where Lang and Hammond were (who are two of the prisoners in this litigation), to which she answered that she had heard they were locked in the fortress of this city; and that then Howard (with such an angry tone and facial expression as to frighten the witness) said, repeating: "The devil take me if in fifteen days they are not here and free" and "I am going to look for complete satisfaction."

That Howard addressed the witness who was warming himself next to the chimney and said: "I think you live on the St. Johns River?" When answered, "yes," he then asked, after the witness stated that he lived sixteen miles from John Forrester:[17] "Do you know if he will soon be coming here to remove his wife and mother-in-law?" To that the witness answered that he had already taken them away, and stated that he did not know if he had come back to the river; and Howard, at this, began swearing and cursing again, revealing his displeasure at the information and his desire to take revenge on Forrester.

That at the end of this conversation Howard left and rejoined seven or eight armed men (among them John Bayley, a resident in the St. Johns River valley); and together they drove a herd of cattle to the river and took it over to the other side.

That this is the substance of the conversation that he told the Governor about and it is truthful in all its parts. He ratifies it now under oath; and having read his statement he said he was in accor-

17. John Forrester was an employee of Panton, Leslie and Company and also performed official duties for the Spanish government. He acted as a magistrate on the St. Marys (Miller, "Quesada," pp. 146, 212, 239).

dance with it and signed with His Lordship, with the Counsellor and with the interpreter, under oath.

> Quesada
> Attorney Ortega
> James McGirtt
> Miguel Iznardy

Before me, José de Zubizarreta.

[AGI, PC, leg. 166, pormenor 16, p. 133—in English]

St. Marys

12th February, 1794

Dear Sir:

I was at Savannah a few days ago where I saw many of your old friends who begged to be remembered to you. I found some letters there for you which I enclose now to you and Mr. McQueen. I am very happy to hear that you have got some of our wortheys of Georgia, namely Mr. Genet's men in keeping. I hope before they come out of the Pen that the[y] will be brave and fat as the[y] left their rations behind them.

Sunday a French privateer brigg, yellow sided [illegible] mounting 16 guns, kept hovering off this bar all day but the pilot would not go near her. I am sure she was to be joined by certain characters which you have now jailed.

I am very poor. I believe you and my old friend Mr. McQueen have forgot me. I hope the[e] won't be long.

Your servant,

> Robt. Seagrove

TEN

Whip the Governor "at a Fair Fite"

CAPTAIN Richard Lang submitted a memorandum on 18 February 1794 to Governor Quesada about a colorful conversation he had had with William Jones and John McIntosh, in which Jones strongly expressed his contempt for the governor. The governor later asked about this conversation when he visited Lang in his prisoner's cell in the fortress. Captain Lang speculated that Jones could have been stirred up by some unpleasant news from his son-in-law Hammond.

Earlier, Lang had explained why he abandoned the fortified house at San José on the St. Marys. There were not enough soldiers there, he said, to hold it against an attack by invaders. He also complained that the "volunteer" dragoons on the St. Marys were not paid for their labor. The sacrifice demanded of them, without pay, was too much to expect from the frontiersmen, who had to struggle to make even a bare living for their families.

[AGI, PC, leg. 166, pormenor 16, p. 132—in English]

February the 18, 1794

Please your Excellency recollect the message[1] that was sent besides the message that Mr. Hammond sent. Mr. William Jones

1. Probably Lang was referring to his letter of 30 December 1793, printed at page 33 in this volume.

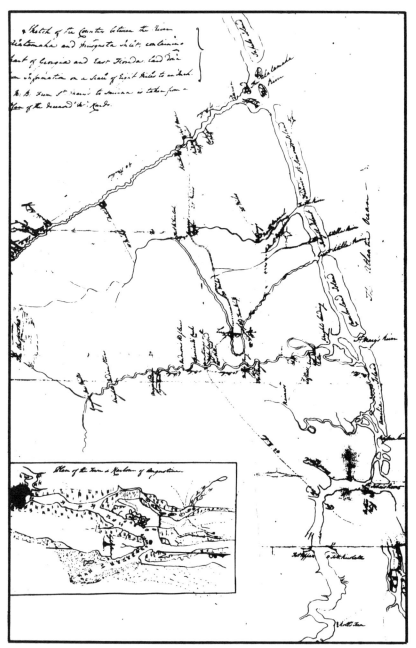

St. Marys River, ca. 1778. Courtesy of the Georgia Department of Archives and History, Atlanta. The frontispiece of this volume is a modern map of the area.

said at the time that he had no business with the Governor and that the Governor might kiss his ass, for he did not value him and that he could whip him at a fair fite and said that you may tell him so. As we was sitting on our horses after riding some distance Colonel MacIntosh said to me, did you notice the words that Jones spoke. I told him yes. Says MacIntosh, I think there must be something at the bottom of that, for I've never heard him speak so openly before. I had answered that I thought so too. These are the words that were spoken, as near as I can recollect.

Richd. Lang

[AGI, PC, leg. 166, pormenor 16, p. 118]

Statement by Richard Lang

St. Augustine, Florida, February 12, 1794.

Richard Lang appeared before the general counsellor, in the cell of the Castillo de San Marcos in which Lang was held prisoner; and he was put under oath by Miguel Iznardy, public interpreter, and before me, the notary, and he took oath before God Almighty and what he believes of the Holy Bible according to his Protestant faith, under which he promised to tell the truth of everything that was asked of him; and so his statements were taken in accordance with the Declaration at the head of these proceedings, and to that end he was asked the following questions:

1st. Asked how long he had been in this province, what position he held under the Spanish government, and if he had taken the oath of loyalty:

He said he had been established in the province long before[2] the coming of the Spaniards; that at the time of the prior governor he had been named judge in the St. Marys district, where his home was; that recently His Lordship had appointed him captain of the militia of the dragoons of that river; and that he has sworn fidelity as a subject.

---

2. The statement that Lang was in Florida before the coming of the Spaniards probably meant only that he had arrived in June of 1784 just a few days before Vicente Manuel de Zéspedes arrived to take over the government from the British. The interval in question was only from 18 June, when Lang was taken from a Savannah jail and subsequently escaped from his captors, to 27 June, when Zéspedes arrived. Alternatively, Lang may have meant that he was in East Florida before Governor Quesada took charge in 1790.

2nd. Asked if before going to jail he had obtained any information (and by what means) of an expedition planned against this province from Georgia prior to the things previously told to Lieutenant Colonel Carlos Howard, commander of the St. Johns River, and afterward to His Lordship secretly, confirming them in a sworn statement that he has given in these proceedings:

He said that on the occasions referred to he forgot to mention that a Doctor Brown[3] was also a leader in the planned expedition, but that he knows nothing more about it.

3rd. Asked as to what day he last left St. Marys, and as to who accompanied him, and as to whose house he visited and for how long, and as to the day he arrived in this city:

He said that on the seventh of last month he had left his home accompanied by Walter Drumman, who stayed with William Lane,[4] with whom they had spent the night; that the next night he stayed with William Jones, and from there he left the next morning to go to Doctor Sterling's, where he stayed for three days, at the end of which he left again for Jones's house, and from there to John McIntosh's, where he spent the night; and that next day, which was a Sunday, he returned to Jones's house accompanied by McIntosh, and there they relaxed for the day; and that next day, Monday, he came to the city with McIntosh and the other captain of the militia on the St. Marys River, Nathaniel Hall.

4th. Asked to name the people he saw in the houses mentioned, the matters discussed, and if any of these people had told the witness that any matter should be communicated to the governor:

He said that when he was in the house of Sterling there were also present Robert Pritchard and MacCay,[5] who spoke to him and Sterling about the expedition being talked about in Georgia; that

3. Jacob R. Brown was appointed lieutenant under William Tate for the western operations of the French intrigue (Louise F. Hays, *Hero of Hornet's Nest; A Biography of Elijah Clark, 1733 to 1799*, p. 243). He was arrested when he tried to join the rebels at San Nicolás (Richard K. Murdoch, *The Florida-Georgia Frontier, 1793–1796: Spanish Reaction to French Intrigue and American Designs*, p. 105).

4. William Lane acquired lands on Trout Creek in 1793 (Pleasant D. Gold, *History of Duval County, Florida*, p. 67). His plantation at Pottsburg Creek on the south side of the St. Johns was the approach point for the attack on San Nicolás in 1795.

5. This was possibly the William McKay who lived across the river from Savannah. A veteran of the patriot cause in the American Revolution, he led eighty men under the command of General Nathanael Green. His wife was tortured by the loyalist troops under Daniel McGirtt (Hays, *Hero of Hornet's Nest*, pp. 85, 150).

everyone gave his opinion on the matter, and that all agreed that it could not succeed; that when he returned with McIntosh to the Jones's home he found his son-in-law Abner Hammond and Nathaniel Hall there; that afterwards several others joined them, but he does not remember all of their names nor the subjects of their conversation; but that the object of this gathering was just relaxation and sociable drinking, which they did all day; and that the next day, Monday the 13th of last month, he came to this city, accompanied by McIntosh and Hall and with a message from Hammond to tell His Lordship, as he did, that he [Hammond] was coming to talk to him on the 15th.

5th. Asked if it were true that not long ago in a conversation with McIntosh he had said he wanted to leave the militia:

He said that not only did he tell McIntosh this, but he also told Lieutenant Colonel Carlos Howard the same thing, telling them that such a commission was too burdensome and took up too much time, time that he should be spending in work to maintain his family; that there was not a month that went by when this duty failed to occupy him five or six days; that since there was no salary this was unbearable; and also that he could never please the lieutenant colonel; and that McIntosh advised him not to leave the company, suggesting that Andrew Alquinson [Atkinson] was also tired of his duty and that if he left the soldiers would not have any leadership left at all.

6th. Asked if, when he had spoken with His Lordship when he last came to the city, he hadn't shown great urgency to return right away, pretending to be needed at St. Marys; and when His Lordship asked him to stay until the arrival of Hammond, which the message brought by the defendant suggested would be by the 15th, allowing the defendant to take the necessary action, he hadn't still insisted on being dispatched right away, and that he didn't agree to stay until he heard Captain Hall, who also witnessed the conversation, and who offered to tarry there himself:

He said that what the question implies is not true; and that the reason he wanted to leave was that he was needed at home; and that Hall, having offered to stay and His Lordship having told him he [Lang] could go, he nevertheless offered to stay in order to return accompanied by Hall, with whom he had come, for any delay could not be too long because Hammond was soon to arrive.

7th. Asked the reason for his insistence to His Lordship, by spoken and written word, that the stockaded and fortified house of

San José be abandoned, because the governor had assured him that, although there was no reason to suspect the Indians, there being complete harmony with them and no belief such a house should be built just for fear of them, but nevertheless it was needed to defend against bad people, whether Indian or white, who were around about, trying to steal, the defendant always insisting on his opinion; but His Lordship trying to persuade him of the usefulness of such a house, mainly because if the invasion took place such a position would be where the enemy would come by on their passage into the province, and the defendant insisting on his opinion against such a reasonable judgment, saying that four pickets were but little defense:

He said that establishing such a house as living quarters for the Commander of the River Lieutenant Colonel Carlos Howard, with a capable military detachment and store for the Indians, was always approved by the defendant because that way there was no basis for his suspicion that the Indians would be dangerous; but that the commander having retired to another post and leaving this one undermanned at a distance of ten miles from the houses of the residents, the defendant thinks that such a fortified house could do no good; rather, on the contrary, the enemy could easily take it in case of invasion and fortify themselves in it and that this could be dangerous; also that the house, because of its location, is exposed to being set afire.

8th. Asked if on the night he was seized he had been playing cards in the house of the innkeeper, Clark; with whom; and if he got up to talk to any of them in secrecy; with whom; and on how many occasions; and what matters were dealt with:

He said that it was true he played cards at Clark's house that night, with two priests and with William MacEnrry, Clark the innkeeper, and sometimes with his wife; and that he thinks John McIntosh came too; that he remembers that he got up two or three times to take a drink although he had drunk quite enough; but that he does not recall if he talked with anyone in particular, and that when it was appropriate he took a candle and went to bed.

9th. Asked if he knows William Howard, and if he came some days ago to ask for a passport to the city, or if William Plowden asked for one for him, stating whether he gave it or denied it, and why:

He said that he knows William Howard because when he was dismissed by the governor and not admitted as a subject, as he told the defendant, Howard presented himself at the defendant's house asking for a pass to go see William Plowden to look for a mare and other things that he had left there when he came to the city; that the defendant did not give him a pass and told him that, since he was coming as one dismissed by the government, he should get a pass from Commander Carlos Howard.

10th. Asked if the defendant was with John Peter Wagnon when he went to Georgia, or if he had found him there; and if he knows the cause of his coming there; and if he came alone or was accompanied by someone:

He said that he traveled with Wagnon, who had told him that he had a pass from the governor, to the other side of the St. Marys River at the Coleraine post; and that with the officer of the post and others they went to Temple with the intention on the part of the witness to go on from there to his house; but that not being able to find a boat he spent the night, and the next day went with Wagnon to Coleraine where he left him and went home; that William Lane, one of those who accompanied him and Wagnon, told him that Wagnon had come on the business of John McIntosh.

And at this point His Lordship suspended the hearing to be continued if needed and the defendant, to whom it was read in the English language by the public interpreter, said he was in accordance with it and he affirmed and ratified it; that he is of the age stated and signed with His Lordship, with the interpreter under oath.

> Quesada
> Attorney Ortega
> Richd Lang
> Miguel de Iznardy

Before me, José de Zubizarreta, court reporter

[AGI, PC, leg. 166, pormenor 16, p. 136]

Statement by Richard Lang

St. Augustine, Florida, February 29, 1794.

In conformity with previous orders His Lordship the Governor and Commanding General came to the underground cell of Richard Lang in the Castillo de San Marcos of this city, and Lang, being sworn by means of the public interpreter, Miguel Iznardy, before God and what he believes of the Holy Bible, promised to tell the truth of what he knew and was asked; and he was asked about the paper filed in folio 132, and if he recognized it as being the one he wrote and sent from this prison, and whether it is in his own handwriting:

He said that the paper[6] shown to him, the one from the folio, is the same one that he wrote to His Lordship and gave to the officer in charge so he could send it on; that all of it is written in his own handwriting as is the signature, which is acknowledged.

1st. After the interpreter read the expressions in said paper relative to conversations with John McIntosh as together they came to this city, wherein they passed judgment on things they had heard William Jones say in disparaging His Lordship, being surprised by them and speculating that he was hinting at something not said, the witness was asked to say what this something might be, or his interpretation of the expressions used so the case can be concluded:

He said that, as Abner Hammond, son-in-law of Jones, had been in Jones's house two or three days before, the defendant guessed that what Jones said could have been the result of displeasure at what Hammond might have told him, and so he burst forth with the terms he had used; that the conversation between McIntosh and the defendant was interrupted by him saying that upon coming back from the city where he was headed, Hammond had promised to stay two or three days at the McIntosh home, and then he said: "McIntosh, I'll try to unravel this and get as much as possible out of him about the matter."

2nd. Asked if he remembers that while talking the day before his imprisonment with His Lordship he had said that the people of St. Marys would take up arms in defense of the province if the expedition took place; but that some would not, and that upon his return there he would write to His Lordship so as to tell which ones they were; please name them now and the reasons for suspicion against each:

He said everything referred to in the question is true; and that the answer of the defendant is completed by the information that John and David Baylei, who had received a letter from their brother in Carolina summoning them, would go away because of that, and that Charles Missley was leaving without this or any other similar

6. The paper referred to was the note from Lang (see page 117 in this volume).

motive and for this reason selling his cattle; and that he had heard many others say they would leave if they continued to be forced to serve without pay.

3rd. Asked who ordered the residents to do service and if the orders he had from His Lordship were compulsory or left up to them:

He said that under orders from the Commander of the River Carlos Howard, they had served after the defendant and other residents agreed with the commander that five men a week were enough for what had to be done; that they operated like that for a time until a settler was scalped, and then the ones from St. Marys River were afraid and would not continue serving, as to which motive His Lordship was notified, and counselled against pressure in the matter even though it was in their own defense.

4th. Asked if it were true that he begged Miguel Iznardy to excuse him with His Lordship because he had delayed in giving information that he now has given and why did he need an excuse:

He said that his oversight consisted of not telling His Lordship on the same day he heard the information, which he gave two or three days later while in prison, having asked to see him for that purpose.

And he answered further that all is the truth under oath; and having read his statement by means of the interpreter, he said he agreed with it, affirms, and ratifies it; that he is as old as he has previously stated and signs under oath with the interpreter.

Quesada

Attorney Ortega

Richd Lang

Miguel de Iznardy

Before me, José de Zubizarreta, court reporter

ELEVEN

Message from Don Juan McQueen

DON Juan McQueen, a loyal Spanish subject originally from South Carolina, held extensive lands in Florida. He wrote a letter from his Amelia Island plantation to Thomas Sterling addressing the major topic of current conversations—the projected rebellion.[1] A discussion at Sterling's house was precipitated by the letter, and that conversation became a subject of the official enquiry.

Other interrogations concerned the temperamental outbursts of John Peter Wagnon after his imprisonment. Wagnon was indignant because he had not been able to complete a philanthropic gesture to a priest (he wanted to give the cleric a good horse in exchange for a poor one). His tactless remarks were questioned as being threats against the government.

1. There are abundant sources of information about McQueen. A pleasing novel, which follows the history very closely, is Eugenia Price, *Don Juan McQueen* (Philadelphia: J. B. Lippincott Co., 1974). Among the best sources are Richard K. Murdoch, *The Georgia-Florida Frontier, 1793–1795: Spanish Reaction to French Intrigue and American Designs*; John McQueen, *The Letters of Don Juan McQueen to His Family, Written from Spanish East Florida, 1791–1807*, ed. Walter C. Hartridge; and Robert MacKay, *The Letters of Robert MacKay to His Wife, Written from Ports in America and England, 1795–1816*, ed. Walter C. Hartridge. Although McQueen's landholdings in Florida included a large portion of the northern extremity of Amelia Island, his principal plantation at this time appears to have been on Fort George Island near the mouth of the St. Johns River, where his tabby plantation house still stands within the boundaries of the Kingsley Plantation State Park. Thomas Sterling, the Spanish official, is not to be confused with Francis Sterling, who married Lang's daughter.

126

[AGI, PC, leg. 166, pormenor 16, p. 140]

Statement by Robert Pritchard

St. Augustine, Florida, March 4, 1794.

The Governor and Commanding General ordered to appear before him Robert Pritchard, who, obeying the order to make a statement, came from the St. Johns River where he had his home, and being placed under oath by Miguel Iznardy, public interpreter, before God Almighty and what he believes of the Holy Bible in his Protestant faith, he promised to tell the truth of what he knew and was asked.

Concerning the interview of Richard Lang relative to the conversations started in the house of Thomas Sterling about the expedition against this province being planned in Georgia, he was [asked]

Don Juan McQueen's house, Fort George Island. Courtesy of Kingsley Plantation State Park, Florida.

to identify each subject on which each participant stated an opinion and to say which was the opinion of each, and everything they talked about:

He said that it was true that he went to the house of Thomas Sterling, where Richard Lang and William McKay were present, and that a little later a conversation was started by Sterling saying he had received a message from Don Juan McQueen on Amelia Island telling of rumors heard about an expedition which they say was projected in Georgia against this province; that each of the persons gathered there said what he thought about the matter, some thinking it practical for a sacking expedition to come, but that Richard Lang made fun of this, saying that none would come about under any circumstance.

He said that is all that happened on what was asked about; and that he has spoken the truth, under the oath he took; and having read his statement with the help of the interpreter he approved of it and ratified it; that he is thirty-five years old and signed under oath with the interpreter.

> Quesada
> Attorney Ortega
> Robt. Pritchard
> Miguel Iznardy

Before me, José de Zubizarreta, court reporter

[AGI, PC, leg. 166, pormenor 16, p. 141]

Statement by John Leslie

On the same day, March 4, 1794, there appeared before us John Leslie, resident and merchant of this city, who, when placed under oath by Miguel Iznardy, public interpreter, before God Almighty and what he believes of the Holy Bible in his Protestant faith, promised to tell the truth of what he knew and was asked.

Asked about the reference which John McIntosh has made to the witness on page 20 [verso] of these proceedings, and told to relate the conversation he had with McIntosh the day he came last to this city relative to the expedition projected against this province from Georgia, the conversation that he witnessed and translated the next day between His Lordship and said McIntosh, and, finally, the promise that McIntosh made to bring in writing the next day the news he had given orally, and any subsequent conversation between the witness and McIntosh relative to the expedition:

He said that one afternoon in January, as to which he does not remember the exact date, he went for a walk with John McIntosh, who had eaten at the witness's house; and, walking along the wharf, McIntosh started a conversation in which he said he was talking to the witness in confidence and friendship about the expedition planned against this province from Georgia. (It was detailed by the witness but is not included here for it repeats what was already said by McIntosh.) And after McIntosh gave an account of the details he was asked if he had advised the governor, and being answered no, the witness told him that he was not doing right in keeping the news from the government (which news could be of interest to them so that they could take precautions in defense of the province); and the witness advised him that he should lose no time, and if he wanted to, the witness could accompany him to the governor's house to serve as an interpreter because the witness had knowledge of the Spanish language and McIntosh did not. He said that McIntosh agreed to what the witness advised and they went together and spoke to the governor, the witness interpreting as best he could what McIntosh said, but since His Lordship was not completely satisfied, he was told to put everything in writing, which he agreed to bring back the next morning.

He said that when he went out in the street with McIntosh, the latter told him that he was going back home the next morning, answering the witness, who reminded him of his promise to the governor to put the information in writing, all that had been said orally, that he could do that in ten minutes.

He said he did not see McIntosh again, nor does he know anything more about what is asked; that all he has said is the truth under oath. And having heard the above statement read by means of the interpreter he said he was in accord with it and ratified it; that he is over twenty-five years old and signed under oath with

> Quesada
>
> Attorney Ortega
>
> John Leslie
>
> Miguel Iznardy

Before me, José de Zubizarreta, court reporter

[AGI, PC, leg. 166, pormenor 16, p. 144]

Statement by Thomas Sterling

St. Augustine, Florida, March 8, 1794

Thomas Sterling, having arrived today from the St. Johns River where he has his home, was made to appear before His Lordship and the general counsellor; and by means of the interpreter, Miguel Iznardy, was put under oath before God Almighty and the Holy Cross, under which he promised to tell the truth of everything he knew and was asked.

He was asked about the statement by Richard Lang on page 120 of these proceedings relating to the conversation in the house of the witness, concerning the expedition planned against this province from the State of Georgia, as to which those gathered there expressed their opinions; he was to say which was the opinion of each, and to identify all those present and to repeat what they said:

He said that he knew that Lang, Robert Pritchard, and William McKay came to his home, but he does not remember that they spoke in his presence about said expedition, because any such conversation was restricted to Lang saying he had received a letter, which he read, from a lieutenant at Fort Coleraine on the American Creek on the other side of the St. Marys River, who wrote that he wanted to come to the St. Johns to destroy a band of thieves who were there; and the witness asked Lang what did that mean and who was being talked about, receiving the answer that he thought it was about the Indians who were with John Forrester, the question being asked by the witness because he knew that Robert Seagrove was also thinking the same and talking the same way about some other Indians who also lived near the witness; and that was the total conversation remembered.

Asked to think carefully about whether the conversation actually did concern the expedition talked about above, since Robert Pritchard, one of those mentioned as being in the house, discussed what was said by Lang, contending that the expedition was spoken of and that the witness initiated the conversation by saying he had received information from Amelia Island, from Juan MacQueen, in which he was told about rumors related to said expedition against this province; and at this did not all those present give their views as to whether it would happen or not:

He said that he remembers that he got a letter from Juan Mac-Queen discussing the proposed expedition and indicating belief that it would not take place; that he also remembers that he read part of the letter to Lang, Pritchard, and McKay, who were then at his house; and with this prompting he remembers that they spoke about the expedition and of the jailing of their leaders by the government of Carolina. That he does not remember anything else being said in the matter and that everything testified is true under oath.

And having read his statement by the help of the public interpreter he affirms and ratifies it. That he is forty-six years old and signed under oath with the interpreter.

Quesada

Attorney Ortega

Thomas Sterling

Miguel Iznardy

José de Zubizarreta, court reporter

[AGI, PC, leg. 166, pormenor 16, p. 145]

Statement by Miguel Iznardy

St. Augustine, Florida, March 13, 1794

There appeared before His Lordship and the general counsellor the public interpreter, Miguel Iznardy, who was by me, the court reporter, sworn before God and the Holy Cross, promising to tell the truth of what he knew; and he was asked about the conversation he had heard on the tenth of this month.

Since he went to prison to visit John Peter Wagnon on orders from His Lordship to accompany the wife of the prisoner, who was to talk with her husband, and after that the witness asked His Lordship to excuse him from then on because he did not want to be involved, please say what this is all about, and his reason for this request:

He said that the preceding Monday he had accompanied John Peter Wagnon's wife, whose name he has forgotten, to the prison where he is held, she having His Lordship's permission to go talk with him, and he, the witness, being under orders to listen to what they talked about; that the official infantry guard of the castle, Juan López, opened the cell of Wagnon and his wife and the witness stayed with [Wagnon] as long as the conversation lasted.

He said in this conversation Wagnon asked the witness if there might be a possibility that the government might release him on bail as he had requested, because he was tired of begging and receiving favors such as allowing his wife to come and talk with him; and that the witness replied that he did not know, nor was it in his authority to have such information; that Wagnon said in a loud voice that he had never been a man to take sides, but that some day he would get out of that prison; that when they were talking about the fact that the order which his wife tried to give the Carmelite priest to get a horse of his could not be carried out, because she told him it had been stolen, Wagnon burst out again and said: "If the government had not arrested me so despotically without telling me why, I could take care of my belongings, and my horses would not have been taken away."

The witness said that he was upset after having heard such statements and at the same time uneasy to see the restlessness of the wife, and the nervousness with which she sought to be left alone with her husband, not having done this before, and that he was afraid she would try to leave him paper and ink, and that afterwards some letter would come out to the government or to some other person that would compromise the witness as an accomplice or as careless.

That with this in mind he told the guard to tell her to finish up because they had already talked enough; and that this is all that happened on the matter inquired upon and the whole truth, he swears.

And having been informed of the above statement as it was read, he affirmed, ratified and signed it under oath with the counsellor.

Quesada

Attorney Ortega

Miguel de Iznardy

Before me, José de Zubizarreta, court reporter

[AGI, PC, leg. 166, pormenor 16, p. 149]

Statement by Juan López

St. Augustine, Florida, March 18, 1794

In explanation of the above statement by Miguel Iznardy, there appeared before His Lordship and the general counsellor one Juan López, ensign of the light companies of Catalana, and before me, the reporter, he took an oath on his word of honor by the Holy Cross to tell the truth on the substance of said matter and stated:

That it is true that he observed the discontent that the said prisoner and wife showed during the time when they were within sight of the witness; that, although he did not understand anything they talked about because it was in English, he observed some movements in the lady that made him think she wanted to leave something in the bed of her husband where she sat while she was there and for this she was searched by the witness, despite the prisoner being very upset, although the witness did not understand what he said.

That he noticed that the interpreter, Miguel Iznardy, was also upset, causing López to ask him what was going on, and although he did not tell him, he told him he was going to ask the governor to excuse him from now on from the task of accompanying that lady when she went to speak to her husband.

That is all he knows about the matter being asked, and all is true under the oath he has taken; and his statement having been read he said he affirmed and ratified it and signed under oath with the counsellor.

Quesada
Attorney Ortega
Juan López

Before me, José de Zubizarreta, court reporter

[AGI, PC, leg. 166, pormenor 16, p. 152]

Statement by John Peter Wagnon

St. Augustine, Florida, April 2, 1794

The governor and commanding general went, accompanied by his lieutenant and general counsellor, to the Castillo de San Marcos and to its dungeon, where John Peter Wagnon is imprisoned, to obtain a statement from Wagnon; and Wagnon having been put under oath by Manuel Rengil to speak the truth before God Almighty and what he believes of the Sacred Bible under his Protestant faith, the following occurred:

1. Asked if, on the last time the public interpreter, Miguel Iznardy, was here to observe what the witness said to his wife, Wagnon had asked if there were any possibility that the government would let him come out on bail and to tell the answer of Iznardy and what he answered:

He said he definitely remembers asking the interpreter, Miguel Iznardy, on said date, if there were any possibility of the Governor setting bail to permit the defendant to be imprisoned at his own home. That Iznardy answered that he did not know, but he thought it would be all right to make a formal request; and with that purpose the defendant talking to his wife said: "Please do me the favor to see the lawyer and talk about the matter"; and that is all he remembers about this.

2. Asked what words the defendant broke forth with when his wife, on the same afternoon, told him it would not be possible by his order for the priest to get back a horse belonging to the witness because it had been stolen, the defendant becoming angry and uttering strong words:

He said that in reference to an agreement the defendant had with the Carmelite priest, who gave him a cheap horse and $20 in exchange for another worth $80, his wife told him his order to give to the Carmelite priest the horse which was kept at Thomas Sterling's house, could not be complied with, because it was very thin, nor could they give him any of the ones left at the Alta Maja River (as he wanted to—a good one which he had brought for that purpose) because his wife told him she had heard that those had been stolen.

That this remark caused the defendant to be upset, he thinking all of this was the invention of his enemies to let it be thought that he had not been truthful in his prior statement in which he affirmed that he left the horses on Black Island at the Alta Maja River, where such could not be stolen, and not at the St. Marys River.

3. Again asked (so that he can think again about the answers previously given) to say if it is not true that, when the interpreter Iznardy said that he did not know if the government would grant him his wish to be set free on bail, that the defendant said that he was not

a man to take sides but that someday he would leave that miserable prison; and asked if, when his wife had told the defendant about the horse, he had answered: "If the government had not arrested me tyrannically without telling me why, I would take care of my belongings and nobody could have taken my horses."

He said that he knows very well what religion compels him to do under oath and consequently, although he does not remember that he said those exact words "that he was not a man to take sides, and someday he would get out of prison," still he may have said it, but in another meaning, that is, that he is not a man to take sides and he thinks he will not be kept there all his life; but he denies having said the other expressions pertaining to the government having arrested him so tyrannically without telling him why.

4. Asked if it is true that on the afternoon in question the defendant and also his wife were insisting on being left alone, showing quite a bit of annoyance because they could not achieve this; and to state the reason that it was so necessary on that occasion and not at other times:

He said that neither directly nor indirectly has he insisted on being alone with his wife while in prison; that on the afternoon stated it is true that Miguel Iznardy having told the defendant and his wife to be brief, because he had other things to do at the fortress, the defendant asked him to go ahead and that he meanwhile leave his wife more time in his company.

At this point His Lordship ordered the hearing suspended to be continued later on if needed; and the defendant, to whom this statement was read by Manuel Rengil, said it is the truth in all its parts and he ratifies it as the truth under oath; that he is of the age stated before and signs with the counsellor and Manuel Rengil.

Quesada

Attorney Ortega

J. P. Wagnon

Manuel Rengil

Before me, José de Zubizarreta, court reporter

TWELVE

Sarah McIntosh, Loyal Wife

WHETHER or not the French "rebellion" in Florida had any heroes, there can be no doubt that its heroine was Sarah McIntosh.

Although left with all the responsibilities of the McIntosh plantations, a family of six young children (the oldest was only twelve), and an aged grandmother, she mounted a fervent campaign to free her husband, eventually securing the intervention of President Washington himself.

Her task was made more difficult because an eye infection had left her almost totally blind. She wrote her letters by placing a ruler on the paper and having her children help to guide her hand.[1]

She wrote to officials in Havana, and specifically to Governor Luis de las Casas, governer general of Cuba, telling him she had laid before Governor Quesada of Florida on 1 April 1794 a petition for the release of John. She wrote: "Suffer, sir, my miserable situation to touch your generous and noble breast with pity and compassion." She described her husband as "one who had been for upwards of fourteen months previous to his captivity laboring under a consumptive habit, whose life has been several times during that period dispaired of. . . . restore to liberty your innocent and suffering prisoner. . . . he has been a warm friend, and upwards of two years a faithful servant of the Spanish gov-

1. George White, *Historical Collections of Georgia*, p. 547 et seq.; Thomas Gamble, *Of Savannah Duels and Duelists, 1733–1877*, p. 20.

ernment, which he served in the office in which he was placed without reward or emolument to the apparent satisfaction of his superiors."[2]

She was allowed to correspond with her husband in his cell at Morro Castle. In October she replied to his letters of 6 July and 2 August: "You flatter me, my dear husband, in saying I would make a good lawyer. I claim no merit; shining abilities are not very necessary to plead well in a good cause."

She also wrote of family matters: "I have sent our son William with $100 to his uncle and requested he should be sent on to New-York. . . . I am sorry I missed your morning gown. I shall send you another." And she mentioned Don Santiago Rodríguez, the man in charge of the commissary at San Vicente Ferrer (today St. Johns Bluff), observing that since he would soon be going to Havana, "I shall furnish him with money to purchase your tobacco."

Here is the petition Sarah filed for her husband, and pertinent supporting documents.

[AGI, PC, leg. 166, pormenor 16, p. 208]

I, Mrs. Sarah Simons McIntosh, lawful wife of John McIntosh, who was formerly Colonel in the National Army of the United States of America, a new settler of this province and a subject to His Majesty, having been admitted with all formalities and sent lately as a prisoner to Havana by order of this government on suspicion of being an accomplice with Frenchmen planning in Georgia an invasion of this province, come before His Lordship, in proper form and with the reservations available to those favoring the cause of my husband, authorized as I am by the laws in such cases to speak for him in defense of his innocence of the crime that is asserted against him, and answering by permission of the Attorney General, say:

To start with, as a safeguard against the false accusations which brought about these proceedings impugning his honor, conduct and reputation while he was in prison and being shipped off to Havana, I present in proper form the documents herewith certified and numbered from one to five, all establishing his honest and upright proce-

2. White, *Historical Collections*, p. 551.

dures before his immigration to this colony from the United States; and so that when His Lordship receives them they will be accurately translated into the Spanish language, being now in English, such translations should be made promptly and put with the originals and this petition in the case file, so that they may have the most appropriate effect, without prejudice to any other evidence which, if necessary, I shall produce in defense of my said husband; and I implore His Lordship to decide with justice; and I implore His Lordship that, after the said translations are executed, I be provided by means of the undersigned notary an account of them, and of this petition, with the fate of it; the account to be certified and attested to formally, and I am willing to satisfy all costs.

Sarah S. McIntosh

Bartolomé de Castro y Ferrer

The said documents having been presented, let them be translated by the public interpreter upon his being approved and sworn, and when the translation has been executed let them be taken to the General Counsellor for his decision as to what to do. So ordered Juan Nepomuceno de Quesada, Colonel of the Royal Army, Governor, Commanding General, Vice Royal Trustee and Subdelegate of Royal House of this Province of St. Augustine, Florida, for His Majesty, who signed the order on April 2, 1794.

Quesada

Before me, José de Zubizarreta, court reporter

[AGI, PC, leg. 166, pormenor 16, p. 211—in English]

No. 1

State of Georgia

City of Savannah

Personally appeared before me, John Berrien,[3] Esquire, one of the Aldermen of said city, Colonel William McIntosh, son of William McIntosh, the Elder and brother of Colonel John McIntosh of Florida, who being duly sworn maketh oath and saith:

3. Berrien was port inspector at Savannah.

That he the deponent never was concerned in any plott, scheem, or expedition against the Province of East Florida, since it was in the Possession of his Catholic Majesty, in any manner whatever, either directly or indirectly. And this deponent further saith, that in December last, being a member of the General Assembly, some information was laid before the House respecting a party of men, which were about to be raised for the purpose of going against East Florida, and that he the deponent reprobated the idea, and was one among the number that got a resolution past [authorizing] the Governor of this state to call any part or the whole of the militia to prevent them proceeding. And the deponent further saith, that he never was and does not believe any of his name ever was concerned with the said party.

Wm. McIntosh

Sworn before me this 22 day of February 1794

That some time in the months of September or October last, he the deponent, wrote to his brother in Florida informing him that he the deponent had sold all Col. John McIntosh's lands in this State and was to receive cattle in payment and that if Col. John McIntosh of East Florida could procure permission from the Spanish Government, he the deponent would drive any part of the said cattle to the St. Marys.

That in December deponent returned from Augusta, that Mr. Wagnon called on the deponent and informed him he was sent in by Col. John McIntosh for four hundred head of cattle agreeable to the deponent's letter. The deponent told Mr. Wagnon the cattle was ready, and that he would deliver them as soon as they could be collected, but at the same time advised Mr. Wagnon of the difficulty of taking them in on account of the great flood of water which then prevailed in all the rivers; on which Mr. Wagnon agreed to leave the cattle until the coming Spring.

The deponent further solemnly declared on his oath that he never intended the cattle for any other use than for the benefit [of] his brother, and the deponent further says that he wrote but one letter by Mr. Wagnon, which he supposes is in the possession of the Spanish Government, nor does the deponent know of any other letters which Mr. Wagnon had.

W. McIntosh

Sworn to this 22nd day, February, 1794

John Berrien, one of the
Aldermen of the City of
Savannah

[AGI, PC, leg. 166, pormenor 16, p. 213—in English]

State of Georgia

City of Savannah

    I, Major General Lachlan McIntosh, of the city aforesaid, do hereby certify upon my honour that I have been intimately acquainted with my nephew Colonel John McIntosh, now of the Province of East Florida, from his infancy, that he served under my command with much honor and reputation to himself during the whole of the late American War in the military line, and afterwards in a high civil department with applause and was ever deemed in his private as well as his public character a man of the strictest honor, truth and integrity, whose word as far as he was able was equal to his bond.

    After our late war, in which he lost the greatest part of his private fortune, he was unguardedly taken in by speculators which involved him in debt and obliged him at length on that account to remove to the Province of East Florida in order to do justice to his creditors without immediate injury to his family;[4] and I am informed that he has taken the oath of allegiance to His Catholic Majesty, which I will wager my life that the whole province would not induce him to forfeit.

    A few months ago Colonel John McIntosh ventured for the first time, sick as he was, to come from East Florida to visit his wife (then under the physician's hand at Savannah) of whom he is passionately fond and kept close in her room the whole time. He stayed on account of his disorder, his creditors admitting very few of his most intimate friends to see him, among whom I was one myself and I must candidly confess that I was astonished to find them both such enthusiastic admirers of the Spanish Government under which they intended to spend their lives.

Lachlan McIntosh
at the voluntary request
of General McIntosh

4. The Georgia law on debts inspired Juan McQueen and other Georgians to do this too.

Sworn to this 22nd day of February, 1794, before

John Berrien, Alderman
of the City of Savannah

[AGI, PC, leg. 166, pormenor 16, p. 215—in English]

State of Georgia

Before me, Joseph Welscher, Notary and Tabellion [reporter] Public for the State aforesaid, duly and by lawful authority admitted and sworn, residing in the City of Savannah in the said State, personally appeared Josiah Tattnall, of the said county of Chatham, Colonel of the Militia of the said county, who being sworn on the Holy Evangelists of Almighty God did depose, declare and say as follows: that is to say: That the deponent has, for ten years past been acquainted with Colonel John McIntosh who hath lately left this state to reside in the Province of East Florida.

That he the deponent hath been in the habits of intimacy during the time aforesaid with the said John McIntosh; that he always found him an honest and upright man and of the utmost integrity and firm in friendship; that the deponent hath several years served with the said John McIntosh in the General Assembly of this state whereby he had the opportunity of observing that he was a man of unshaken fidelity, ever attentive to the true interest of the country which he represented, and justly possessing the confidence of his countrymen; that he knew him when he served as Sheriff of the County of Chatham and always understood that he faithfully discharged the trust reposed in him.

That after the said John McIntosh had left Georgia and moved to East Florida, Mrs. McIntosh was compelled to return here to advise with physicians about her eyes, being at that time almost blind; that the said John McIntosh, anxious to see her, followed her some weeks afterward to Georgia and stayed several days with the deponent, during which time the deponent asked Col. McIntosh how he liked the Spanish government, their customs and practices; to which he replied that he had found as warm a reception as imaginable, that he was strongly attached to the government and the people, that every privilege possible had been afforded him and others; and finally that he never wished to leave the country; so upon the whole and from the well known honesty and integrity of said John McIntosh the deponent can hardly believe it probable that he would enter into or be in any wise concerned in conspiracy against the Spanish Government or in any other treasonable act whatever.

Josiah Tattnall, Jun[ior].

Sworn before me, the said notary at Savannah, aforesaid this twenty second day of February, in the year of Our Lord one thousand seven hundred and ninety four. In testimony of the truth whereof I have hereunto set my hand and seal notarial.

Joseph Welscher

[AGI, PC, leg. 166, pormenor 16, p. 217—in English]

State of Georgia

City of Savannah

We the Mayor and Aldermen of the city aforesaid, do certify, that we have long been acquainted with Colonel John McIntosh, formerly of this State and now of the Province of East Florida, & have always believed him to be possessed of the strictest principles of honor & political integrity, & we conceive that he could not be guilty of so base a conduct as to plot against the welfare of a country from which he has received the highest marks of friendship, confidence and protection.

We further certify that among the number of persons who are said to have engaged in an expedition against the Floridas (an enterprise not only unauthorized by our State government, but all acts of the kind positively prohibited & forbidden by the President of the United States) that we never heard the name of Colonel John McIntosh mentioned as being a party or any other person of that name being concerned in the business & we verily believe that he has no concern in the matter.

Given under our hands & the seal of the said city this twentieth day of February, one thousand seven hundred and ninety four.

W. Stephens, Mayor

Aldermen:

Joseph Clay, Jr.[5]

5. Clay was active in political support of the American Revolution and was a merchant with wide business connections (Wilbur H. Siebert, *Loyalists in East Florida, 1774 to 1785*, 1:51, 53, 54).

John Berrien
Geo. Jones
John Cunningham[6]
Andrew McCredie
Wm. Lowden

These are to certify to all whom it may concern that I am well acquainted with the Mayor and Aldermen of the City of Savannah who have signed the foregoing certificate and that full faith and credit is due to their signatures as such, the same having been inscribed in my presence.

I further certify that I never heard the name of Colonel John McIntosh mentioned as being concerned directly or indirectly in the Party said to be collecting in this State under the influence of French emissaries with hostile intentions against the flag and territories of His Catholic Majesty.

I also certify that I am personally acquainted with Colonel McIntosh and have in no instance had occasion to impeach his honor or integrity, either from my own knowledge or the information of others.

Witness my hand and seal at Savannah, this 20th day of February, 1794.

John Wallace,[7] His Britannic Majesty's
Vice Consul for Georgia.

I do hereby certify that John Berrien, esq. is an alderman of the City of Savannah, and that Joseph Welscher, esquire is a Notary Public within the County of Chatham and State aforesaid and that full faith and credit is due to their signatures and to the several certificates hereunto annexed, the same having been executed in my presence.

Witness my hand at Savannah this 20th day of February, 1794

John Wallace,
Vice Consul

6. Cunningham fought as a lieutenant in the American Revolution and was the subject of controversy after his retreat in an attack by Indians. He fought under his friend Elijah Clark in that war (Louise F. Hays, *Hero of Hornet's Nest; A Biography of Elijah Clark, 1733 to 1799*, pp. 39, 125, 149).

7. Wallace cooperated with Governor Quesada during the French intrigue (Janice Borton Miller, "Juan Nepomuceno de Quesada: Spanish Governor in East Florida, 1790–1795" [Ph.D. diss.], p. 238).

[AGI, PC, leg. 166, pormenor 16, p. 219—in English]

No. 2

State of Georgia

City of Savannah

Personally appeared before me John Berrien, Esq., one of the aldermen of said city, Daniel Course, of the city aforesaid, auctioneer, who being duly sworn saith:

That he is a near connection in the family of Col. Samuel Hammond of this State & that he the said Colonel Hammond is at present & has been for some time past in the upper country & that he is not expected down that country or in Savannah in less than two weeks hence. The deponent yesterday received a letter from Col. Hammond dated at Augusta the 14th instant in which he informed him, the deponent, that he (Col. Hammond) was just taking his departure from Augusta for Wilkes County & should not be in Savannah for some time—and further saith not.

Daniel Course

Sworn to the 22nd of February, 1794, before:

John Berrien, Alderman
of the City of Savannah

[AGI, PC, leg. 166, pormenor 16, p. 220—in English]

No. 3

State of Georgia

County of Liberty

We the subscribers being called on to testify what to us is personally known respecting the character of Colonel John McIntosh, late an officer in the Armies of the United States of America and now an inhabitant of East Florida do in the presence of Almighty God:

Declare that during an acquaintance of many years we have known him without reproach, either in public or private life; of manners truly inoffensive, we have found him to possess the universal esteem of a numerous and respectable acquaintance in the several circles he has lived. That his mind naturally bent to domestic pursuits suffered him to engage but little in the affairs of government since his retirement from the army; and from what we know of the man we are well assured that nothing could induce him to betray any trust reposed in him or take any measures unfriendly to the interest of the government under which he lived.

> F. Oneal, Col.[8]
>
> J. Armstrong,[9] late col. of the State Troops
>
> Lach. McIntosh, Cap. in the Armies of the United States

Sworn to before me this 19th February, 1794

> John Mitchell,[10] J.P.

I have known Col. John McIntosh and from my knowledge I feel myself pleased in an opportunity to testifying to his merits and I wish it serve when I say, I know the witness respecting him to be founded in truth.

> February 19, 1794
>
> John Mitchell

[AGI, PC, leg. 166, pormenor 16, p. 221—in English]

No. 4

State of Georgia

County of Glynn

These are to certify that I have been long acquainted with Colonel John McIntosh, originally of this state but now of East

8. Ferdinand O'Neal fought under Elijah Clark during the American Revolution (Hays, *Hero of Hornet's Nest*, p. 132).

9. Armstrong fought under Elijah Clark in the American Revolution. He was critical of Spanish Florida (ibid., pp. 138, 288).

10. John Mitchell was one of a group critical of U.S. efforts to protect Indian claims during difficulties in the Oconee area in 1794 (ibid., p. 259).

Florida; that I ever found him a man of the most [obliged?] honor and integrity. And that I am well acquainted with his brother Col. Wm. McIntosh; that I served with him in the General Assembly of this State in November last and that on a communication being laid before the House of Assembly by the Governor of South Carolina respecting a party which was about to be raised under the influence of French emissaries, and that Col. William McIntosh was much opposed to the measure and interested himself considerably in getting a resolution passed authorizing the Governor of this State to call out any part or the whole of the militia to prevent any such party going forward; and I do further certify that I am well convinced that neither Col. William McIntosh nor any of his family was ever concerned either directly or indirectly with the said party.

Given under my hand & seal at Frederica in Glynn County, this 8th day of March, 1794.

Samuel Wright, Asst.
[Judge]

[AGI, PC, leg. 166, pormenor 16, p. 220—in English]

No. 5

St. Marys, 10th March, 1794

I hereby certify that in all conversation I ever had with Col. John McIntosh I never heard him say anything against the Spanish Government and that he always appeared perfectly satisfyed with that government; and that I believe him to be [a] gentleman of strict integrity.

Henry Gaither, [11] Majr.,
Commandt., Federal
Troops, Georgia

11. President Washington sent Henry Gaither to Georgia in 1793 with two assignments: to protect the Georgia frontier against Indians and to calm down Elijah Clark, who was overzealous in subduing the Indians' retaliation against the westward expansion of whites into Indian-claimed lands. One hundred federal troops accompanied Gaither. Forts were established by the federal troops, largely to restrain the whites, and by the Georgia militia, largely to subdue the Indians (ibid., p. 229).

[AGI, PC, leg. 166, pormenor 16, p. 223]

To advise His Lordship in compliance with his communication, of the second of this month, I [Ortega] have certified these papers which have this morning been presented on request of Mrs. Sarah Simons McIntosh, placing the originals and translations together in these proceedings against her husband John; and they are sought to be admitted as testimony.

I find this request justified in all its parts, and hope His Lordship agrees to it and adopts my decision in this process made on the seventh of this month to send me to Havana to continue the matter with McIntosh who is in jail there; because in this case I do not believe these proofs are useful in this matter without being studied in McIntosh's presence; and that we should try to continue this case until that opportunity arises. This is my way of thinking and I sign in St. Augustine, Florida on the 26th of April 1794.

Attorney José Ortega

Decree

Florida, April 28, 1794

I agree to comply with the foregoing.

Quesada

Before me, José de Zubizarreta, court reporter

THIRTEEN

Path of the Peddler

AMONG the most interesting men of eighteenth-century America were the Indian traders. They, along with the government Indian agents like James Seagrove, maintained active ties with the natives. Some Indian agents were sent to live among the Indians, and some earned the Indian sobriquet "beloved man."[1]

The traders, for their part, were business venturers. They traded manufactured goods—mostly European—to the Indians for the pelts of North American wild animals, highly prized in Europe at the time. The Indians greatly coveted the guns and ammunition they gained in trade—not only for hunting but for combat with white neighbors, particularly the more aggressive ones.

In Florida the dominant trading firm during the British and later Spanish occupations was Panton, Leslie and Company. Its home bases were in St. Augustine and Pensacola, and at the more rustic midway location of St. Marks, near the mouth of the Wakulla River.

1. The chiefs assembled at Coleraine made repeated requests that a "beloved man" be sent from the U.S. government to their towns to explain the things that the chiefs had agreed to but which would be unpopular. Washington appointed the well-liked Benjamin Hawkins to undertake this responsibility. McGillivray said of one of the other, less successful Indian agents: "They had sent up an agent; and for what I know not, without it was to play the fool, which he performed with considerable insolence." The agent was Daniel McMurphy, whose testimony appears in this chapter. James F. Doster, *The Creek Indians and Their Florida Lands, 1740–1823*, pp. 93, 218; John W. Caughey, *McGillivray of the Creeks*, p. 28.

Samuel and Abner Hammond's Indian-trading firm, Hammond and Fowler, was headquartered at Savannah. It was frequently observed at the time that a strong motive for Samuel Hammond's leadership in the French republican thrust against East Florida was to substitute his Indian trading business in Florida for the Scottish-based firm of Panton, Leslie and Company.

For Hammond to accomplish this maneuver, the sovereignty of Florida had to be shifted from Spain to the United States, to France, or to a new and independent local republic. Spain was obviously dependent upon her Indian allies to protect her boundaries; and the key to that alliance was the operation of the house of Panton, Leslie and Company. The firm was needed both for organizing Indian leadership and for commerce. Panton, Leslie and Company relied heavily on Alexander McGillivray, part Scot and part Indian, who had his headquarters at Little Tallassie in what is now Alabama.

In the same area there was also another trading firm, owned by George Galphin. His headquarters were at Silver Bluff below Augusta on the Savannah River,[2] and he traded widely in the Indian-occupied lands that today are part of Alabama, Georgia, and Florida. In 1775 he was appointed by the Continental Congress to be Indian Commissioner in the South; and he worked vigorously during the Revolution to keep the Creeks and other Indians friendly, or at least neutral, toward the colonies. Galphin's principal competition came from the Tory firm of Panton, Leslie.

One of Galphin's agents in the old Southwest (east of the Mississippi) was Daniel McMurphy,[3] whom the Indians called "Yellow Hair." As could be expected from his Whig background and his business affiliation with the patriot Indian trader Galphin, he was greatly disliked by McGillivray—particularly when, in 1786, he came as an agent of Georgia to live among the Creeks and

2. David H. Corkran, *The Creek Frontier, 1540–1783*, p. 238.
3. Doster states that while McGillivray was away during the summer of 1786 "a Georgia agent named Daniel McMurphy came into the Creek nation to preserve peace, control trade, and demand satisfaction for recent depredations." He "fled the nation before McGillivray's return" (*The Creek Indians*, p. 93).

to attempt to enforce Georgia's new Indian trading license laws. At one point McGillivray believed that McMurphy sought to kill him and observed, "I had the satisfaction to make that scoundrel McMurphy run off as hard as he could for his life."[4]

This Irishman McMurphy finally settled down in the Augusta area and then decided because of his debts to move to Florida, making his living as a peddler along the way. This chapter recounts the story of his journey to Florida and what he found out about the projected rebellion en route.

[AGI, PC, leg. 166, pormenor 16, p. 163—in English]

Charles Howard, Esq. Lieu. Colonel of his Majesty's Armys, Capt. of Grenadiers of the Third Battalion of the Regiment of Cuba & temporary Commandant of the Spanish frontier on the rivers of St. Marys and St. John in this Province of East Florida:

Whereas a person calling himself Danl. McMurphy arrived at this post of St. Vincente, on the aforesaid river, St. Johns, announcing himself to have come from the State of Georgia & laterally from the stockade of Temple, situated on the river St. Marys in said state & whereas it is notorious that in said state & also at Temple designs are carrying on by evil minded persons unauthorized by the executives of the United States against the tranquillity of this province. I, in consequence, have thought proper to summon before me the said Daniel, in order to take his declaration in form, regarding the above mentioned designs, & having duly sworn him in the presence of two assisting witnesses upon the Holy Evangelists, he promised by virtue of said oath, to answer truely & faithfully to the best of his knowledge to such questions as shall be put to him regarding said designs:

Being asked his name, his country, profession or calling, whence he came & what his business is in this country he saith:

That his name is Daniel McMurphy, that he was born in Ireland & came to New York in the 1760's, has ever since lived in America; that at the time of the Revolution he became and actually now is a resident of the United States; & has resided since twenty years in Georgia, where he lives & now has a wife and four children; and

4. Caughey, *McGillivray of the Creeks*, p. 32.

further saith that he lived about eight years near Fort St. Marks at Apalache as agent for Mr. George Galphin, the Elder, who is now deceased; that trained to no particular trade but he took the calling of a peddler. That he came back into this province from Georgia, & that his business in this country was to see if he could be allowed to settle in it.

Being asked what enducement he had to leave Georgia & to leave his wife & family, saith:

That his enducement to come to this country was to avoid being imprisoned for debt & in hopes of a recovery of some hundreds of pounds due him by John Peter Wagnon, an inhabitant of this province, & also a sum of money by Capt. Andrew Atkinson; by the recovery of which debts he hoped to be enabled to send for his wife & family & make out a livelihood for them in Florida. Deponent intended moreover to dispose of the lands of which he is still possessed of in Georgia & also a house, horses, horned cattle & sheep in the County of Richmond,[5] State of Georgia.

Being asked how it happened that being a man of such property having an intention to come back and settle in this province, has come into it with barely the clothes upon his back, saith:

That his intention has been for more than two years to settle in this province as will appear by a passport issued by the late Governor of Georgia, Telfair, by which he presents (and I take to be genuine); but not being able at that time to settle his affairs, he has delayed his purpose & that when he sett out from his house in Richmond on the 23rd or 24th of last February, he did not then sett out with an intention of putting his designs of coming into this province into execution, having only gone to Savannah with a design to dispose of some timber & being about to return home an express arrived to him from his friends to inform him by word of mouth that the suits depending against him in the courts of Augusta had been given (in) favor of his creditors & that he in consequence would be clapt in jail, upon which notice he struck off for Florida, with the clothes he had then on himself and two shirts.

Being asked if before he left home or at any time before or since he heard or knew of any designs, carrying on by citizens of the State of Georgia under the sanction of French authority or commissions to invade this province, or any of his Catholic Majesty's dominions;

5. Richmond County included Augusta.

what were the names of such citizens, what their forces & what their intentions, saith:

That immediately upon the arrival of the French ambassador Genet at Charleston that the deponent heard it rumored & suspected amongst his own neighbors that commissions for said purpose had been issued by Genet even previous to his going to Congress & deponent further saith that many citizens of Georgia (indeed the whole of the people of the back country of which the County of Richmond is a part) seemed to rejoice at it in the notion that the Floridas would soon become a French or English government, that is, the Torys in favor of the latter & the Whigs of the former. However some months afterwards the deponent understood that the people who had formed the Yazoo Company & Torys were those who had chiefly embraced Genet's proposals.

That some day after the 20th of Dec., that is the 21st, 22nd, 23rd or 24th, deponent cannot clearly remember which, the day he was present at Augusta in the House of Assembly when a motion was made (the same had been previously produced in the Senate but not yet carryed), that resolution similar to those adopted in the Assembly of South Carolina should take place against citizens accepting commissions or raising men under foreign powers, that is that the governor should be authorized to call out the whole or any part of the militia to put down the enlistments then carrying on.

This motion was made in the Senate, deponent understands, by a Mr. Milledge & is certain that it was made in the lower house by Mr. Wallburgh and seconded by Mr. Jones of Chatham County. This was agreed to in said house but rejected by the Senate when returned but at any rate it was resolved that the Governor should be authorized to issue his proclamation forbidding any armed force to embody itself in the State, which proclamation however was delayed & not issued when deponent left home, nor had it ever reached St. Marys when he was laterally there.

That regarding the intentions of Genet's party they were twofold, one directed against this province, the leader of which was said to be (deponent speaks by what he has heard) Samuel Hammond, called Colonel & now reported to have a General's commission in the French service. Deponent also heard that Abner Hammond had a commission in the same. Deponent also recollects that a few days before the Assembly broke up he had met the said Abner about four miles this side of Augusta in company with another man, a

Frenchman as deponent was told. Abner told the deponent he was going home, to which deponent replied he believed he would soon be down there himself. Hammond replied deponent would be welcome.

A few days afterwards deponent happened to be at a tavern ten miles on this side of Augusta, kept by one Valenton, where there was an entertainment; that plenty of bread, meat, drinks and salt pork was there for the company of militia commanded by Capt. Nowland; where deponent heard General Twiggs,[6] Commander-in-Chief of the Militia of Georgia, say smiling to Capt. Nowland & Valenton who were together, "Remember you will be brought to account for all this by the Governor" as its given in favor of Genet's men. Deponent further adds that he heard some time ago that Col. Armstrong[7] was to be one of the Genet leaders; but he knows the contrary since, as said Armstrong has raised, and been appointed under the authority of Congress, Capt. of a troop of horse.

Deponent has likewise heard & believes that a Mr. Ross is a captain under Sam'l Hammond. Deponent has also heard the names of others of Hammond's officers but does not recollect them & observes that, in general, all the Genetists endeavor to keep themselves private and to avoid the enquirings of government untill they could get beyond the bounds of the state.

As to the expedition against West Florida & the Mississippi, deponent has always heard & verily believes that General Clarke of Georgia was to be one of the leaders & General Clarke of Kentuckee the other, both with commissions of French Major General, but he heard of none other in Georgia; but in South Carolina that Stephen Drayton, Mr. Scorcon and some others have embraced Mr. Genet's party to march to the Westward. That these made so little secret of it that they publicly wear the French National cockade in Charles-

6. General John Twiggs was a patriot officer in the American Revolution, an Indian fighter, and a peace commissioner who became a general in the Georgia service. He was sent by the Georgia governor to persuade Elijah Clark to cease his revolutionary activities after the war. In 1796 he was asked to act as governor of Georgia but refused. Twiggs was the ranking Georgia military officer at the time of the French intrigue (Louise F. Hays, *Hero of Hornet's Nest; A Biography of Elijah Clark, 1733 to 1799*, pp. 51, 69, 168, 192, 209, 222, 232, 270, 277, 286; Wilbur H. Siebert, *Loyalists in East Florida, 1774 to 1785*, 2:329; Richard K. Murdoch, *The Georgia-Florida Frontier, 1793–1796: Spanish Reaction to French Intrigue and American Designs*, p. 160).

7. Armstrong fought as a patriot in the American Revolution and was also an Indian fighter in Georgia (Hays, *Hero of Hornet's Nest*, p. 138, 288, 348).

town, to which town two separate deputations arrived from Kentuckee to settle their plan of operations.

As to the part of the question which regards the force which the Genetists can collect in Georgia and Carolina, deponent believes that they may raise a thousand men in Georgia & about the same number in Carolina, however, the Genet followers count on many more than that; and deponent has no doubt that if a French fleet appears to defend them the number of people following them would increase, in which case it is very possible that some of the State troops would join up, because some have been six months without pay and others twelve without getting any pay.

That all who were raised in the States would have to be mounted because the defendant knows for sure that they will not find any men who will join up to march on foot.

Asked if he can estimate how long a time and for what distance horses can stand up to the fatigue of a march when fed only grass, and no corn:

Deponent said by his own experience at this season of the year, & particularly in the heat of summer, that of a thousand horses only one hundred would be apt to survive & at the end of eight days surely not even fifteen would survive and that this has been demonstrated by Georgians in their frequent expeditions against the Indians; and that in the last war in the expedition they made against this province [1778 expedition by patriots into the Jacksonville area], as to which the declarant was a witness, of the fifty carts that came from the Altamaha to the St. Marys not even one came back again because of the incapacity of the horses.

Asked when the deponent determined to leave Savannah and come to this province to avoid arrest, by which places did he pass on his way, and what did he hear with respect to the "Genetists":

Deponent said that from Savannah he left with a Captain Baker of the militia with whom he travelled fifteen miles to the ford of the Ogeechee River; that there the deponent found a neighbor of his, Mr. Beale, and in a conversation heard him say that a man had come to the settlement of Midway[8] (he could not say his name but he had only one eye), who apparently had a lot of money and was believed to belong to Genet's organization, which very much upset the people of

8. Midway, Georgia, was named after Medway, England, and originally was spelled Medway.

this settlement, because all this could bring about war; and it was observed that this man was very reserved in his speech and that he never gave very satisfactory answers.

That Beale also told the deponent that Major West had marched to St. Marys with a group of people, supposedly with the intent of sacking Florida; that Beale asked the deponent to come to his house with him but that the deponent answered that he could not do this until he had first contacted Captain Atkinson who owed him some money.

That then the deponent and said Baker crossed the river and went eight miles to the Foster's Tavern, where the deponent found his old neighbor Andrew Berrihill, who told the witness that he had found out at Williamsburg (previously called Williamstown), on the Altamaha, that Major West was crossing the river with twenty-four or twenty-five men & with Christie, a cowboy of Governor Telfair; and that Christie said to Berrihill that he was going to Florida to reclaim some Blacks who had been stolen from the Governor; that the deponent remembers that he heard Berrihill say that West or some of his men had told him that they were to be followed in three weeks by a thousand five hundred men and also by a French fleet that would soon be in Florida to provide them with arms and all necessary things; and that also Berrihill had said to the deponent that West and Smither had guns and swords, and two of the other men had guns, but that these were all the arms that were then among them; and that Baker had remarked that if this plan against Florida were to be executed it would bring ruin to the settlements along the coast because if West looted Florida the Spaniards would arm their ships and would capture all their Negroes along the coast.

That from Foster's Tavern the deponent and Baker went seven miles to Midway where they separated; that the deponent continued on to North New Port where at an inn he found some of Captain Armstrong's men in uniform. Deponent heard these say, speaking of West's expedition, that it was a wild enterprise & that the consequence would be that West & his men would be cut to pieces or else be clapped in a Spanish calaboose.

From No. Newport deponent proceeded nineteen miles to the widow McDonald's near Sapelo Bridge, where he lay that night where he heard nothing commentable except general conversation about West, which was the common talk everywhere. Deponent from McDonald's went to Darien, twelve miles. There he learnt he could pass no further by land; & remained there that night at one Lesly's who engaged him to carry him in a boat to Newtown on the St. Marys, but could not the next day as there was to be an election for county officers: Inspector, Clerk, Surveyor, & Sherriff. There also, deponent sold his horse for his passage to St. Marys & a paper certificate for eight pounds; and the next day Lesly set off for the election voting at Sapelo Bridge & returned that same night, late. Next morning he (Lesly) informed deponent that he had been in company with Col. Armstrong, who told him that he had received a letter from Major West importing that he had at Temple all kinds of provisions & particularly of rum, as much as he could use & further that he (West) would not return without he had his own scalp or took those of others. Lesly further mentioned that he heard Col. Oneale and other gentlemen at the election say that if West did mischief in Florida they did not see which way he could turn to, for that he dare not return to the States & where else could he go to.

The next day it blew so hard that the boat deponent was to sett off in could not start. About 12 o'clock Capt. Flournoy,[9] formerly of the State troops, arrived at Lesly's & with him a lawyer, James Wood. Lesly had been a soldier with Capt. Flournoy in the State Troops in the Indian Alarm of the year '88, for which service sixty pounds was due to Lesly. However, the deponent present, Lesly agreed to sell his right to Flournoy for seven pounds, who closed on that. That evening a boat belonging to Major Pierce Butler[10] happened to pass by there. Deponent weary of staying there sett off in her for Frederica & arrived there the same evening, twenty miles. Next morning Lesly arrived with a canoe & with him deponent set off.

Now the deponent recollects he had walked that day to Col.

9. Captain Robert Flournoy, of Huguenot descent, served the patriot cause in the American Revolution, coming from Virginia to Georgia shortly after the war. He was a very substantial landowner in Georgia. In Chatham County he owned the plantations Chatham, Cedar Grove, and Bonnabelle, his principal residence. He died in 1825 at age 62 (see Ellis Merton Coulter, *John Jacobus Flournoy, Champion of the Common Man in the Antebellum South*, pp. 1–3; Lucian Lamar Knight, *Georgia's Bicentennial Memoirs and Memories . . .*, 3:411).

10. Major Pierce Butler came to the Darien, Georgia, area from South Carolina. He purchased the island in the Altamaha River delta next to Darien and made "Butler's Island" one of the great rice plantations in the country. He was extremely wealthy and had extensive landholdings in Georgia (see Bessie Lewis, *They Called Their Town Darien*, p. 39).

Hillary's,[11] & dined there where all the general talk was about West & his men, & Colonel Hillary said that if West carried his plans into execution all the settlers must quit Frederica Island as retaliation would be looked for from the Spaniards. Deponent further recollects that when he called upon the way at Darien he met with three men who said they were going to join West at St. Marys & asked deponent if there were a great many men raising for to join him, to which deponent replied that he knew of none and believed that none would. One of the three seemed very anxious to go forward & supposed that West would go thro' the Indian Nation to fall upon the river St. Johns, to which deponent replied that he knew the country well & that he believed it would be impossible or at least very difficult. This seemed to stagger those men very much & probably induced them to return, as he knew for a certainty that they did not join West.

Returning to where deponent says he set off with Lesly, they followed on towards St. Marys untill they arrived at Mr. Jno. King's,[12] the Senator at Crooked River about five miles from Cumberland Sound. King told deponent that Colonel Howard had broke up his station, that West was at Temple & that he, Mr. King, had taken a number of affidavits concerning said West, which he had forwarded to Governor Mathews & that if the said Gov. did not come to St. Marys as he told him he would then the Gov. was not the man he [King] took him to be but that he did not doubt that the Gov. would come as soon as he received the express. King further added that the 16th of March he, Major Gaither, Major Burrows[13] & other

11. Christopher Hillary was born in 1755 and lived in Glynn County, Georgia. He was a Revolutionary War soldier and a surveyor for Glynn and Camden counties, served in the Georgia legislature from Glynn County (1787–89), and was a member of the Georgia militia. He made the motion to adopt the federal Constitution in the Georgia convention and was collector of customs for Frederica and Brunswick. He died in Savannah on 18 February 1796. His daughter married William McIntosh, son of John and Sarah. His widow, Agnes, married John after the death of Sarah (see Margaret Cate, *Our Todays and Yesterdays: A Story of Brunswick and the Coastal Islands*, p. 187).

12. King is believed to have been born in North Carolina about 1740. He served as an enlisted man in the Continental troops in Georgia during the American Revolution. He was one of the five commissioners of the town of St. Marys when it was founded and served as justice of the Inferior Court of Camden County in 1794–1804. He was also a state senator and a port collector and one of the largest landowners of the county (Marguerite G. Reddick, *Camden's Challenge: A History of Camden County, Georgia*, p. 403).

13. John Burrows was a justice of the peace for Camden County, to whom Governor Quesada addressed complaints about Georgia citizens involved in insurrection in Florida (Hays, *Hero of Hornet's Nest*, p. 290).

gentlemen of Newtown had had an interview with Capt. Atkinson on Roses Bluff[14] & that he, King, was of opinion that all designs against this province would come to nothing, let what would be the case with the other province of West Florida & further added that West would be obliged to quit Temple as soon as the Gov. arrived. King also told deponent, & also understanding that he wanted to see Capt. Atkinson, that he might easily do this from Newtown.

Deponent remained two days at Mr. King's and then sett out afoot eight miles for Newtown where he lodged at Mr. Carn's, where he saw Major Burrows & learned from him that he had been just copying a couple of letters from West to Major Gaither. Major Burrows added that he would go up to Roses Bluff where he expected to see Captain Atkinson; upon which deponent prayed him to apply to Major Gaither[15] to go with him; which Burrows promised to do before the tide lowered. Burrows did speak but let that tide slip by.

Next morning deponent seeing Major Gaither walking at the landing, went up & spoke to him, in consequence of Major Burrow's promise. Major Gaither replied it was true Major Gaither spoke to him about deponent & that he might go with Burrows & as consequence would need no pass. However something hindered Major Burrows from going up & of consequence the deponent was detained at Newtown where deponent observes he had arrived the 22nd March & remained there until the 28th.

The 26th Mr. Jno. King, aforesaid, came to Newtown where deponent saw him, Major Gaither and other gentlemen at Maclary's store where the conversation in general was upon West. Mr. King was of opinion that West ought to be drove out from Temple by force, but Major Gaither replied that would only be giving the fellows a higher idea of their own consequences, and whilst they behaved peacefully it would be better to take no notice of them untill the Govr. arrived.

From this conversation they proceeded to speak pretty warmly on Indian affairs. Major Gaither and King agreed in opinion that Governor Telfair was the promoter of Genl. Twiggs' expedition the beginning of last fall against the Indians. Major Gaither further said that it was true he had furnished Twiggs' men with beef & all the flour

14. An impressive bluff near Amelia Island on the Florida side.
15. Gaither was commander of all federal troops in Georgia (Murdoch, *The Georgia-Florida Frontier*, p. 35).

he had in his stores on the Oconee, except two barrels, but he would never do such a thing again without order from Congress & to his certain knowledge the white people had burned two Indian villages without the least provocation being given by the Indians since McGillivray's peace at New York; & called to deponent if he was a positive witness to the fact; to which deponent replied with great truth he was.

Major Gaither further told Mr. King that he had written the whole proceeding to the Secretary at War & both King and Gaither agreed finally in opinion that Gov. Telfair had acted diametrically contrary to the orders of Congress.

The next day, 27th, deponent seeing that Maj. Burrows declined going up the river, called upon Major Gaither for a pass at Mr. Seagroves; where the Major always passed the day tho' he slept in the fort at night. Upon this application the Major told deponent that he would give him a pass but that he had lately received a letter from Col. Howard signifying that as times were troublesome it was no time for people to come into this province but upon special business: & further Major Gaither questioned that were he even to see Capt. Atkinson if it would be to any effect, but that the deponent might go up with Capt. Randolph[16] & stay at Coleraine until the Florida Scout would appear & then deponent might either send his name to Capt. Atkinson or run the risque of crossing over himself. Major Gaither further told deponent that as soon as he heard of West's arrival at Temple he had written to him to know what his business was there & by what authority he had hoisted the American flag in the stockade & that West in his answer expressed that he was sent there by Col. Sam Hammond to take care of the house & stores, West signing himself Capt., that upon this he Gaither wrote a second letter to West desiring him to explain who authorized Col. Hammond to send him on. To this West answered in an evasive manner and signed himself Temporary Captain.

After this Major Gaither asked deponent if he was acquainted with West, who replied he was extremely well during the whole course of the war [American Revolution] & since. Upon which Major Gaither then told deponent that he had another letter ready to send West & that he would be glad that he would lay hold of the

16. Captain John F. Randolph was in charge of the U.S. cavalry at Coleraine. It was testified that he ordered Indians killed and scalped (Hays, *Hero of Hornet's Nest*, pp. 234, 356).

Samuel Hammond. Courtesy of the Library of Congress, Washington, D.C.

opportunity of going up with Capt. Randolph who was to be the bearer of the letter, to get into private conversation with West & let him know, as from deponent himself, how all his friends & relations were alarmed and disgusted about his wild enterprise against Florida. Deponent promised he would do his endeavors; but at the same time said that West, he well knew, was a man that a notion he had once taken could never be drove out of his head. Deponent then again requested a pass but received the same answer as before; & before deponent left the room another man came to ask likewise for a pass, which the Major declined giving, aledging Col. Howard's letter as above.

Next day, being 28th of March, he set off in a boat for Temple with Capt. Randolph, who was charged as above with a letter to Mr. West. Slept that night at old Cryer's on the Georgia side & sett off next morning, the 29th, when deponent arrived at Temple in company with Randolph around 10 o'clock; & upon inquiring for West understood he was drunk & abed. About an hour after hearing that West was a'stirring, deponent went up upon the strength of being an old acquaintance & was kindly received by West, who shook hands & asked what brought him there; to which deponent replied his object was to get over to Florida; & little further passed as West appeared still dosed with the fumes of liquor. Randolph upon his arrival had given the letter to one of the Temple men who, it seems, finding West asleep had left it on a table in the room. This man now came in, took up the letter & handed it to West, who upon reading it flew into an amazing passion, stompt about the room & cursed Gaither & immediately passed into the next room where most of his people were—with the letter in his hand. There the letter was read over again & this deponent could hear who was in the next room. They were all in as great a passion as West & talked very big, loud; & turned to the room where deponent was; & Capt. Randolph came in. West told Randolph that he had received a letter from Major Gaither, he did not know to what purpose as he had answered him sufficiently already. Then he gave Gaither's letter to Captain Randolph so he could read it, saying he wanted to give an answer to Gaither but he did not want to give him satisfaction in the manner he enquired.

Deponent here recollects that the men upon hearing Gaither's letter read in the next room cried out that they could raise eighty or ninety men in a few hours, or more than was sufficient if they pleased to take one or both of Cap. Atkinson's battalions. Capt. Randolph, seeing that West would not answer Major Gaither's letter by him but would send the answer himself, set off for Coleraine. Randolph, being about to depart, Deponent wanted to go with him; but West insisted on him to stay to dine, to which Deponent agreed, the sooner in hopes of giving compliance to what Major Gaither had encharged him. When dinner time came on, those that sat down to table appeared to be officers, in all five or six including Commisary Jones & a Frenchman who sat at the head of the table; & spoke so bad English that the deponent could not well understand what he said.

Being asked who he imagined said Frenchman to be & who was the person that he calls Commisary——saith:

That he was a tall fairskinned young man & that he appeared to be of consequence among them, that he was in his shirt sleeves and overalls; that the commissary's name was Jones; & as he learnt next morning brother to another boy called Jones who lives in Florida; & both sons to a man also of the name Jones, who as deponent likewise understood, was confined in Augustine.

Deponent returning to what happened at the dinner saith:

That nothing in particular occurred there, nor was a single word spoken of future plans or intentions of the Templetonians. Deponent here adds that the dinner consisted of excellent salt beef & pork with plenty of wheat bread, but not a drop of liquor. When they were finished then a bottle [of] rum was put on the table, of which West took the best part to himself & soon got drunk & went to sleep in which condition he remained till after sunset. Soon after sunset a man of the name of Pitcher, one of those who acted as officer placed a sentry at the gate but deponent cannot say whether within or outside; but recollects to have heard them challenge in the night & fire once. At the shot West & everyone turned out; but deponent lay still & heard the people return soon laughing & saying that the fellow said he did not know what he had fired at. Deponent further adds that when West recovered from his afternoon doze he told deponent that he should sleep with himself & so it happened.

Next morning they both got up early & deponent perceiving that West was then perfectly sober spoke to him in the manner Major Gaither had encharged him & advised him, in the most earnest manner as an old friend & acquaintance, to return home. To all which West replied that he knew his own business & that he supposed deponent was sent to pump him & that he had a good mind to put him upon the guard. Deponent replied that he only gave good advice, that he was a citizen as well as West & had as good a right to speak his sentiments, & that his doing so was no reason for West to arrest him.

This happened when West & deponent were alone; but immediately Pitcher & some other men came in & at the same [time] deponent, being vexed at the obstinacy of West, made use of an Indian expression in signifying it would be better if you went home; that this was understood by one of those present who also spoke Indian, and he said in a loud voice that deponent had no business to give such advice. Upon this deponent wanted to sett off for Coleraine but Pitcher swore he should not till after breakfast. Deponent did stay & after breakfast Pitcher told him, smiling, you have been now well treated upon republican provisions.

Deponent here recollects that when he arrived at Temple he saw at the landing a sailing boat that had brought six bushels & twelve half bushels of rice for the use of Temple. Deponent had seen the same boat pass Newtown, where the master said he came from Savannah & that the rice he brought was for the people of Clarke's Bluff. Said people are six or eight families that came from this side.

Soon after breakfast, deponent heard somebody cry out below there was the Florida Scout. Upon which he went downstairs where, meeting Pitcher, he asked if he would permitt him to go over, who replied he would, but asked deponent if he was resolved to go, for good & all. Deponent answered yes good & all, at all risques. A boat was then getting ready, on which Pitcher & four or five more got; also Deponent. On the boat's pushing over the Florida Scout cryed out to them not to approach the land. Deponent then requested Pitcher to bring him but so near that he could leap on shore. This was done.

While the deponent was at the landing at Temple he heard a youth from this side, who he was told was Commissary Jones's brother (deponent frequently heard the two call one another brother during the conversation) call out at Temple for his brother & on his appearing told him he came for their sister's Mrs. Hammond's cloathes. After deponent had got on shore he sat on the bank & there he saw the Georgia Jones come over in a little canoe, asking his brother among other things if he thought him being in Temple would bring any prejudice to his father & if it was known in Florida that he was at Temple; to which the youth from this side answered that it was very well known that he was there & that it did much harm to their father who probably would have been long ago out of confinement.

Georgia Jones then asked if the officer of the Spanish Scout was there. The other answered that he was; but out of sight but within hearing. Upon this, Capt. Hall walked to the beach & was asked by the brother in the canoe if he could send a letter to his mother to which the Capt. replied that he might but that every letter not directed to the Governor must be sent open. Deponent then asked Capt. Hall whether he could go forward. The Capt. answered to stay a little & then he would tell him.

Temple Jones then returned to that stockade & deponent heard said Jones tell his brother that there was what clothes he could find of the sister, tho' they were not all there for the trunk had been broke open before he came to Temple. Upon this Capt. Hall came riding down on horseback & Pitcher, who was near the shore, pushed off crying out to Hall you can not seize me for I have not touched rum. Shortly before this, while the Scout & Pitcher were in conversation the deponent heard Pitcher swear and damn himself that there was not a commission of any kind among them. Deponent had heard

West, Pitcher & indeed the most of the people at Temple declare the same the day before in the presence of Capt. Randolph.

Capt. Hall upon riding down told deponent that, pass or no pass, he must go to the camp to Capt. Atkinson, to whom he was accordingly conducted & by him sent forward to this place [San Vicente].

Being asked what number of men he saw or believes to be altogether in Temple, saith:

That he does not imagine West had with him of people properly called his men above twelve or thirteen including Commissary Jones & the Frenchman, but that these men gave to understand that they could have a great many men at a short notice & that they would be over in Florida sooner than was expected. Deponent adds that he heard Pitcher say that he knew everything that passed in Florida as also that Capt. Atkinson had not above seventy or eighty men with him. Besides West's men, so called, deponent saw at Temple one Wright, a Justice of the Peace, also one Baillie & one Drummond. Deponent further adds that he recollects to have heard more threats against the fore mentioned Senator King than against any other person, Spanish or American. They concluded to him that when gathered together they would destroy everything he had; & that, for his taking so much pain in fishing out affidavits against them & to find their intentions to the end of informing government of same; & further deponent wishes to include with this his declarations a list of Title Deeds of land property he has in Georgia & Carolina, which deponent left in possession of Mr. Carnes at New Town.

And further deponent saith not; but that all he has declared above is true in virtue of the oath he is taken & he is fifty-two years of age. In Testimony whereof he signs this his declaration, having first read it, word by word to his own satisfaction in the presence of the two aforesaid assisting witnesses: Thomas Sterling, Esq. & Don Joseph Sainz.[17]

Dated in San Vicente on the above-mentioned River of St. Johns this eighth day of April, One Thousand Seven Hundred & Ninety Four.

Daniel McMurphy
Charles Howard
Thomas Sterling
Joseph Sainz

17. Sainz was foreman of slaves in St. Augustine (Janice Borton Miller, "Juan Nepomuceno de Quesada: Spanish Governor of East Florida, 1790–1795" [Ph.D. diss.], p. 76).

[AGI, PC, leg. 166, pormenor 16, p. 204]

That to the above he [McMurphy] adds that there is common conversation all over America about a desire to break ties with Spain, people being persuaded that it is the only way to control the Indians, because by taking away the benefits and arms given by the Spaniards and British, and by attacking them from both sides of the province the Indians would be compelled to surrender.

2nd. Asked whom else did he know in this province other than the ones named to Lieutenant Colonel Howard; and if he brought any letter of introduction to anyone:

He said that from Charlestown one John Sanders, a Mr. Carter, and a Mr. John Peter Wagnon, and a Mr. Hammond, whom he knows to be in Havana, but that he did not bring any letter of introduction to anyone.

3rd. Asked if he knew why they came to this province, the ones named; and explain where he had made friends so quickly with Parkinson and Backuse:

He said that Sanders came because of forging papers and counterfeits, being exposed by his companion, Major Washington;[18] that Wagnon came because of having circulated counterfeit money and for his debts; and that Carter came only for this last reason; that his friendship with Backuse and Parkinson came about from eating at the house of the first one, where he had been told he could eat cheaply and that he was joined there by the second one who came for the same purpose.

At this point His Lordship ordered the statement suspended to be continued if necessary; and the defendant to whom this was read says he affirms and ratifies it; that he is as old as he has stated and signs with His Lordship and the interpreter.

Quesada

Daniel McMurphy

Miguel Iznardy

Before me, José de Zubizarreta, court reporter

---

18. Tom Washington was one of the directors of the South Carolina Yazoo Co., a land speculation company which failed. Tom O'Fallon, another director, referred to him as "poor Tom Washington" when Tom was hanged in South Carolina for counterfeiting. Arthur Preston Whitaker, *The Spanish American Frontier, 1783–1795* . . ., p. 129. See also Hays, *Hero of Hornet's Nest*, pp. 119, 125; Siebert, *Loyalists in East Florida*, 1:83.

FOURTEEN

Conclusions of the 1794 Investigation
of the Rebellion in Florida

ON 25 April 1794 Attorney José de Ortega submitted to Governor Quesada a twelve-page legal brief on the facts and applicable law in the case against John McIntosh, Abner Hammond, Richard Lang, William Plowden, John Peter Wagnon, and William Jones "on suspicion of involvement in a conspiracy to invade East Florida from Georgia under French commissions."

Ortega concluded that the evidence was not strong enough to warrant the continued imprisonment of Lang, Plowden, Wagnon, and Jones. He said that the cases against McIntosh and Hammond were also weak but that in those two cases there might be some political reason or "reason of state" that might warrant a different handling, at the governor's discretion.

The attorney observed that "there is no penalty for the crime of thought"; and that "one who repents before taking any evil action is not to be punished"; and that "crimes must be proved openly by witnesses, letters or confessions, not by suspicions only." (He cited as authority Elizondo, volume 4, plenary suit, page 244, paragraph 25.)

The governor on 7 May released William Plowden, after the prisoner's brief formal request under bond.[1] The then governor

1. Plowden's testimony appears at page 104 in this volume. He wrote the Spanish governor from St. Marys, 19 June 1795, asking that his family be permitted to join him in Georgia (collections of the Georgia Department of Archives and History).

166

received the more detailed petitions of Lang, Wagnon, and Jones, presented in this chapter. These three were freed after some months of delay.

The McIntosh and Hammond cases were resolved more slowly. The Spanish authorities accepted promptly Sarah McIntosh's offer to post bond in connection with her petition for her husband. As a result, his slaves were seized (as shown in the last document in this chapter). Both his and Hammond's cases were sent to Madrid for review; both men were then returned to St. Augustine and finally freed. In making this decision the Council of State at Madrid stated that McIntosh was guilty of giving moral support to the French revolutionary plans in Florida, but added no further penalty to the many months he had already spent in prison.

[AGI, PC, leg. 166, pormenor 16, p. 254—in English]

St. Augustine, 12th of May, 1794

To His Excellency the Governor, Etc., Etc.

The memorial of Richard Lang, a citizen of the Province of East Florida humbly sheweth:

That whereas your memorialist was on the night of sixteenth day of January last arrested and put in close confinement in the fort of this place by order of Your Excellency where he remained three months and twenty-five days, deprived of all sort of communication untill the evening of the twenty-ninth day of April, at which time he was conveyed to another appartment in the fort in company with three other prisoners, without yet being informed of the cause of his confinement; in consequence of which his family[2] was left exposed (as they were informed and had sufficient reason to believe) either to savage cruelty or the mercy of a set of lawless plunderers imbodied in a neighboring state as was generally believed in order to make a de[s]cent on this province, at the same time receiving orders from

2. Lang married Sarah Benson and they had seven children: Elizabeth, b. 1773; Mary, b. 1775; Rebecca, b. 1777; William, b. 1780; Lydia, b. 1782; David, b. 1786; and Eady, a daughter, b. 1790 (Folks Huxford, *Pioneers of Wiregrass Georgia: A Biographical Account of Some of the Early Settlers* . . ., 5:256).

government for all inhabitants of St. Marys to move in ten days to the south of the River St. Johns through a desert of forty miles distance. Being without horses or boats it was entirely out of her power to comply with the orders of government. In this distressed situation she was induced to move across the River St. Marys into the State of Georgia, which procedure was without the knowledge or approbation of your memorialist as it left her amongst a set of people whose mode of government he from principle has uniformly opposed.

And whereas your memorialist being conscious of never having disobeyed your Excellency's orders or being guilty of any crime injurious either to his King or country, and Your Excellency having been lately pleased to give one of his fellow prisoners his liberty on his giving security to appear whenever called upon[,] your memorialist humbly begs that Your Excellency will be pleased to grant him also his liberty on giving security in like manner, which will enable your memorialist to adopt some method of getting his family again settled in such part of this province as Your Excellency may think most advisable; and your memorialist will ever pray, etc.

Richd. Lang

[AGI, PC, leg. 166, pormenor 16, p. 249—in English]

St. Augustine, 13th May, 1794

To His Excellency the Governor, Etc., Etc., Etc.

The memorial of William Jones, a citizen of the Province of East Florida, humbly sheweth:

That whereas your memorialist was on the 17th of January last by Your Excellency's order arrested at his plantation on the St. Johns, his arms secured fast behind his back with a rope, & compelled to get on a very lame, tired horse, by which his frequent stumbling caused a hurt in one of his arms, which has terminated in the loss of the use of it, & in that situation conveyed to St. Augustine & close confined in the calabooce, the floor of which was always wet & whenever it rained covered in water, in that cold season not allowed fire to keep him warm, deprived of the benefit of the light & all sort of communication, scarcely allowed air enough to keep life; & in that situation labored under a lingering indisposition till the 29th day of April, being three months & twenty-four days; without ever yet being informed the cause of his confinement & was then conveyed to an apartment in the fort in company with three other prisoners; his wife & four small children turned out of doors; ordered off from their place of abode, a place surveyed by order of Your Excellency for your petitioner; that his property has naturally wasted each day because of his absence, being left to the care only of a helpless wife & four small children in a strange country far from any relations exposed to the insults of a malicious world; destitute of any friend of whom she can with any degree of propriety ask assistance.

And whereas your memorialist being conscious of never having either disobeyed Your Excellency's orders or having been guilty of any crime injurious either to his King or Country & Your Excellency having been pleased lately to grant Mr. William Plowden one of the prisoners confined with us, his liberty on given security to appear before Your Excellency when called upon, your memorialist therefore most humbly beggs that your Excellency will of your great goodness, be pleased also to grant him his liberty on his giving sufficient security to appear before Your Excellency whenever called upon; and your memorialist as in duty bound will ever pray.

William Jones

[AGI, PC, leg. 166, pormenor 16, p. 244—in English]

St. Augustine, 13th of May, 1794

To His Excellency the Governor, Etc., Etc.

The memorial of John Peter Wagnon, a citizen of the Province of East Florida, humbly sheweth:

That whereas your memorialist was on the night of the sixteenth of January last arrested in this town and conducted to prison by Your Excellency's orders where he has been close confined in an uncommon filthy room for three months and twenty-five days, deprived of all sort of communications untill the evening of the twenty-ninth of April without ever yet being informed of the cause of his confinement and then conveyed to another appartment in company with three other prisoners.

By which means the little property he has is dailey wasting and what is still more distressing a young, tender and affectionate wife reduced to the utmost difficulties, deprived of all her friends and relations, without even a female companion living under the same roof to alleviate her miseries, exposed to the insults of a malicious world; without money or resources as all his papers were seized the same night and are still detained, amongst which were accounts and obligations against people of this province, for considerable sums; for want of collections that could have been made from such papers, she has been obliged to sacrifice for her own and your memorialist's support, while in confinement, part of the household furniture.

Your memorialist therefore being conscious of never having committed any crime injurious either to his King or the country he lives in, most humbly requests that, as Your Excellency has been pleased to grant one of our fellow prisoners his liberty on giving security, that Your Excellency in your great goodness may be pleased also to grant your memorialist liberty of the town on his giving sufficient security to appear when called for to answer any complaint that may be lodged against him, and your memorialist, as in duty bound, will ever pray, etc.

                                                      J. P. Wagnon

The final document in these 1794 legal proceedings was a recitation of seizure, pending further order, of the slaves of John McIntosh and the placing of them in the custody of one Thomas Sterling:

[AGI, PC, leg. 166, pormenor 16, p. 260]

On May 27, 1794, I, Santos Rodríguez, Keeper of Supplies and Lieutenant to the Royal Agent at San Vicente Ferrer, following orders of April 28 from the Governor and Commanding General of this Province of East Florida, did enter the home of Sarah McIntosh, wife of John McIntosh, accompanied by José Sainz and Salvador García as witnesses, and also Domingo Fernandez, as interpreter, to make the inquiry provided for in said orders and to record the conversation with the lady; and she, being in said home after having been informed of said order by the interpreter in the presence of the witnesses, intelligently answered that she was ready to comply with the order and that, as permitted by law, she could post bond and was now willing to provide it.

So, I proceeded to comply with the order which I executed on the following property since there was nothing else available; five Negroes called Carolina First, Steven, London, Romeo and Carolina Second and ten Negresses named Giky, Dinah, Sarah, Judil, Carlotta, Isabel, Penda, Diana, Ginda and Flora, whom I immediately placed in trust with Thomas Sterling, resident of this river valley; that he gave a receipt and accepted charge of them for his supervision as a trustee, committing himself to return them or their value but in the meantime to maintain them in his possession as a deposit of property responsive to His Majesty in compliance with any sentence passed by legal authority.

Santos Rodríguez
Thomas Sterling
Domingo Fernandez
Salvador García
José Sainz

Before the end of 1794 Colonel Howard learned that Plowden and some of the others involved in the 1794 rebellion activities were still plotting a major Florida invasion. Lieutenant Colonel Henry Gaither promised to be on the alert for any questionable activity discovered in Georgia. Richard Lang and Elijah Clark, both then in Georgia, were the men chiefly suspected of plotting renewed efforts from that state for a French-supported revolution in Florida.

FIFTEEN

Capture of Juana, 1795

WHILE the influential relatives of John McIntosh, professing his innocence, sought his freedom through diplomatic means, Samuel Hammond tried to use McIntosh's incarceration to strengthen the forces of rebellion. He appealed to the McIntosh family in Georgia to give substantial aid to the rebellion as a means of revenge. Hammond at about the same time explained to Mangourit his plans for stepping up the military supplies and personnel of the revolutionaries; he emphasized the need for Indian allies and naval support.[1] However, only minor increases in supplies and personnel resulted from these efforts and no overt help from the McIntosh family was forthcoming. The McIntosh clan considered that only careful diplomacy gave John, imprisoned in faraway Morro Castle, any reasonable chance for freedom. Storming the castle at St. Augustine seemed to them an impractical enterprise that would endanger the safety of their kinsman.

The disclosure of the preparations for rebellion in 1794 had understandably produced a generally deflating effect on the revolutionaries' morale. With all chance of surprise eliminated, the French warship *Las Casas* pulled away from the St. Marys River in April of 1794. She left behind on Amelia Island a cadre of Frenchmen and a store of weapons for future use.

Within the following week General Elijah Clark called his

1. Hammond to Mangourit, 5 March 1794, Samuel Hammond Papers, Boston Public Library.

172

men together at Temple. He told them that, since their plans had been exposed, they were all free to return to their homes or they could join him in a new project to set up a republic in the Indian lands to the west of the Oconee River. He still felt secure in the use of the French military commissions, though they had long since been announced by French officials to be no longer in effect.

Most of the men followed him to the Oconee. They set up a chain of forts in a ten-mile swath of land on the western banks of the Oconee. Officials of the United States and of Georgia were critical of Clark's actions, claiming that they were illegal. Quickly

Elijah Clark. Courtesy of Agnes Bacon.

the old general submitted himself voluntarily to local judges in Wilkes County, Georgia, who just as quickly decreed that they could not find anything he had done contrary to federal or state law.[2] Clark, with this official blessing, went vigorously forward with his republican operations in the Indian lands.

The Trans-Oconee affair was well under way by May of 1794; and so was persistent opposition to it from the federal capital at Philadelphia. On 5 June a federal law was enacted making criminal the use of foreign commissions in a war against a third nation. Many people in Georgia saw the Trans-Oconee operations as some protection against Indian belligerents along the border; so Georgia's Governor George Mathews was at first reluctant to do much in the matter. When it became clear, however, that if Georgia did not send troops to put down these activities the federal government would do so, the governor at last acted. On 28 July he issued a proclamation discrediting the project. Clark nevertheless stayed on until it became obvious that Georgia troops would in fact fight to oust him if necessary. Finally, on 28 September, Clark vacated his landholdings and surrendered his troops to the Georgia militia.[3] Nor did Samuel Hammond bring his troops to Florida as planned. Thus the Oconee project as well as the Florida project faltered and stalled in 1794.

On 27 November 1794 an impressive group of East Florida leaders, including Francis P. Fatio, Antonio Pelicer, and Manuel Solana, drafted a letter to the Spanish court stating in strong language why they felt the liberalized Spanish immigration policy had failed in Florida. The letter[4] said of Spain: " . . . in vain has it granted permission to foreigners to settle in this province, for as we see it, it is doubtful whether anyone will dare to come here now."

It was explained in this document that those who came from the American states had been "bred under a government and laws that never deprive even the most unfortunate of his rights," yet

2. Louise F. Hays, *Hero of Hornet's Nest; A Biography of Elijah Clark, 1733 to 1799*, p. 267.

3. Ibid., p. 277.

4. Arthur Preston Whitaker, *The Spanish American Frontier, 1783–1795* . . ., p. 195.

the immigrants to Florida were charged high taxes and deprived of basic rights. The letter concluded:

"But what drove the rest of them out was the imprisonment, in January of this year, of five or six inhabitants on the St. Johns River, two of whom were sent to Havana, and the others are still in jail. Who can think of the losses and misery that they and their families are suffering, without being moved to pity. And perhaps they are innocent, as many people think. God grant that your Majesty may remedy this and make them full amends if they are not guilty."

It was shortly thereafter that Lang, Wagnon, and Jones were freed. Abner Hammond and John McIntosh were both released just under a year from the time of their arrest and incarceration.[5]

Back on Amelia Island the cadre of Frenchmen and their protected cache of weapons remained. The island was so large and the cadre so wily that the tiny garrison of Spanish soldiers originally stationed on the island could never make a capture. By early 1795 the entire Spanish garrison had withdrawn to Talbot Island, a smaller island that did not require the military strength needed to defend Amelia. Elijah Clark knew of the virtual abandonment of Amelia and that numerous of his co-revolutionaries still resided in the St. Marys Valley and had never gone very far afield from their original locations or plans. He also knew that Abner Hammond still had quantities of war materials stored at Temple, accumulated under the banner of France. It was not surprising, therefore, that the Spanish authorities at St. Augustine received a report in May of 1795 that Clark had recently been at Coleraine arranging for a fresh attack on East Florida, still relying on the French commissions and assuming continued French approval.

Richard Lang spent nearly two months in the hospital in St. Augustine after he had been released from his cell in the Castillo

---

5. "In a little less than a year Colonel McIntosh was released without trial" (George White, *Historical Collections of Georgia*, p. 548). See also Richard K. Murdoch, *The Georgia-Florida Frontier, 1793–1796: Spanish Reaction to French Intrigue and American Designs*, p. 157.

de San Marcos. He was soon observed at Temple and Coleraine in long conversations with well-known revolutionaries.

On 18 May 1795 Lang wrote the Spanish governor a letter, which Carlos Howard told the governor was probably the result of recent meetings between Clark and Lang. If this were the case it may have been that Lang wanted to disguise his real plans for the conquest of East Florida as a paltry revenge for his imprisonment— presenting a much less alarming prospect that would give little cause for substantial reaction from the Spanish. Following is the Lang letter:[6]

May the 18th, 1795

Sir,

   With patience I have waited for your answer to my account presented to your Excellency, which is justly due me; but finding instead of answering my account, presented a copy of my Letter to the Governour of the State; but I will have your Excellency to know, that I am not yet become a citizen of the United States; but am a subject of the King of Spain. I further wish to inform your Excellency that at the receipt of this, you will without delay, or at any rate by the 1st of June next, you will send my full amount of the account presented to your Excellency by me, which will be the only means of preventing me from cohorting myself with all my power to pull off the yoke of despotism, and spread abroad the liberty and freedom that God has bestowed to all mankind. I can assure your Excellency that no one can wish more for peace than I do; but that unjust confinement your Excellency laid on me, and being so ill treated by your Excellency's orders, which distress'd a large, and helples family to almost a morcell of Bread and Water, which I cannot forgit it, which I hope God will wash away all strife, which after I will pledge you my word of honour that I never will interfere with your Government. I have the honour, Sir, to be your humbel servant.

Richard Lang

His Excellency the Governour of
East Florida at St. Augustine

6. Lang to Quesada, 18 May 1795, Georgia Department of Archives and History.

Governor Quesada promptly contacted the Spanish representative in Philadelphia to make complaint about the threatening activities of Clark and others on the St. Marys. The Spanish authorities also noted the ominous presence of two French corsairs at the mouth of the St. Marys and at the bar of St. Augustine.

On 29 June 1795 a rebel force of over sixty men under orders from Richard Lang and perhaps from General Clark destroyed the Spanish fort at Juana, capturing the entire garrison, which consisted of the commander, Lieutenant Isaac Wheeler, and fourteen enlisted men. The rebels also appropriated the more than 100 head of cattle at the stockade. A 1795 document[7] signed by Juan de Araoz described the event and stated that the attack was led by Richard Lang and William Plowden. Although Araoz merely stated that Juana was "between the St. Johns and the St. Marys rivers," correspondence of about the same date reveals that Juana was where the road from Savannah to St. Augustine crossed the narrow headwaters of the Trout River. It was not only a military outpost but also a collection and inspection point for cattle driven from the north to feed the people of East Florida. During the American Revolution British troops had temporarily occupied the same spot.[8]

On 5 July 1795 Bartolomé Morales, acting temporarily as governor during the illness of Quesada, wrote[9] excitedly and indecisively to the governor general in Havana, Luis de Las Casas y Aragorri, as follows (and in part):

7. Murdoch, *Georgia-Florida Frontier*, pp. 86, 87; HM 9462, Juan de Araoz, 21 August 1795, minutes of Council of War, MS., Huntington Library, San Marino, Calif.

8. Bruce Chappell, paleographist and linguist at the P. K. Yonge Library of Florida History, University of Florida, Gainesville, advises that correspondence to and from Juana pinpoints its location at the headwaters of the Trout River and is to be found in "Correspondence of Governors, 1794–1795, St. Johns River," in Reel 40 of the microfilm of the East Florida Papers at the P. K. Yonge Library. Most of the cattle taken at Juana belonged to Captain George Fleming, who was in the Spanish militia (Murdoch, *Georgia-Florida Frontier*, pp. 86, 87; Pleasant D. Gold, *History of Duval County, Florida*, pp. 65, 93, 96). Colonel Thomas Brown during the American Revolution stated that the British regulars were ordered to take post "at the head of Trout Creek" (Charles E. Bennett, *Southernmost Battlefields of the Revolution*, p. 9; see also pp. 13, 15, 16).

9. Morales to Las Casas, July 5, 1795, Archivo General de Indias, Papeles Procedentes de Cuba, legajo 1438. The papers referred to in the subsequent pages are from this letter and its enclosures. The materials are available in the Library of Congress.

[AGI, PC, leg. 1428]

In an official letter yesterday I informed you that the dragoons detachment located between the St. John's and St. Mary's rivers, intended to patrol the frontier and to report everything that happened on that side, was attacked and taken prisoner by Richard Lang and William Plowden, with an uncertain number of followers of these insurgents. That they destroyed and burned the redoubt named Fort Juana, in which they were sheltered; that they took along one hundred fourteen head of horned cattle with their drivers; and that I would advise you of the outcome of the reconnaissance of this attempt, which Don Carlos Howard had made, as soon as this officer lets me know the result.

Yesterday evening Don Carlos' letter reached my hands, which I am enclosing for you [illegible], and seeing by its contents that the rebel and traitor Richard Lang, with his companion William Plowden, have situated themselves in this Province's territory, accompanied by the American, Abner Hammond, and up to about seventy-two other scoundrels, I intended to attack them at their camp before they joined with a great many others of their same character, of which there is an abundance in the State of Georgia, and also those in this Province who are opposed to the Spanish government, of which there are more than a few, all of them new settlers, but before I made up my mind I wanted to hear the opinion of the Council of War; for which purpose I immediately called a meeting of it. The opinion of all the members was contrary to mine with regard to attacking the rebels, and even though the observations they made to me to the contrary were solid and founded, as you may see by the copy of that which was agreed upon which I am enclosing, I had with a great deal of repugnance to go along with this consensus: I was almost resolved to put mine into execution, urged by the desire to inflict an exemplary punishment on the traitor Lang but I was restrained by the consideration that in case of some hapless event all the burden of responsibility would fall upon me because I would be working against the dictates of all the members of the council, and I have made up my mind without a doubt that the action might have had bad consequences, for today I have learned from the prisoner whom Lang set free, (by giving him the paper herewith enclosed) that when Lang struck camp it was because of word received from Newton and it was to join fifty Frenchmen and some American rebels who were joining up with Lang.

It all appears, Sir, as if there are not enough forces here to dislodge Lang from where he has stationed himself and that undoubtedly a great many people will be gathered together with whom he can attempt the crossing of the St. Johns River at different points, which are little defended or not defended at all.

The Council of War referred to by Acting Governor Morales had met in St. Augustine and had found that Lang, Plowden, and Abner Hammond were in East Florida in a rebellion then supported by seventy-two men, expecting strong reinforcements under General Clark. They found that many whom Lang had taken as prisoners were now his allies; and they observed that it was not to be presumed that "once Richard Lang had raised up the standard of rebellion and unsheathed his sword against the sovereign to whom he had sworn obedience, that he would sheath it again or cease to go ahead with his evil plan." The council summarized its recommendations as follows:

[AGI, PC, leg. 1428]

1. To arm all the free Negroes and Mulattoes in the province; for, being fugitives from the State of Georgia, they will be loyal and will defend themselves to the death in order not to return to their former slavery; that as great a number as possible of Indian warriors be sought; that to these people, so suited and fit for passing through the flooded places and marshes, add the dragoons who have good mounts and are not suspected of disloyalty; and crossing over to the other side of the St. Johns River let them attack the enemy and pursue him if they encounter a measure of success; and if not, let them divert and engage the enemy until the Captain General, promptly informed of this predicament, may determine to send succor, or whatever he deems suitable;

2. To reinforce the battery detachment at the shoal with eight men more than what they already have.

3. To look for two launches, boats or rafts to put in order, and mount on them the only two small-bore cannon there are at this fort so as to use them to bar the enemy from crossing the river when he comes to attempt it at one of the many spots offered him along the banks of its extensive course.

4. That for the same purpose, by the schooner which was captured by the English brigantine, in case the captain wants to sell it, and through these, the only means afforded us by the situation we find ourselves in, prolong and stretch out our defenses until the arrival of succours from Havana.

Shortly after the fall of Fort Juana, John McIntosh and Peter Wagnon protested their innocence to Colonel Howard and Captain Hall and volunteered to help in the pursuit of the rebels. But their sincerity was seriously doubted by the Spanish authorities.

The report by Colonel Carlos Howard mentioned by Morales was dated at midnight on 3 July and was signed aboard the *San Simeon* anchored at San Nicolás. It included the following comments:

[AGI, PC, leg. 1428]

At this instant Militia Sergeant Francisco Cain has just arrived here, having been dispatched with a letter from Captain Hall for me which I am enclosing for you in its original form and which I won't set about translating in order not to lose time. The militia man Jonathan McCoullogh,[10] and his Indian confidant, Sam, came with the sergeant; the former in the nature of a prisoner released on parole by Richard Lang; as shown by the paper which I know to be in his handwriting, with a letter from Lt. Wheeler,[11] a prisoner of Lang. He also wrote me one to his wife, which I have seen and it is of no consequence.

Hall says in his letter that Lang is undoubtedly (as the aforementioned Jonathan and the Indian affirm) at this side of St. Marys

10. Sergeant Jonathan McCoullogh, second in command at Juana, was in charge of the thirteen enlisted men there (Murdoch, *Georgia-Florida Frontier*, pp. 87, 166).
11. Cornet Wheeler was the commanding officer at Juana (ibid., p. 87).

Harbor with from forty to fifty men (the Indian assures me through the above-mentioned sergeant that there are sixty-two and that he counted them three or four times); and that Col. Johnson is expected with four hundred men and also General Clark with another gang. That Hall, in agreement with Lieutenants Summeral and Hogan, have stopped and are awaiting my reply about eighteen miles from here, until tomorrow afternoon; and if they don't hear from me by then he will return to this river because he does not think he has enough forces to go ahead, and because of having two tired horses already, and finding it necessary to walk slowly, otherwise the same thing would happen to all of them; and that he would prefer to take a chance with his people on foot rather than mounted on sick horses.

That his opinion is that the Indians will be useful to us now, along with the rest of the militia and all or part of the townspeople and that then it might perhaps be possible to drive off the French band which is grouping; and the sooner this is undertaken, the better, for it is expected that the enemy will keep getting bigger and bigger in number. He concludes by saying that it would be wise to build a fort on the northern strip of this command.

Wheeler tells me in the letter he wrote me with the permission of Capt. Lang, the French republican of whom he is prisoner, that the greater part of the military prisoners have placed themselves under Lang's protection; that he, Wheeler, will appreciate it very much if I will have him exchanged as soon as I can because he finds himself very unfavorably situated there; that Lang says that there are French prisoners in St. Augustine and that he will agree to a formal exchange in conformity with the rules of war. That Mr. James McGirtt and son are prisoners too, with strong desires of being exchanged also.

The aforementioned McCoullogh has informed me that Lang had changed his mind by virtue of a notice which came to him this morning from Newton, and that when they let him loose they were almost all already mounted and headed for Roses Bluff, where, according to what he heard told to Abner Hammond, they were going to assemble about fifty Frenchmen with some people from a certain town and that within a short time five hundred more Frenchmen would arrive, and all that I have been able to learn is confined to this.

In view of everything I mean to write to Capt. Hall and tell him to wait with his people at the spot where he is now, or some other immediate site that looks good to him until he receives your decision through me; for, of course, it seems certain that he does not have enough forces to attack the enemy until reinforcements come to him.

Where these will be found is a difficulty which I am unable to overcome. On the opposite bank I have collected sixteen soldiers on foot because they have no horses, or because some of them are weak; so all the strength I have on the other side of the river comes down to forty men.

What Hall proposes about having Indians come is not a bad idea, but I doubt if there are sufficient provisions to furnish them if they should come, and they would not be satisfied with a little. Also, use could be made of the free Negros, but it will be necessary to put them on rations, too. Building a fort on this northern bank is desirable, but I don't know where to find the materials. That which is pressing is the construction of the battery on the shoal, and since for the time being and without express orders from you this gunboat cannot leave here, I think that it might be convenient to employ Juan McQueen's Negroes to carry the necessary woods in rafts, by commissioning Santos Rodríguez[12] for the purpose.

McCoullogh added that the rumors among Lang's people (it is true that he has a bad leg, but he doesn't stop getting around) is that they do not wish to harm anyone, but they will take over the Province or die. I will have McCoullogh continue there as soon as he can. Right now he is tired and out of commission.

Howard enclosed in his report a paper signed by Richard Lang as "Commander of St. Marys, East Florida." Headed "Republican Territory, Mills's Ferry, Headquarters, July 3, 1795," it stated: "On this day I have freed on parole Jonathan MacCullough, a Spanish subject who has promised and agreed to remain a prisoner of war until he is exchanged in accordance with the articles of war."

On 6 July Morales wrote to Governor Mathews of Georgia complaining of the capture of Juana, and particularly that some of the invaders were federal troops stationed at Coleraine.[13]

12. Rodríguez was in charge of supplies at San Vicente Ferrer.
13. Morales to Mathews, 6 July 1795, Georgia Department of Archives and History, Atlanta.

My dear Sir:

From the enclosed copy of the letter that I directed to the magistrates of Camden County, established in the town of Newton, you will inform yourself of the offense that has been committed by the people of that state in the territory of G. M. [Governor George Mathews] in this province, attacking a fortified town, surrounded by the king's troops, taking them and the official at the head prisoners, and then proceeding to rob one hundred head of cattle. These deeds of depreciation seem to announce a break of those states with my soverign; and I would believe it true seeing the violators accompanied by some of the soldiers of the Federal troops which guard the town of Coleraine, if not made evident by a firm resolution of the Supreme Government of those states to invariably preserve its neutrality in the present war, and your good intentions to contribute to the proper purpose; but in spite of all these good intentions the insults continue, producing fatal consequences, and the ones committing the crimes continue being armed with apparent signs of continuing.

Your prudent resolves were able to stop consequences which the first insult would have brought about under the authority of Captain Randolph, and hardly was that attempt settled than one of greater consequence is committed. You know that there is in that State a considerable number of French immigrants thrown out of their Island[14] and many other strayed men who are idle and have no fixed homes; if these come near, as is expected, to those upon whom these attempts were made, the affair may take on unbounded limitations; I hope that you will think this over and will decide that it is necessary to stop the malignant cancer by dissecting away the infected membrane.

I consider your personal appearance necessary on this border to stop such deadly designs.

The seriousness of this affair has placed me in a tight spot to send you an official for a personal interview with an interpreter to discuss the damage done. I recommend the said official, not only for his merits but also for the sovereign whom he serves, and I beg that you help him to make a comfortable return.

14. The slave revolution of 1791 in France's Santo Domingo created Haiti, a black republic, and many white colonists fled to the United States (see Kenneth G. Goode, *From Africa to the United States, and then . . .; A Concise Afro-American History*, p. 23).

May our Lord guard you for many years.

I have the honor to subscribe myself your most attentive servant

Bartolomé Morales

St. Augustine, Florida

July 6, 1795

Most Excellent George Mathews

Probably Acting Governor Morales had little real expectation that Governor Mathews would or could do very much to stop the rebellion. After the capture of Juana the rebels settled down at Mills's Ferry. This indicated to the Spanish that Lang's men would await reinforcements from General Clark before undertaking any new offensive.

Captain Andrew Atkinson of the Spanish militia dragoons meanwhile reported to the governor about a banquet he had attended at St. Marys where a number of Frenchmen and American supporters of Lang spoke of plans to capture first San Nicolás and then St. Augustine and to take possession of the province. They declared that they would be joined at the St. Johns by local rebels.

Governor Quesada went quickly forward with plans to augment the Spanish defenses. He ordered continuous land patrols on the south bank of the St. Johns. He strengthened his small fleet by purchasing the French schooner *Micaela* from her captor, the *Conquest*, a British privateer; both ships were then at the bar at St. Augustine. He renamed the schooner *Santa Mónica*.

SIXTEEN

Capture of San Nicolás and End of the Rebellion, 1795

WHEN John McIntosh returned to Florida after his imprisonment in Cuba, he found himself under persistent suspicion as a
result of the events of 1794, particularly the official adverse opinion of him expressed by the Council of State at Madrid. He
therefore found it prudent not to advertise his presence at his
strategically located plantation at Cowford; instead he visibly
concerned himself with properties closer to St. Augustine and
resided at Spring Hill on the south side of the St. Johns, eight
miles east of San Nicolás. But he did not abandon his plantation at
Cowford. He kept some obviously agricultural work going on
there—to justify the presence of horses, men, and boats, things
that could be useful in a time of rebellion. Surely July of 1795 was
such a time.

Despite the official 1794 order to burn all buildings north of
the river, the McIntosh buildings at Cowford were still intact in
July of 1795. So were those of Juan McQueen on Fort George
Island.[1] McQueen, however, had the complete confidence of the
Spanish authorities. Like McIntosh, he had come to Florida as a
Protestant Anglo-Saxon; but he soon embraced Catholicism,

---

1. McQueen acquired Fort George Island in 1792 (Carita Doggett Corse, *The Key to the
Golden Islands*, p. 109). He fitted up a sawmill to exploit its timber resources and built a
residence at the north end of the island. He already had a substantial residence on St. George
Street in St. Augustine (John McQueen, *The Letters of Don Juan McQueen to His Family . . .*, p. xxix).

demonstrated complete fidelity to the king, and even changed his name from "John" to "Juan." We have seen how McQueen's presence and his slaves were in fact relied upon in the Spanish defense of the St. Johns Valley. But the holdings of Richard Lang at Mills's Ferry and those of McIntosh at Cowford were wisely considered to be vulnerable spots in the defense lines of the provinces. Of course, the McIntosh plantation at Cowford was under constant observation from across the river at San Nicolás, giving Spanish authorities a sense of reassurance.

Despite all of the Spanish defense precautions, a rebel force of fifty or more men under Richard Lang crossed the St. Johns River, undetected, on the evening of 9 July. Instead of coming from the McIntosh plantation buildings[2] across from San Nicolás, they hid their approach by crossing downstream a mile and more away. Most of them landed at William Lane's plantation, just west of the mouth of Pottsburg Creek. Some reached the spot by swimming their horses across the river, and others used John McIntosh's boats. At the Lane plantation they captured some of the Spanish militia who were there on a patrol commanded by Lieutenant Timothy Hollingsworth.

The rebels continued southwest to the William Jones plantation, then headed north to the Spanish fort at San Nicolás on the regular road from St. Augustine to Cowford.[3] Enroute they met a large group of Floridians ready to assist in seizing the fort, including John McIntosh, John Peter Wagnon, William Plowden, and William Jones.

The rebels in a combined force of more than 100, speaking Spanish and appearing to be a relief force, deceived the sentries and entered the fortifications before being recognized as enemies.

2. See location 13 on map at page 189 of this book. The notation on the 1794 map at this point reads *Casas del Plantase viejo de MacIntosh*, "Old plantation buildings of McIntosh" (Archivo General de Indias, Papeles Procedentes de Cuba, legajo 2564, p. 1425, in East Florida Papers, Reel 129, B294P12, p. 1425, Manuscript Division, Library of Congress).

3. The source of information here and throughout this chapter about the conflict at San Nicolás is Las Casas to Campo Alange, 25 August 1795, Archivo General de Indias, Papeles Procedentes de Cuba, legajo 2564, with enclosures. The material is on microfilm at the Library of Congress in the Manuscript Division as Reel 129, B294P12, East Florida Papers. The microfilm was utilized in this preparation.

The combat that ensued was fierce and swift. Three Spaniards were killed and several wounded. The commander of the artillery, Lieutenant José Alfredo, died after leaping from a window of the barracks. The rest of the garrison, including its commander, Lieutenant Ignacio López, were taken prisoner. Thus twenty-eight men—all members of the prestigious Catalán Light Infantry Company—were taken captive, and not a rebel was injured.

As the night was dissolving in the first rays of the morning light of 10 July, the land conquest of San Nicolás was complete; but there still remained at the waterfront the royal gunboat *San Simeon*. The republicans, partly shielded by the edge of the woods, shouted loudly to the ship the capitulation order: "Strike the colors!" This was achieved after another half-hour of fighting, but no other lives were taken. In the turmoil there were shouts of "Viva la libertad y la República Francesa!" The crew of one officer and seventeen men surrendered, mainly because the ship was in no position to defend itself. The captain, against his better judgment, had previously acceded to the request of the fort's commander to bring the ship so close to shore that it was within pistol shot of the riverbank. Still worse, in completing the move, one of its lines had become fouled; the ship had swung even closer to shore than planned and was partly grounded and no longer maneuverable. Thus misplaced and immobilized, the gunboat could not effectively use its weapons, particularly on account of the nearby woods, which offered excellent cover to the rebels.

A contemporary map of the battle is reproduced here for the first time. It is the earliest known map of present-day downtown Jacksonville to show more than one building.[4] The events are clearly shown by the original numbering. The top of the map is the north and shows plantation buildings of John McIntosh at 13. Number 12 is the mouth of Pottsburg Creek. Number 11 is the William Lane plantation and Number 10 is the plantation house of William Jones. Number 9 is the location of other plantation build-

4. See Pleasant D. Gold, *History of Duval County, Florida*, p. 52, for 1772 map showing ferry house; for 1795 map, see Archivo General de Indias, Papeles Procedentes de Cuba, legajo 2564, p. 1425; in East Florida Papers, B294P12, p. 1425, Manuscript Division, Library of Congress.

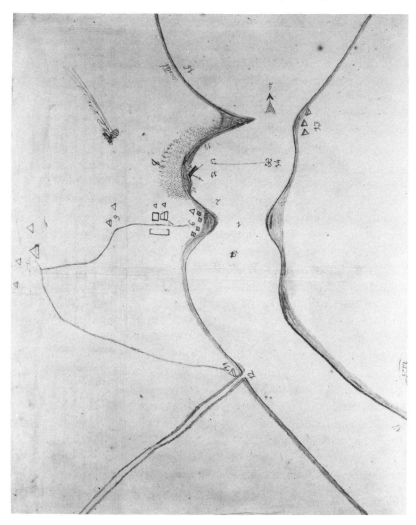

San Nicolás battle map, 1795 (B294P12, p. 1425, Reel 129, East Florida Papers, Library of Congress, Washington, D.C.). Today this land is part of downtown Jacksonville, Florida.

ings on the regular route from St. Augustine to San Nicolás. Number 7 is the location of the officers' quarters and guard house. Number 6 is the battery of the fort. Number 8 is a dense woods. Number 4 is the grounded gunboat *San Simeon* on the edge of the woods. Number 3 was where the fort's commandant wanted the ship placed. Number 15 is where the ship's commander wanted it

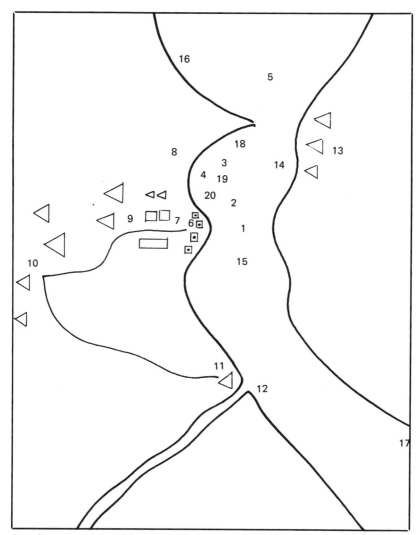

A modern reproduction of the map at left. See text below for key to numbered locations.

placed. Number 20 is where the republicans shouted to the ship: "Strike the colors!" Numbers 16 and 17 show where the channel ran. The word on the bank of the river at 16 indicates the pasture. The other numbers (1, 2, 5, 14, 18, 19) indicate the ship's placement of anchors at different times.

News of the fall of San Nicolás soon reached Santa Ysabel,

the next outpost toward the ocean. It was six miles from San Nicolás, at today's Reddie Point. The fifteen men in the garrison there promptly spiked their single cannon and abandoned their post. They moved out to consolidate their forces with those at the principal defense post of the St. Johns River, San Vicente Ferrer. The twenty-man force sent by the rebels at San Nicolás to take Santa Ysabel was thwarted by necessary delays in getting across the broad waters of Pottsburg Creek, and the Spaniards easily escaped to reach San Vicente Ferrer.

Colonel Howard, upon hearing of the capture of San Nicolás, immediately sent out reconnaissance personnel to determine the strength of the enemy. One of those who reconnoitered, Luis Maas, spoke English well and managed to penetrate the celebration party of some of the victors of San Nicolás. He reported that he had joined the party at 11:30 on the evening of 10 July "en la casa del rebelde Don Juan McIntosh inmediata a dicha Bateria" ("in the house of the rebel John McIntosh, next to the said fort"). Since the fort primarily mentioned in Maas's report was Santa Ysabel, apparently the plantation where McIntosh was acting as host was not the one at Cowford but rather the one the Spanish called Cerro Fuente, a mile or so beyond the little battery of Santa Ysabel. Maas told Colonel Howard that the rebels were all drinking, singing, and bragging.

Since the events at San Nicolás had revealed that some of the Spanish Florida militia had fought there against the Spanish regulars, the Spanish military command was understandably uncertain about how many of the Florida militia could now be relied upon. One militiaman, accused of being involved in the capture of San Nicolás, raised the point that the only evidence against him was that a man with a scarred or crushed nose, like his own, was present with the rebels. That was no proof at all, he said, since "this is a common thing among American backwoodsmen who, when they fight and come in hand-to-hand combat, bite the nose of their opponent or gouge the eyes with their thumbs."[5]

5. Las Casas to Campo Alange, 25 August 1795, Archivo General de Indias, Papeles Procedentes de Cuba, legajo 2564, p. 1425; in East Florida Papers, Reel 129, B294P12, p. 1293, Manuscript Division, Library of Congress. For another mention of eye gouging see Eugene Perry Link, *Democratic-Republican Societies, 1790–1800*, p. 64.

The information gathered from Maas made it clear to Howard that his own forces could greatly outnumber the rebels if he struck back quickly, before reinforcements from General Clark could be brought in and before local dissident plantation owners could be organized. This reasoning prompted immediate action by the Spanish commander. A reconnaissance of San Nicolás from the decks of the cruising *Conquest* was made on the afternoon of 11 July; a decision to strike quickly seemed well advised.

Besides San Vicente Ferrer the only Spanish outposts in the area were a small battery at the bar of the St. Johns and a small battery on Talbot Island, defending the southern shore of the entrance to Nassau Sound. Colonel Howard immediately ordered the abandonment of the battery on Talbot Island, Dos Hermanas, in order to consolidate its men at San Vicente Ferrer for counterattack on San Nicolás. He quickly put together an impressive force for this operation. A small Spanish gunboat, the *Santo Tomás,* was already at the headquarters. The garrison at Dos Hermanas, after spiking their guns, came with their launch, the *San Agustín de Patrón.* The British privateer *Conquest* had been persuaded to join the operation and had come from St. Augustine with its prize, the *Santa Mónica;* the two vessels had come into the St. Johns River on Saturday afternoon, 11 July. It should be remembered that there was at the time an alliance between Britain and Spain, reason enough for the *Conquest* to join the fight.

In the task force to retake San Nicolás, Colonel Howard came as the commander of the *Conquest,* accompanied by his staff, as well as forty veteran infantrymen, forty-two free mulattoes, and thirteen local militiamen. The *Santa Mónica* carried Juan McQueen and thirty soldiers. The *Santo Tomás* carried Captain José de los Remedios, heading the St. Augustine reinforcements, together with twenty men from the Catalán Company. The *San Agustín de Patrón* carried supplies and ammunition. They were all on their way by midday of Sunday, 12 July. That same morning a letter was written from San Nicolás, summarizing the events as observed by a rebel.[6]

6. *Federal Intelligencer and Baltimore Gazette*, 1 September 1795, in collections of the Jacksonville Historical Society, Jacksonville, Fla.

I have but just time to inform you, that on Thursday night, the 9th instant, the French in Florida crossed St. John's River, a little below the Cow-Ford. The night was far advanced in crossing the men, 50 in number, under the command of Capt. Richard Lang.

On their arrival on this side they took three Spanish militia officers prisoners of the following rank and names, viz., captain Holansworth, lieutenant Summerlin, and ensign Hogan, together with a small militia guard.

The day approaching very fast, they with all possible speed marched for the battery of St. Nicholas, alias Cow-Ford, containing two eighteen pounders, and without hesitation, proceeded to storm it. The conflict was short, the Spaniards had two men killed and one wounded, who has since died of his wounds; twenty-eight taken prisoners, together with commandant Ignacio Lopez, a cadet, about one hundred stand of arms, and a plenty of provisions and stores.

The subsequent morning, they attacked the king's launch, and after an engagement of half an hour she struck; they took prisoners on board, capt. Don Manuel, and seventeen seamen—her prow contained a twenty four pounder, a number of swivels, plenty of ammunition, a quantity of rum, pork, beef, bread, etc.

Saturday a party of twenty men was ordered to go and attack Noleses battery; however on their approach the Spaniards discovered them, and before our men could get over the Potsburg ferry, that intercepted their march, the Spaniards spiked their cannon and fled, leaving their arms and everything behind them.

There was lying in this port a British 20 gun brig, a small schooner of 10 guns, & a Spanish galley, & the republicans were apprehensive of being attacked by them should they discover their numbers. The Spanish inhabitants are joining them hourly—but they are much in want of men to man the battery and galley, & are quite inexperienced in gunnery. The militia officers have generally given themselves up and received paroles. The express is just going off to general Clark by whom I sent this.

The commander of the federal troops in Georgia at this time was Colonel Henry Gaither. He wrote to Governor Mathews from his Fort Fidius headquarters at Rock Landing on Georgia's Oconee River, discussing the taking of San Nicolás:[7]

7. In collections of the Georgia Department of Archives and History.

I am inform'd that the subjects of His Catholic Majesty in E[ast] Florida in conjunction with Citizens of this and Other of the U[nited] States are now in arms against the Government of that Province. They have already taken a Fort near the Cowford on the River St. Johns, in which they kill'd three Spanish Soldiers and made fourteen prisioners, part of Capt. Randolph's Troop have Join'd them, I have just sent orders to Capt. Dickinson to demand, or to have a demand made, by one of his Commission'd officers, of all Soldiers belonging to the Service of the United States that may be found in arms in the Province of Florida, and by no means attempt to take any such deserter that may be found without the Consent of the Commanding Officer there.

When the little Spanish armada came to San Nicolás on that bright Sunday afternoon, reality could no longer be evaded. Colonel Howard ordered the firing of a couple of cannon balls and a round of small arms. It seemed hardly necessary. The size of the Spanish task force was so impressive that the rebels quickly left behind forty horses grazing in the pasture at the fort and made their separate ways into the marshes and across the river. After securing the fort, Howard sent out a party to fight the republicans at Mills's Ferry; but they had gone instead to Amelia Island, and the Spaniards returned empty-handed after burning Lang's fort on the St. Marys. The fort was probably located at the site of the British Fort Tonyn, which had been captured by the patriots in 1778, about 1.3 miles east of the ferry.[8]

The French had built a crude fort on the northwestern shore of Amelia Island in early July of 1795—in part, perhaps, to divert Spanish attention from the planned operations at San Nicolás, and in part because the absence of a Spanish garrison on the island had allowed the rebels to use it as a permanent location. The French tricolor was reported to have been flying in the breeze since the very beginning of construction of the fort.[9] The rebel forces fleeing San Nicolás on 12 July came naturally to this fort

8. Richard K. Murdoch, *The Georgia-Florida Frontier, 1793–1796: Spanish Reaction to French Intrigue and American Designs,* p. 92.
    9. Ibid., p. 95.

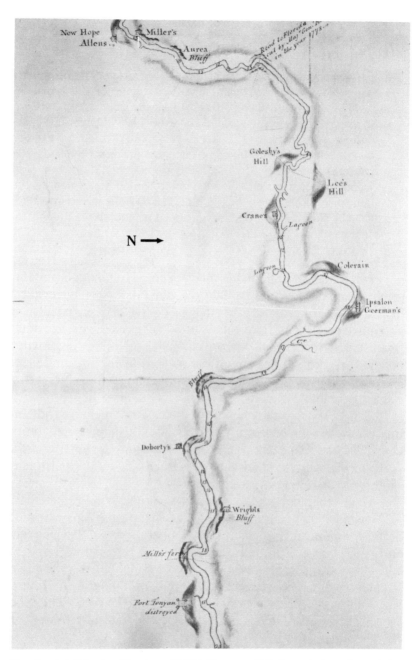

Map showing Coleraine, Temple, and Mills's Ferry, ca. 1780. From the Peter Force Collection, courtesy of the Library of Congress, Washington, D.C.

since it was easily accessible by canoes and small boats; thus a consolidation of all the revolutionaries under arms in Florida took place here.

On 18 July the revolutionary forces on Amelia Island petitioned the new French minister to the United States, Pierre Auguste Adet, to ask the French government for naval and other aid to succor their republic in Florida. Adet had already expressed concern over the conservative policy of his predecessor, Fauchet, and his failure to assist the American revolutionaries under the French flag when France and Spain were enemies in a ongoing war. The new minister mounted a prompt and strenuous program of aid, assisted largely by the Popular Society of Charleston. Substantial supplies were secured; very few were delivered, however, because it immediately became apparent that France and Spain were soon to sign a treaty of peace.[10]

On 2 August the Spanish government in Florida, with reinforcements sent from Cuba, mounted an offensive against the French on Amelia Island. On that date the brigs *Flecha* and *San Antonio*, along with the schooner *Santa Mónica* and two gunboats, came to the St. Marys in a task force headed by Colonel Carlos Howard, assisted by Juan McQueen. The *Santa Mónica* and the gunboats promptly ran aground, giving the French ample time to see the impossibility of defending against the force that approached them. So, before battle could be joined, the revolutionaries retreated, heading for Georgia in canoes and leaving behind them twenty-two Spanish prisoners previously taken at San Nicolás.

On 8 October Governor Quesada wrote to Georgia's Governor Mathews again, this time expressing concern over a rumor that General Clark, then in Georgia, was mounting another French revolutionary invasion of Florida. Quesada asked Mathews for cooperation in putting down the revolutionaries in Georgia before they left the state.[11]

10. Ibid., p. 96.
11. In collections of the Georgia Department of Archives and History. Note that the letter reveals that the McIntosh family were furnished a vessel in which to go to Newton and that the French rebels on Amelia Island captured it.

My dear Sir:

On April fifth of this year you answered my letter of March the tenth written to the magistrates of Camden County, that they take the necessary steps to prevent the diabolic menaces of the two Blunts and Lang. I expected favorable consequences but instead there was a repetition of the insults by Lang and also by Plowden in the two territories which you will take notice of from the two copies of the letters which these two rebels directed to me. I enclose them numbered 1 and 2.

Those threats were followed by robberies of which Colonel Bartolomé Morales gave you an account, who had authority in the province, and for that reason I, on the sixth of last July by a copy of the official letter to the said magistrates, asked that they intercept the devastation begun—all this with no favorable result—but instead a repetition by the citizens of that state mixed with rebel vassals of G. M. [George Mathews] who were led by Richard Lang and John Peter Wagnon and early in the morning on the tenth of July pretending to be militia-men who were going as reinforcements from that Plaza they attacked a Battery situated on the south border of St. John's River, took possession of the passage named Cowford, taking the officer and troop prisoners and killing three men; also they imprisoned a gun boat and its crew; and gave liberty to the officer and others of the company under oath to give up their arms and gave them papers saying this, some signed by Lang and others by General Clark.

Cast out from the said Battery by Lieutenant Colonel Carlos Howard, Commander of the Border; they went to that state where they found protection, and they took possession of Amelia Island where they stationed themselves. There they secured prisoners, the master and sailors of a boat sent out by me to conduct John McIntosh's family to Newton; they prepared themselves for new insults commanded by a French captain; but in the same way they were cast out of that island and again were protected in Newton, Temple, and Coleraine where they publicly proclaimed themselves French people waiting for General Clark who is already with them to get up a sufficient number of people to renew the invasion, and in the meantime some secretly do damage and return to that State where they remain unpunished. I have given an account of these acts to the Magistrates of Newton of which I am enclosing a copy for you. The justification that I have made on the passing of rebel vassals of G.M.

[George Mathews], William Ashly[12] and William Downs[13] from Temple to the St. John's River and robbing an inhabitant of that province of three slaves and threatening him with death is that the stolen property be returned, and that the rebel vassals of G.M. be delivered as offenders of the State and well deserved punishment to be given to those citizens of Georgia who have joined them; having found out of the arrival of Lieutenant Colonel Sebastián Kindelan[14] to this port sent out by the Captain General of Cuba and this province to talk to you about the disagreeable occurrences, I gave him this official letter so that the contents may serve as instructions besides those given by Thos. Jefe.[15] and then giving it to you.

I see with much resentment that the rebel vassals of G.M. who are real offenders of the State find protection in Georgia; that united with citizens of that state make hostile attempts in this province; that these attempts are disguised; that they are preparing themselves for greater ones; and this procedure unfortunately can compromise the Supreme Government of the United States of America with the King, my master: It is in your hands to stop the deadly consequences which are to be expected and I trust that you will do it efficiently.

May God keep you for many years.
I have the honor to subscribe myself
Your most humble servant,

Juan Nepomuceno de Quesada

St. Augustine, Florida October 8, 1795

His Excellency, George Mathews

Captain Andrew Atkinson of the Spanish East Florida militia reported early in October[16] that he had just discovered General Clark and a sizable force of revolutionaries—among them John

12. Ashley ran a ferry on the St. Marys, and James Seagrove considered him a desperate character. See Roger C. Harlan, "A Military History of East Florida during the Governorship of Enrique White, 1796–1811" (Ph.D. diss.), p. 200.
13. William Downs was a judge in Wilkes County, Georgia, in the early part of the American Revolution and later a commissioner for Houston County. He went to Florida and participated in the rebellion and in 1795 fled back to Camden County, Georgia. He took a party from Temple to raid the Plummer plantation in 1795 (Louise F. Hays, *Hero of Hornet's Nest; A Biography of Elijah Clark, 1733–1799*, pp. 68, 172, 289, 290).
14. Kindelan later became governor of East Florida (Gold, *Duval County*, p. 82).
15. Possibly Thomas Jefferson.
16. Murdoch, *Georgia-Florida Frontier*, pp. 125, 127.

McIntosh—occupying a large hummock in a swampy area south of the St. Marys River. On 20 October there was a rebel ambush against Atkinson's men on the road to St. Augustine from Mills's Ferry, but the attackers dissolved into the swamps after a short skirmish without injury to either side. When Colonel Howard reached the hummock later in the month to attack Clark in full force, nothing was found but the ashes of many campfires. This was the last appearance of General Clark in Florida. The door had finally slammed shut on the "French" revolutionary movement in Florida, although not on all hopes for its revival.

The Spanish authorities made every effort to punish the revolutionaries of 1795, but the real leaders all escaped to Georgia, notably Elijah Clark, Richard Lang, John McIntosh, and John Peter Wagnon. Sixty-eight cases were brought before the Spanish courts, including those of the thirty-five who had escaped to Georgia. Most of them had their property confiscated. Those who were captured were imprisoned; their trial began in January 1796 and concluded on 22 February 1798. Some sentences were dramatic: the defendants were to be dragged by the tail of a horse to the plaza at St. Augustine and there hanged; their bodies were then to be quartered and their heads and arms erected in the vicinity of San Nicolás and the pass of the St. Johns "to serve as a warning to others." McIntosh and Lang were among those thus severely sentenced, in absentia. However, no evidence has come to light indicating that any were actually executed. Defendants still living in Florida in 1800 were pardoned.[17]

There were many reasons for the fading of the "French" rebellion after the attack on San Nicolás. Lack of substantial success was, of course, reason enough. Further, in Basle, Switzerland, Spain and France finally concluded a treaty of peace in August 1795, after which Elijah Clark and others could not successfully pretend that they were acting any longer under French military commissions. Suares, the French consul at St. Marys, appeared on 1 October before a justice of the peace to state that there were no longer any authorized French troops in the United States.[18] Clark might reason that his troops, while in Indian lands

17. Janice Borton Miller, "The Rebellion in East Florida in 1795," p. 185.
18. Murdoch, *Georgia-Florida Frontier*, pp. 130, 175.

to the west or in Spanish Florida lands to the south, were outside the jurisdiction of the United States; but he obviously had no foundation for any further assertion of French support. Just as in the Trans-Oconee affair in 1794, both Georgia and United States troops were ready to force an end to his operations. He shelved his guns and returned to Georgia.

In 1796 and 1797 an attempt was made by the British to revive the Florida rebellion, this time under the British flag. The project was historically known as the Blount conspiracy, after the brothers William and Thomas Blount, who devised it.[19] Elijah Clark was asked by the British to operate against the Spanish in Florida as well as in the western lands, with the English to acquire sovereignty in any lands taken. Britain was then at war with Spain. Clark coolly turned the proposal down. When the old general died two years later at his plantation in Wilkes County, Georgia, the commander of the Georgia militia announced his death in a general order: ''The gallant old veteran, the late Major General Elijah Clark of Georgia, whose name ought to be so dear to this state and to the United States for his truly heroic exploits, is dead.''[20]

Richard Lang returned to Georgia ahead of Clark. He took the oath of American citizenship in 1799. On 15 October 1800 John King wrote from St. Marys to Georgia's Governor James Jackson: ''On the day of election here Lang got drunk and left the letter now sent, on the counter of Colonel Green's store.''[21] The letter that Lang had dropped was from William Augustus Bowles, soliciting the help of Lang and Clark for a rebellion in Florida under the leadership of Bowles. Actually Lang had already informed the governor of Bowles's overtures, as is shown by a letter of 12 July of that year from the governor to the U. S. Department of State.[22] King understood that Lang had contacted the governor about Bowles, but he was still suspicious of him.

19. *Biographical Directory of the American Congress, 1774–1971* (Washington: U.S. Government Printing Office, 1971), p. 605; Hays, *Hero of Hornet's Nest*, p. 289; J. Leitch Wright, Jr., *Florida in the American Revolution*, p. 151.

20. Hays, *Hero of Hornet's Nest*, p. 296.

21. In collections of the Georgia Department of Archives and History.

22. Ibid.

A patrol was sent to capture Bowles. Discovered near Traders Hill, he escaped, but left behind a letter which threw further suspicion on Lang. The letter was from William Jones to Bowles, dated 17 August, and it gave the impression that Lang was working with Bowles and Jones for a newly planned Florida rebellion.[23] In the letter, Jones proposed a rendezvous of the three men south of the St. Marys; he said, of himself and Lang, "I am certain that we can lead men enough to bid defiance to all the forces that Florida can produce. . . . I have lately seen a number of our friends in Florida and nothing prevents them from joining you but the appearance of a force sufficient to protect them from a small scout . . . of about twelve or fifteen men."

Lang was soon arrested for disturbing the peace and for new revolutionary activities but shortly thereafter was listed as "at large."[24] He was not punished and continued to live in Georgia. In 1804 he became justice of the peace at St. Marys, a post he continued to hold until his death. His Florida plantation, Casa Blanca, was sold to his friend William Drummond in 1816, and in that year Lang died.[25] Whether or not he had anything to do with other revolutionary activities that took place in Florida in 1812 and 1816 is not known. It seems improbable that he could have missed the events of 1812, since his old friend John McIntosh at one time commanded all the troops in that rebellion. Perhaps with Lang's advancing years he turned his back not only on his previously avowed Tory political views but also upon confidence in rebellion as a method of settling problems. The fact that he continued his responsibilities as a justice of the peace lends credibility to this conjecture.

John McIntosh, who was by almost any standard the most

23. Ibid.
24. Ibid. Lang's arrest is shown in a letter of 16 October 1800 from John King, probably to the governor. In the same collections is the 29 October 1800 letter from Thomas King to the governor stating that "Lang and Tally are at large."
25. The deed, dated 24 February 1817, is recorded in "Spanish Land Grants in Florida," Florida Department of Agriculture, 3:30. Apparently the Pigeon Creek lands of Lang were approximately 3,000 acres and were disposed of by grant application on the basis of default by the "rebel" Lang (see ibid., 2:300). For further details about Lang and his family, including his justice of the peace service in Georgia and his death, see Folks Huxford, *Pioneers of Wiregrass Georgia . . .*, 5:256.

notable man in events of the years 1793 through 1795 in Florida,
continued his unusual career. The Spanish authorities, recogniz-
ing his impressive leadership qualities, made it easy for him to
leave Florida after the events of 1795. They did try to attach his
property, but his wife, Sarah, took much of it with her to Georgia.
A Spanish inventory of the McIntosh chattels that were seized
listed four mahogany tables, a mahogany chest of drawers richly
gilded, a walnut desk similarly decorated, a mahogany armchair,
and seven straight chairs. Of course, all of the McIntosh real
estate in Florida was forfeited to the crown.[26]

McIntosh continued his revolutionary and military adventures. In 1797 he entered into negotiations with the British government at their instigation. He was offered the command of an
expeditionary force to be raised in Georgia for the capture of
Florida. The first step planned was for Britain to capture Amelia
Island as a base for operations. Many details were settled upon
and McIntosh accepted the proposal, but British authorities eventually decided to abandon the idea.[27]

In April of 1812 McIntosh was back in Florida leading rebel
troops against the Spanish authorities in an effort to set up a
republic which would turn itself over to the United States for
annexation. In this rebellion McIntosh cooperated with George
Mathews, who had been Georgia's governor during the events of
1793–95 and who, in 1812, claimed to have the support of the
Federal government in Washington. John's cousin John Houston
McIntosh was chosen political leader of the Patriot Republic of
East Florida; but the project collapsed when the expected support
of the United States was withdrawn. Sebastián Kindelan, East
Florida's Spanish governor, offered one thousand dollars for the

26. For the listing of McIntosh chattels found at Spring Hill, see East Florida Papers,
Reel 129, B295, pp. 11–12, Manuscript Division, Library of Congress. Other McIntosh
property is listed ibid., Escrituras 1784–1821, Reel 170, B269, 1793–94, p. 41, Manuscript
Division, Library of Congress (the Sarah McIntosh will). The will lists 2,700 acres of Florida
lands but not legal descriptions.

27. Cochrane Papers, Memorandum of 1797, National Library of Scotland, noted in J.
Leitch Wright, Jr., *Britain and the American Frontier, 1783–1815*, p. 112. This material has
been duplicated and placed in the Bennett Collection, Manuscript Division, Library of
Congress.

scalp of John Houston McIntosh and ten dollars for the scalp of each follower.[28]

John McIntosh capped his career in the service of his country when he served in the latter part of the War of 1812 as a major general under Andrew Jackson at Mobile. He died on 12 November 1826 at his plantation, Fair Hope, in McIntosh County, not far from his place of birth. Sarah had predeceased him in 1799 on St. Simons Island, and he had then remarried. The widow he left was Agnes McIntosh, who had been the widow of his longtime friend Christopher Hillary of Glynn County, Georgia.[29]

General Mathews, as we have noted, played an important part in the abortive efforts of 1812 to take Florida away from the Spanish and form a new republic that would revert immediately to the United States. He wrote to President Madison mentioning John Houston McIntosh as a possible U.S. governor for Florida and recommended that John Peter Wagnon, also a prominent participant in the 1793–95 revolutionary activities in Florida, be made either surveyor general or registrar of public lands for the new territory under U.S. sovereignty.[30] Wagnon, on leaving Florida after the failure of the French revolutionary activities, had settled in Sumner County, Tennessee, where he was a greatly respected citizen and where he died in 1828.[31]

As late as 1797 Samuel Hammond was agitating in Georgia for an attack on Spanish Florida with the assistance of the French, suggesting that a separate state be created in the area between the St. Marys and the St. Johns rivers, to act as a buffer between the United States and Spanish Florida. He reasoned that, with sufficient pressure applied on Spanish Florida, Spain might find such a state an appropriate solution to continuing problems of rebellion in that area. His pleas fell on deaf ears, but he went on to greater accomplishments. He was elected to Congress in 1802 and in 1805 was appointed governor of Upper Louisiana (Missouri), succeed-

28. Rembert W. Patrick, *Florida Fiasco: Rampant Rebels on the Georgia-Florida Border, 1810–1815*, pp. 112, 155, 182.
29. Margaret Cate, *Our Todays and Yesterdays: A Story of Brunswick and the Coastal Islands*, pp. 187–89.
30. Patrick, *Florida Fiasco*, p. 155.
31. Pension Papers, Archives of the United States.

Fair Hope, final home of John McIntosh. Courtesy of the Georgia Department of Archives and History, Atlanta.

ing General James Wilkinson at that post.[32] He was later secretary of state for South Carolina, where he died in 1842. His brother, Abner, went back to the mercantile business in Georgia. Abner was also state senator from Jefferson County from 1803 until 1809 and secretary of state for Georgia from 1811 until 1813. He lived his last years in retirement at Milledgeville, Georgia.[33]

The occurrences recorded on these pages are today not widely known even in the areas where they happened—the chief reason why this book was written. It would be a mistake to overstate the importance of these events by ascribing to them a major part in the "manifest destiny" of American expansion or a major part in the pressures exerted toward the opening of the Mississippi to United States commerce. Nevertheless, these activities in Florida did demonstrate the inability of Spain to maintain its boundaries securely and to resist effectively the turbulent Anglo-Saxons in their demand for navigation rights on the Mis-

32. *Biographical Directory of the American Congress*, p. 1060; *Webster's Biographical Dictionary*, s. v. "Hammond, Samuel"; Murdoch, *Georgia-Florida Frontier*, p. 151.
33. Hays, *Hero of Hornet's Nest*, p. 359; Pension Papers, Archives of the United States.

sissippi. The treaty of San Lorenzo el Real, ratified in 1796, not only settled boundary lines between the United States and Spanish America but also secured for the United States the freedom of navigation of the Mississippi to its mouth.

The events of the last decade of the eighteenth century had a permanent effect on the domestic political life of America. The two-party system was born. It probably would have come anyway; but the events described herein assisted in the unfolding of the process. The intellectual justification for the American political system could not be better stated than in the eighteenth-century resolution of the Patriotic Society of Newcastle that "the collision of opposite opinions produces the spark which lights the torch of truth."[34] On the remote and thinly populated Florida frontier of those days, however, the events of the Florida rebellion were generated more from territorial concerns than from ideology or national and international matters.

This period of history was one in which the newly formed federal government of the United States asserted its national character to limit the powers of states to act independently, thereby making a fitful but clear transition from the chaos of the earlier confederation. The new 1787 Constitution specifically provided that the president of the United States would be commander-in-chief of the state militia when it was called into service, thus dampening enthusiasm for state military actions. Further, President Washington insisted that the Constitution properly implied that only the central government could make treaties and hence that the Georgia treaties with Indians were improper. One of the earliest foreign policy statutes of the United States came as a direct reaction to the French revolutionary activities that are the subject of this work. This 1794 statute (found today in somewhat modified form in Sections 958–962 of the *United States Code,* 1970 edition) made it a crime for an American citizen to attempt to handle international affairs independently of the direction of the national government.

Finally, the happenings in Florida in 1793–95 were part of a series of similar events that pressed inexorably to the ultimate entry of Florida into the Union.

34. Link, *Democratic-Republican Societies*, p. 211.

APPENDIX

Hammond's Recollections of French Proposals

The original copy of the French proposals made to Colonel Samuel Hammond appears in chapter 8 of this volume. While the Spanish authorities were seeking this document at the William Jones plantation, Abner Hammond wrote out his recollections of the document from memory. The recollections, reproduced here, are of some importance, since they prove that Colonel Hammond was the American who was being approached and they verify the signature of the French agent, which is not very legible in the original document.

In consequence of instructions & authorizations from Citizen Consul Mangourit of the French Republic, I, the subscriber, have set down the following proposals for the consideration of Col. S. Hammond.

Col. Hammond will endeavor to raise a number of men who are to be marched into East Florida and there in the name of the French Republick to attempt the reduction of that province.

The said Col. Hammond & the officers & soldiers engaging in said expedition shall be under French pay from the moment they enter the service which shall be continued to them so long as the war lasts or so long as their service may be wanted.

When a sufficient number of men shall be engaged, proper measures will be taken for their support and supplies furnished in due time by said republick.

All publick property taken by the said troops in the said expedition shall be equally devided among the officers & troops.

Every person engaging in the said expedition shall be entitled to a lot or lot and house in the Town of St. Augustine so far as the publick lots will go; the officers to take choice by seniority; and should there not be a sufficient numbers the remainder to be subdivided in such a manner as to afford every man a share.

Should the Province of West Florida & Louisiana shake of [f] the yoke from their present masters they together with East Florida will be at liberty to form a Federal government.

The province of East Florida during the war will be considered as a part of the Republick of France and, as such, be under its immediate protection and at the end of the war the said province will be at liberty to form a government of their own which must be a strictly democratical republican government, the rights of man to form the basis of their constitution.

In order to protect the coast & Inland Navigation from the Havannah & Bahama pirates it will be necessary to have several armed vessels for which purpose all such vessels taken in the said province shall be appropriated to that service.

Every person engaging in said expedition shall be entitled to a generous bounty in land the quantity to be ascertained hereafter, which shall be laid out to them in any of the unappropriated lands in said province.

Proper encouragement will be held out to the neighboring & other governments, to such as wish to become citizens & engage during the war in defense of said province.

At the end of the war should said province be given up to its former owners, provision shall be made by the Republick of France to those engaged in the expedition equal to the sacrifices they may severally have made.

As nearly the above as I can recollect at present. Is signed C. M. F. Bert

The above is as nearly as I recollect to the best of my knowledge, an abstract of the articles & proposals hinted by me in my declaration given by me before Col. Charles Howard on the 5th, Inst.; and for the best ends that may be for the better of this government, I sign the present in St. Augustine on the 27th January 1794—

A Hammond

Selected Bibliography

1. Manuscript Sources

Archives of the United States. Pension Papers; particularly "Florida Private Land Claims." Washington.

Archivo General de Indias (AGI). Papeles Procedentes de Cuba (PC); particularly legajos 166, 167, 1428, 2354 (Seville), and legajo 2564 (Santo Domingo).

Archivo General de Simancas. Particularly legajo 7235. Simanca.

Archivo Historico Nacional. Particularly legajo 923. Madrid.

Archivo Nacional de Cuba. Particularly legajos 1, 3, 14, 21, 34. Havana.

Boston Public Library. Samuel Hammond Papers.

Florida Department of Agriculture. "Spanish Land Grants in Florida." 5 vols. Historical Records Service, Works Progress Administration, 1941. Tallahassee.

Georgia Department of Archives and History. Particularly the letterbook of Governor George Mathews, 1793–96. Atlanta.

Georgia Historical Society. Joseph Bevan Papers. Savannah.

Library of Congress, Manuscript Division. East Florida Papers; particularly boxes 293–96. Washington.

National Library of Scotland. Cochrane Papers. Edinburgh.

2. Printed Materials

Abernethy, Thomas P. *The South in the New Nation, 1789–1819*. Baton Rouge: Louisiana State University Press, 1961.

American State Papers. Documents, legislative and executive, of the Congress of the United States. . . . 38 vols. Edited by Asbury Dickins and James C. Allen. 38 vols. Washington: Gales & Stratton, 1832–61.

Bennett, Charles E. *Laudonnière and Fort Caroline: History and Documents*. Gainesville: University of Florida Press, 1964.

———. *Southernmost Battlefields of the Revolution*. Bailey's Crossroads, Va.: Blair, 1970.

———, trans. *Three Voyages*, by René Goulaine de Laudonnière. Gainesville: University Presses of Florida, 1975.

Brevard, Caroline Mays. *A History of Florida from the Treaty of 1763 to Our Own Times*.

Edited by James Alexander Robertson. 2 vols. Deland: Florida State Historical Society, 1924–25.

Candler, Allen D., comp. *Revolutionary Records of the State of Georgia.* 3 vols. Atlanta: Franklin-Turner Co., 1908.

Cash, W. T. *The Story of Florida.* 4 vols. New York: American Historical Society, Inc., 1938.

Cate, Margaret. *Our Todays and Yesterdays: A Story of Brunswick and the Coastal Islands.* Rev. ed. Brunswick, Ga.: Glover Press, 1930.

Caughey, John W. *McGillivray of the Creeks.* Norman: University of Oklahoma Press, 1938.

Coleman, Kenneth. *The American Revolution in Georgia, 1763–1789.* Athens: University of Georgia Press, 1958.

Corkran, David H. *The Creek Frontier, 1540–1783.* Norman: University of Oklahoma Press, 1967.

Corse, Carita Doggett. *The Key to the Golden Islands.* Chapel Hill: University of North Carolina Press, 1931.

Coulter, Ellis Merton. "Elijah Clark's Foreign Intrigue and the Trans-Oconee Republic." *Mississippi Valley Historical Review,* Supplement (November 1921), pp. 260–79.

———. *John Jacobus Flournoy, Champion of the Common Man in the Antebellum South.* Savannah: Georgia Historical Society, 1942.

Crane, Verner W. *The Southern Frontier, 1670–1732.* Ann Arbor: University of Michigan Press, 1956.

Davis, T. Frederick. *History of Early Jacksonville, Florida; Being an Authentic Record of Events from the Earliest Times to and Including the Civil War.* Jacksonville: H. & W. B. Drew Co., 1911.

———. *History of Jacksonville, Florida, and Vicinity, 1513 to 1924.* St. Augustine, Fla.: Record Company Press, 1925.

Doster, James F. *The Creek Indians and Their Florida Lands, 1740–1823.* 2 vols. New York: Garland Publishing, Inc., 1974.

DuPree, Mary M., and Taylor, G. Dekle. "Dr. James Hall, 1760–1837." Pamphlet. Bennett Collection, Library of Congress, Manuscript Division, Washington.

Federal Intelligencer and Baltimore Gazette, 1 September 1795. Collections of the Jacksonville Historical Society, Jacksonville, Fla.

Fletcher, M. S. "French Consular States Agents in the United States, 1791–1800." *Franco-American Review* 1:85–90.

"Florida Private Land Claims." Pension Papers. Archives of the United States, Washington.

Folmer, Henry. *Franco-Spanish Rivalry in North America, 1524–1763.* Glendale, Calif.: A. H. Clark Co., 1953.

Fuller, Hubert Bruce. *The Purchase of Florida, Its History and Diplomacy.* 1906. Reprint. Gainesville: University of Florida Press, 1964.

Gamble, Thomas. *Of Savannah Duels and Duelists, 1733–1877.* Savannah, Ga.: Review Publishing and Printing Co., 1923.

Gold, Pleasant D. *History of Duval County, Florida.* St. Augustine, Fla.: Record Company Press, 1929.

Goode, Kenneth G. *From Africa to the United States and then. . .; A Concise Afro-American History.* Glenview, Ill.: Scott, Foresman & Co., 1969.

Hays, Louise F. *Hero of Hornet's Nest; A Biography of Elijah Clark, 1733 to 1799.* New York: Stratford House, Inc., 1946.

Hill, Roscoe R., editor. *Descriptive Catalogue of the Documents Relating to the History of* the United States in the *Papeles Procedentes de Cuba* Deposited in the Archivo *General de Indias at Seville*. Washington: Carnegie Institute of Washington, 1916.

Huxford, Folks. *Pioneers of Wiregrass Georgia: A Biographical Account of Some of the Early Settlers of That Portion of Wiregrass Georgia Embraced in the Original Counties of Irwin, Appling, Wayne, Camden, and Glynn*. 5 vols. Waycross, Ga.: Herrin's Printing Shop, 1951-1967.

Johannes, Jan H. *Yesterday's Reflections, Nassau County, Florida: A Pictorial History*. Edited by Kay S. Pedrotti. Callahan, Fla.: Florida Sun Printing, 1976.

Jones, Charles C. *The History of Georgia*. 2 vols. Boston: Houghton, Mifflin Co., 1883.

Kinnaird, Lawrence, ed. *Spain in the Mississippi Valley, 1765-1794*. Washington: U.S. Government Printing Office, 1949.

Knight, Lucian Lamar. *Georgia's Bicentennial Memoirs and Memories: A Tale of Two Centuries, Reviewing the State's Marvelous Story of Achievement, since Oglethorpe's Landing in 1733*. 3 vols. Atlanta: privately printed, 1931-32.

Laudonnière, René Goulaine de. *Three Voyages*. Translated by Charles E. Bennett. Gainesville: University Presses of Florida, 1975.

Lewis, Bessie. *They Called Their Town Darien: Being a Short History of Darien and McIntosh County, Georgia*. Darien, Ga.: The Darien News, 1975.

Link, Eugene Perry. *Democratic-Republican Societies, 1790-1800*. New York: Columbia University Press, 1942.

MacKay, Robert. *The Letters of Robert MacKay to His Wife, Written from Ports in America and England, 1795-1816*. Edited by Walter Charlton Hartridge. Athens: University of Georgia Press, 1949.

McQueen, John. *The Letters of Don Juan McQueen to His Family, Written from Spanish East Florida, 1791-1807*. Edited by Walter Charlton Hartridge. Columbia, S.C.: Bostick & Thornley, 1943.

Miller, Janice Borton. "The Rebellion in East Florida in 1795." *Florida Historical Quarterly* 57 (October 1978):173-86.

Minnigerode, Meade. *Jefferson, Friend of France, 1793; The Career of Edmond Charles Genêt, Minister Plenipotentiary from the French Republic to the United States, as Revealed by His Private Papers, 1763-1834*. New York: Putnam, 1928.

Mowat, Charles L. *East Florida as a British Province, 1763-1784*. Berkeley: University of California Press, 1943.

Murdoch, Richard K. "Citizen Mangourit and the Projected Attack on East Florida in 1794." *Journal of Southern History* 14 (1948):522-40.

―――. *The Georgia-Florida Frontier, 1793-1796: Spanish Reaction to French Intrigue and American Designs*. Berkeley: University of California Press, 1951.

Norman, Charles. *Discoverers of America*. New York: Thomas Y. Crowell Co., 1968.

Patrick, Rembert W. *Florida Fiasco: Rampant Rebels on the Georgia-Florida Border, 1810-1815*. Athens: University of Georgia Press, 1954.

Reddick, Marguerite G. *Camden's Challenge: A History of Camden County, Georgia*. Jacksonville, Fla.: Paramount Press, 1976.

Siebert, Wilbur H. *Loyalists in East Florida, 1774 to 1785*. 2 vols. Deland: Florida State Historical Society, 1929.

Tanner, Helen H. "Zéspedes and the Southern Conspiracies." *Florida Historical Quarterly* 38 (1959):17ff.

―――. *Zéspedes in East Florida, 1784-1790*. Coral Gables, Fla.: University of Miami Press, 1963.

Turner, Frederick J. "The Mangourit Correspondence in Respect to Genêt's Projected Attack on Louisiana and the Floridas." *American Historical Association Report*, pp. 569–75. Washington: Government Printing Office, 1898.
———. "The Origin of Genêt's Projected Attack on Louisiana and the Floridas." *American Historical Review* 3 (1898):650ff.
Ward, James, and O'Neal, Peggy. "Time Traveler." *Florida Times Union*, 28 March 1977.
Whitaker, Arthur Preston. *Documents Relating to the Commercial Policy of Spain in the Floridas, with Incidental Reference to Louisiana*. Deland: Florida State Historical Society, 1931.
———. *The Spanish-American Frontier, 1783–1795; the Westward Movement and the Spanish Retreat in the Mississippi Valley*. New York: Houghton, Mifflin, 1927.
White, George. *Historical Collections of Georgia*. New York: Pudney and Russell, 1854.
Wright, J. Leitch, Jr. *Britain and the American Frontier, 1783–1815*. Athens: University of Georgia Press, 1975.
———. *Florida in the American Revolution*. Gainesville: University Presses of Florida, 1975.
———. *William Augustus Bowles, Director General of the Creek Nation*. Athens: University of Georgia Press, 1967.

3. Unpublished Materials

Arana, Luis, and Manucy, Albert. "The Building of Castillo de San Marcos." Eastern National Park and Monument Association, St. Augustine, Florida, 1977.
Harlan, Rogers C. "A Military History of East Florida During the Governorship of Enrique White, 1796–1811." Ph.D. dissertation, Florida State University, Tallahassee, 1971.
Miller, Janice Borton. "Juan Nepomuceno de Quesada: Spanish Governor of East Florida, 1790–1795." Ph.D. dissertation, Florida State University, Tallahassee, 1974.

Index

Adet, Pierre Auguste, 195
Alfredo, José, 187
Allen, Diego, 50, 82–83
Alligator Bridge, battle of, 3, 15, 23
Altamaha River, 10, 110, 134, 155, 156
Amelia Island, Fla., ii (map), 15n, 30, 47, 59, 73, 76, 89, 126, 130, passim; garrisoned by Spanish, 11, 175; fortified by French, 172, 193; abandoned by French, 195
Armstrong, Colonel, 145, 153, 156
Arons, George, 53–54; testified, 57–60
Ashly, William, 197
Atkinson, Andrew: land claims of, 13n; mentioned, 21, 81, 151, 157, 159, 161, 164, 197; biog. note, 61–62; in McIntosh's testimony, 81–83; in Lang's testimony, 121; in McMurphy's testimony, 151, 155, 158, 159, 161; reported plans to capture San Nicolás, 184; ambushed, 198
Ayllón, Lucas Vásquez de, 1

Bailey, David, 124
Bailey, John, 61, 71, 115, 124, 164
Bernal, Manuel: signed documents, 43, 54, passim

Berrien, John, 138–44 passim
Berrihill, Andrew, 155
Berrio, Pedro, 47, 49, 73, 75
Bert, C. M. F. de: biog. note, 25n; as leader in Genét affair, 25, 28; wrote to French consul, 29; identified by A. Hammond as French agent, 40; signed French proposals to S. Hammond, 37, 86, 92, 97
Blount, Thomas, 199
Blount, William: land speculation of, 8; Blount Conspiracy, 196, 199
Bowles, William Augustus, 6, 7 (illus.), 199–200
Brackin, Daniel, 105, 106
Brown, Jacob R., 43, 120
Brown, John, 5
Burnett, Daniel, 61
Burnett, David, 61n
Burrows, John, 157, 158, 159
Butler, Pierce, 156

Cain, Francisco, 180
Carr, Thomas, 8
Cartier, Jacques, 2
Charles IX, 2
Clark, Elijah: a party to Genét's plans,

211